LET SLEEPING VETS LIE

I have long held the notion that if a vet can't catch his patient there's nothing much to worry about . . . It's not all chasing livestock around fields, though — James Herriot is also kept busy judging the Family Pets contest at the Darrowby village show (discovering the cut-throat, backstabbing politics seething beneath the fête's surface), and attempting to calve a cow whilst drunk (on a farm full of strict Methodists). And he's over the moon after proposing successfully to Helen Alderson — even if it looks like they'll be spending a romantic honeymoon travelling around farms tuberculin testing cattle . . .

JAMES HERRIOT

◆

LET SLEEPING VETS LIE

Complete and Unabridged

ULVERSCROFT
Leicester

First published in Great Britain in 1973 by
Michael Joseph Ltd
London

This Ulverscroft Edition
published 2018
by arrangement with
Pan Macmillan
London

A catalogue record for this book is available
from the British Library.

ISBN 978–1–4448–3658–5

Published by
F. A. Thorpe (Publishing)
Anstey, Leicestershire

Set by Words & Graphics Ltd.
Anstey, Leicestershire
Printed and bound in Great Britain by
T. J. International Ltd., Padstow, Cornwall

This book is printed on acid-free paper

To my Wife
with love

1

As the faint rumbling growl rolled up from the rib cage into the ear pieces of my stethoscope the realization burst upon me with uncomfortable clarity that this was probably the biggest dog I had ever seen. In my limited past experience some Irish Wolfhounds had undoubtedly been taller and a certain number of Bull Mastiffs had possibly been broader, but for sheer gross poundage this one had it. His name was Clancy.

It was a good name for an Irishman's dog and Joe Mulligan was very Irish despite his many years in Yorkshire. Joe had brought him into the afternoon surgery and as the huge hairy form ambled along, almost filling the passage, I was reminded of the times I had seen him out in the fields around Darrowby enduring the frisking attentions of smaller animals with massive benignity. He looked like a nice friendly dog.

But now there was this ominous sound echoing round the great thorax like a distant drum roll in a subterranean cavern, and as the chest piece of the stethoscope bumped along the ribs the sound swelled in volume and the lips fluttered over the enormous teeth as though a gentle breeze had stirred them. It was then that I became aware not only that Clancy was very big indeed but that my position, kneeling on the floor with my right ear a few inches from his mouth, was infinitely vulnerable.

I got to my feet and as I dropped the stethoscope into my pocket the dog gave me a cold look — a sideways glance without moving his head; and there was a chilling menace in his very immobility. I didn't mind my patients snapping at me but this one, I felt sure, wouldn't snap. If he started something it would be on a spectacular scale.

I stepped back a pace. 'Now what did you say his symptoms were, Mr Mulligan?'

'Phwaat's that?' Joe cupped his ear with his hand. I took a deep breath. 'What's the trouble with him?' I shouted.

The old man looked at me with total incomprehension from beneath the straightly adjusted cloth cap. He fingered the muffler knotted immediately over his larynx and the pipe which grew from the dead centre of his mouth puffed blue wisps of puzzlement.

Then, remembering something of Clancy's past history, I moved close to Mr Mulligan and bawled with all my power into his face. 'Is he vomiting?'

The response was immediate. Joe smiled in great relief and removed his pipe. 'Oh aye, he's womitin' sorr. He's womitin' bad.' Clearly he was on familiar ground.

Over the years Clancy's treatment had all been at long range. My young boss, Siegfried Farnon, had told me on the first day I had arrived in Darrowby two years ago that there was nothing wrong with the dog, which he had described as a cross between an Airedale and a donkey, but his

2

penchant for eating every bit of rubbish in his path had the inevitable result. A large bottle of bismuth, mag carb mixture had been dispensed at regular intervals. He had also told me that Clancy, when bored, used occasionally to throw Joe to the ground and worry him like a rat just for a bit of light relief. But his master still adored him.

Prickings of conscience told me I should carry out a full examination. Take his temperature, for instance. All I had to do was to grab hold of that tail, lift it and push a thermometer into his rectum. The dog turned his head and met my eye with a blank stare; again I heard the low booming drum roll and the upper lip lifted a fraction to show a quick gleam of white.

'Yes, yes, right, Mr Mulligan,' I said briskly. 'I'll get you a bottle of the usual.'

In the dispensary, under the rows of bottles with their Latin names and glass stoppers I shook up the mixture in a ten ounce bottle, corked it, stuck on a label and wrote the directions. Joe seemed well satisfied as he pocketed the familiar white medicine but as he turned to go my conscience smote me again. The dog did look perfectly fit but maybe he ought to be seen again.

'Bring him back again on Thursday afternoon at two o'clock,' I yelled into the old man's ear. 'And please come on time if you can. You were a bit late today.'

I watched Mr Mulligan going down the street, preceded by his pipe from which regular puffs rose upwards as though from a departing railway engine. Behind him ambled Clancy, a picture of massive calm. With his all-over covering of tight brown curls he did indeed look like a gigantic Airedale.

Thursday afternoon, I ruminated. That was my half day and at two o'clock I'd probably be watching the afternoon cinema show in Brawton.

★ ★ ★

The following Friday morning Siegfried was sitting behind his desk, working out the morning rounds. He scribbled a list of visits on a pad, tore out the sheet and handed it to me.

'Here you are, James, I think that'll just about keep you out of mischief till lunch time.' Then something in the previous day's entries caught his eye and he turned to his younger brother who was at his morning task of stoking the fire.

'Tristan, I see Joe Mulligan was in yesterday afternoon with his dog and you saw it. What did you make of it?'

Tristan put down his bucket. 'Oh, I gave him some of the bismuth mixture.'

'Yes, but what did your examination of the patient disclose?'

'Well now, let's see.' Tristan rubbed his chin. 'He looked pretty lively, really.'

'Is that all?'

'Yes . . . yes . . . I think so.'

Siegfried turned back to me. 'And how about you, James? You saw the dog the day before. What were your findings?'

'Well it was a bit difficult,' I said. 'That dog's

as big as an elephant and there's something creepy about him. He seemed to me to be just waiting his chance and there was only old Joe to hold him. I'm afraid I wasn't able to make a close examination but I must say I thought the same as Tristan — he did look pretty lively.'

Siegfried put down his pen wearily. On the previous night, fate had dealt him one of the shattering blows which it occasionally reserves for vets — a call at each end of his sleeping time. He had been dragged from his bed at 1 AM and again at 6 AM and the fires of his personality were temporarily damped.

He passed a hand across his eyes. 'Well God help us. You, James, a veterinary surgeon of two years' experience and you, Tristan, a final year student can't come up with anything better between you than the phrase 'pretty lively'. It's a bloody poor thing! Hardly a worthy description of clinical findings is it? When an animal comes in here I expect you to record pulse, temperature and respiratory rate. To auscultate the chest and thoroughly palpate the abdomen. To open his mouth and examine teeth, gums and pharynx. To check the condition of the skin. To catheterize him and examine the urine if necessary.'

'Right,' I said.

'OK,' said Tristan.

My employer rose from his seat. 'Have you fixed another appointment?'

'I have, yes.' Tristan drew his packet of Woodbines from his pocket. 'For Monday. And since Mr Mulligan's always late for the surgery I

5

said we'd visit the dog at his home in the evening.'

'I see.' Siegfried made a note on the pad, then he looked up suddenly. 'That's when you and James are going to the young farmers' meeting, isn't it?'

The young man drew on his cigarette. 'That's right. Good for the practice for us to mix with the young clients.'

'Very well,' Siegfried said as he walked to the door. 'I'll see the dog myself.'

★ ★ ★

On the following Tuesday I was fairly confident that Siegfried would have something to say about Mulligan's dog, if only to point out the benefits of a thorough clinical examination. But he was silent on the subject.

It happened that I came upon old Joe in the market place sauntering over the cobbles with Clancy inevitably trotting at his heels.

I went up to him and shouted in his ear. 'How's your dog?'

Mr Mulligan removed his pipe and smiled with slow benevolence. 'Oh foine, sorr, foine. Still vomitin' a bit, but not bad.'

'Mr Farnon fixed him up, then?'

'Aye, gave him some more of the white medicine. It's wonderful stuff, sorr, wonderful stuff.'

'Good, good,' I said. 'He didn't find anything else when he examined him?'

Joe took another suck at his pipe. 'No he

didn't now, he didn't. He's a clever man, Mr Farnon — I've niver seen a man work as fast, no I haven't.'

'What do you mean?'

'Well now he saw all he wanted in tree seconds, so he did.'

I was mystified. 'Three seconds?'

'Yis,' said Mr Mulligan firmly. 'Not a moment more.'

'Amazing. What happened?'

Joe tapped out his pipe on his heel and without haste took out a knife and began to carve a refill from an evil looking coil of black twist. 'Well now I'll tell ye. Mr Farnon is a man who moves awful sudden, and that night he banged on our front door and jumped into the room.' (I knew those cottages. There was no hall or lobby — you walked straight from the street into the living-room.) 'And as he came in he was pullin' his thermometer out of its case. Well now Clancy was lyin' by the fire and he rose up in a flash and he gave a bit of a wuff, so he did.'

'A bit of a wuff, eh?' I could imagine the hairy monster leaping up and baying into Siegfried's face. I could see the gaping jaws, the gleaming teeth.

'Aye, just a bit of a wuff. Well, Mr Farnon just put the thermometer straight back in its case turned round and went out the door.'

'Didn't he say anything?' I asked.

'No, divil a word. Just turned about like a soldier and marched out the door, so he did.'

It sounded authentic. Siegfried was a man of instant decisions. I put my hand out to pat

Clancy but something in his eyes made me change my mind.

'Well, I'm glad he's better,' I shouted.

The old man ignited his pipe with an ancient brass lighter, puffed a cloud of choking blue smoke into my face and tapped a little metal lid on to the bowl. 'Aye, Mr Farnon sent round a big bottle of the white stuff and it's done 'im good. Mind yous,' he gave a beatific smile, 'Clancy's allus been one for the womitin', so he has.'

★   ★   ★

Nothing more was said about the big dog for over a week, but Siegfried's professional conscience must have been niggling at him because he came into the dispensary one afternoon when Tristan and I were busy at the tasks which have passed into history — making up fever drinks, stomach powders, boric acid pessaries. He was elaborately casual.

'Oh by the way, I dropped a note to Joe Mulligan. I'm not entirely convinced that we have adequately explored the causes of his dog's symptoms. This womiting . . . er, vomiting is almost certainly due to depraved appetite but I just want to make sure. So I have asked him to bring him round tomorrow afternoon between two and two thirty when we'll all be here.'

No cries of joy greeted his statement, so he continued. 'I suppose you could say that this dog is to some degree a difficult animal and I think we should plan accordingly.' He turned to me.

8

'James, when he arrives you get hold of his back end, will you?'

'Right,' I replied without enthusiasm.

He faced his brother. 'And you, Tristan, can deal with the head. OK?'

'Fine, fine,' the young man muttered, his face expressionless.

His brother continued. 'I suggest you get a good grip with your arms round his neck and I'll be ready to give him a shot of sedative.'

'Splendid, splendid,' said Tristan.

'Ah well, that's capital.' My employer rubbed his hands together. 'Once I get the dope into him the rest will be easy. I do like to satisfy my mind about these things.'

★ ★ ★

It was a typical Dales practice at Darrowby; mainly large animal and we didn't have packed waiting rooms at surgery times. But on the following afternoon we had nobody in at all, and it added to the tension of waiting. The three of us mooched about the office, making aimless conversation, glancing with studied carelessness into the front street, whistling little tunes to ourselves. By two twenty-five we had all fallen silent. Over the next five minutes we consulted our watches about every thirty seconds, then at exactly two thirty Siegfried spoke up.

'This is no damn good. I told Joe he had to be here before half past but he's taken not a bit of notice. He's always late and there doesn't seem to be any way to get him here on time.' He took

9

a last look out of the window at the empty street. 'Right we're not waiting any longer. You and I, James, have got that colt to cut and you, Tristan, have to see that beast of Wilson's. So let's be off.'

Up till then, Laurel and Hardy were the only people I had ever seen getting jammed together in doorways but there was a moment when the three of us gave a passable imitation of the famous comics as we all fought our way into the passage at the same time. Within seconds we were in the street and Tristan was roaring off in a cloud of exhaust smoke. My employer and I proceeded almost as rapidly in the opposite direction.

At the end of Trengate we turned into the market place and I looked around in vain for signs of Mr Mulligan. It wasn't until we had reached the outskirts of the town that we saw him. He had just left his house and was pacing along under a moving pall of blue smoke with Clancy as always bringing up the rear.

'There he is!' Siegfried exclaimed. 'Would you believe it? At the rate he's going he'll get to the surgery around three o'clock. Well we won't be there and it's his own fault.' He looked at the great curly-coated animal tripping along, a picture of health and energy. 'Well, I suppose we'd have been wasting our time examining that dog in any case. There's nothing really wrong with him.'

For a moment he paused, lost in thought, then he turned to me.

'He does look pretty lively, doesn't he?'

2

This was my second spring in the Dales but it was like the one before — and all the springs after. The kind of spring, that is, that a country vet knows; the din of the lambing pens, the bass rumble of the ewes and the high, insistent bawling of the lambs. This, for me, has always heralded the end of winter and the beginning of something new. This and the piercing Yorkshire wind and the hard, bright sunshine flooding the bare hillsides.

At the top of the grassy slope the pens, built of straw bales, formed a long row of square cubicles each holding a ewe with her lambs and I could see Rob Benson coming round the far end carrying two feeding buckets. Rob was hard at it; at this time of the year he didn't go to bed for about six weeks; he would maybe take off his boots and doze by the kitchen fire at night but he was his own shepherd and never very far from the scene of action.

'Ah've got a couple of cases for you today, Jim.' His face, cracked and purpled by the weather, broke into a grin, 'It's not really you ah need, it's that little lady's hand of yours and right sharpish, too.'

He led the way to a bigger enclosure, holding several sheep. There was a scurry as we went in but he caught expertly at the fleece of a darting ewe. 'This is the first one. You can see we

11

haven't a deal o' time.'

I lifted the woolly tail and gasped. The lamb's head was protruding from the vagina, the lips of the vulva clamped tightly behind the ears, and it had swollen enormously to more than twice its size. The eyes were mere puffed slits in the great oedematous ball and the tongue, blue and engorged, lolled from the mouth.

'Well I've seen a few big heads, Rob, but I think this takes the prize.'

'Aye, the little beggar came with his legs back. Just beat me to it. Ah was only away for an hour but he was up like a football! By hell it doesn't take long. I know he wants his legs bringin' round but what can I do with bloody great mitts like mine.' He held out his huge hands, rough and swollen with the years of work.

While he spoke I was stripping off my jacket and as I rolled my shirt sleeves high the wind struck like a knife at my shrinking flesh. I soaped my fingers quickly and began to feel for a space round the lamb's neck. For a moment the little eyes opened and regarded me disconsolately.

'He's alive, anyway,' I said. 'But he must feel terrible and he can't do a thing about it.'

Easing my way round, I found a space down by the throat where I thought I might get through. This was where my 'lady's hand' came in useful and I blessed it every spring; I could work inside the ewes with the minimum of discomfort to them and this was all-important because sheep, despite their outdoor hardiness, just won't stand rough treatment.

With the utmost care I inched my way along

12

the curly wool of the neck to the shoulder. Another push forward and I was able to hook a finger round the leg and draw it forward until I could feel the flexure of the knee; a little more twiddling and I had hold of the tiny cloven foot and drew it gently out into the light of day.

Well that was half the job done. I got up from the sack where I was kneeling and went over to the bucket of warm water. For the other leg I'd use my left hand and I began to soap it thoroughly while one of the ewes, marshalling her lambs around her, glared at me indignantly and gave a warning stamp of her foot.

Turning, I kneeled again and began the same procedure and, as I once more groped forward, a tiny lamb dodged under my arm and began to suck at my patient's udder. He was clearly enjoying it, too, if the little tail, twirling inches from my face, meant anything.

'Where did this bloke come from?' I asked, still feeling round.

The farmer smiled. 'Oh that's Herbert. Poor little youth's mother won't have 'im at any price. Took a spite at him at birth though she thinks world of her other lamb.'

'Do you feed him, then?'

'Nay, I was going to put him with the pet lambs but I saw he was fendin' for himself. He pops from one ewe to t'other and gets a quick drink whenever he gets chance. I've never seen owt like it.'

'Only a week old and an independent spirit, eh?'

'That's about the size of it, Jim. I notice 'is

13

belly's full every mornin' so I reckon his ma must let him have a do during the night. She can't see him in the dark — it must be the look of him she can't stand.'

I watched the little creature for a moment. To me he seemed as full of knock-kneed charm as any of the others. Sheep were funny things.

I soon had the other leg out and once that obstruction was removed the lamb followed easily. He was a grotesque sight lying on the strawed grass, his enormous head dwarfing his body, but his ribs were heaving reassuringly and I knew the head would shrink back to normal as quickly as it had expanded. I had another search round inside the ewe but the uterus was empty.

'There's no more, Rob,' I said.

The farmer grunted. 'Aye, I thowt so, just a big single 'un. They're the ones that cause the trouble.'

Drying my arms, I watched Herbert. He had left my patient when she moved round to lick her lamb and he was moving speculatively among the other ewes. Some of them warned him off with a shake of the head but eventually he managed to sneak up on a big, wide-bodied sheep and pushed his head underneath her. Immediately she swung round and with a fierce upward butt of her hard skull she sent the little animal flying high in the air in a whirl of flailing legs. He landed with a thud on his back and as I hurried towards him he leaped to his feet and trotted away.

'Awd bitch!' shouted the farmer and as I

turned to him in some concern he shrugged. 'I know, poor little sod, it's rough, but I've got a feelin' he wants it this way rather than being in the pen with the pet lambs. Look at 'im now.'

Herbert, quite unabashed, was approaching another ewe and as she bent over her feeding trough he nipped underneath her and his tail went into action again. There was no doubt about it — that lamb had guts.

'Rob,' I said as he caught my second patient, 'why do you call him Herbert?'

'Well that's my youngest lad's name and that lamb's just like 'im the way he puts his head down and gets stuck in, fearless like.'

I put my hand into the second ewe. Here was a glorious mix up of three lambs; little heads, legs, a tail, all fighting their way towards the outside world and effectively stopping each other from moving an inch.

'She's been hanging about all morning and painin',' Rob said. 'I knew summat was wrong.'

Moving a hand carefully around the uterus I began the fascinating business of sorting out the tangle which is just about my favourite job in practice. I had to bring a head and two legs up together in order to deliver a lamb; but they had to belong to the same lamb or I was in trouble. It was a matter of tracing each leg back to see if it was hind or fore, to find if it joined the shoulder or disappeared into the depths.

After a few minutes I had a lamb assembled inside with his proper appendages but as I drew the legs into view the neck telescoped and the head slipped back; there was barely room for it to come through the pelvic bones along with the shoulders and I had to coax it through with a finger in the eye socket. This was groaningly painful as the bones squeezed my hand but only for a few seconds because the ewe gave a final strain and the little nose was visible. After that it was easy and I had him on the grass within seconds. The little creature gave a convulsive shake of his head and the farmer wiped him down quickly with straw before pushing him to his mother's head.

The ewe bent over him and began to lick his face and neck with little quick darts of her tongue; and she gave the deep chuckle of satisfaction that you hear from a sheep only at this time. The chuckling continued as I produced another pair of lambs from inside her, one of them hind end first, and, towelling my arms again, I watched her nosing round her triplets delightedly.

Soon they began to answer her with wavering high-pitched cries and as I drew my coat thankfully over my cold-reddened arms, lamb number one began to struggle to his knees; he couldn't quite make it to his feet and kept toppling on to his face but he knew where he was going, all right; he was headed for that udder with a singleness of purpose which would soon be satisfied.

Despite the wind cutting over the straw bales into my face I found myself grinning down at the scene; this was always the best part, the wonder that was always fresh, the miracle you couldn't explain.

★　★　★

I heard from Rob Benson again a few days later. It was a Sunday afternoon and his voice was strained, almost panic-stricken.

'Jim, I've had a dog in among me in-lamb ewes. There was some folk up here with a car about dinner time and my neighbour said they had an Alsatian and it was chasing the sheep all over the field. There's a hell of a mess — I tell you I'm frightened to look.'

'I'm on my way.' I dropped the receiver and hurried out to the car. I had a sinking dread of what would be waiting for me; the helpless animals lying with their throats torn, the terrifying lacerations of limbs and abdomen. I had seen it all before. The ones which didn't have to be slaughtered would need stitching and on the way I made a mental check of the stock of suture silk in the boot.

The in-lamb ewes were in a field by the roadside and my heart gave a quick thump as I looked over the wall; arms resting on the rough loose stones I gazed with sick dismay across the pasture. This was worse than I had feared. The long slope of turf was dotted with prostrate sheep — there must have been about fifty of them, motionless woolly mounds scattered at intervals on the green.

Rob was standing just inside the gate. He hardly looked at me. Just gestured with his head.

'Tell me what you think. I daren't go in there.'

I left him and began to walk among the stricken creatures, rolling them over, lifting their

17

legs, parting the fleece of their necks to examine them. Some were completely unconscious, others comatose; none of them could stand up. But as I worked my way up the field I felt a growing bewilderment. Finally I called back to the farmer.

'Rob, come over here. There's something very strange.'

'Look,' I said as the farmer approached hesitantly. 'There's not a drop of blood nor a wound anywhere and yet all the sheep are flat out. I can't understand it.'

Rob went over and gently raised a lolling head. 'Aye, you're right. What the hell's done it, then?'

At that moment I couldn't answer him, but a little bell was tinkling far away in the back of my mind. There was something familiar about that ewe the farmer had just handled. She was one of the few able to support herself on her chest and she was lying there, blank-eyed, oblivious of everything; but . . . that drunken nodding of the head, that watery nasal discharge . . . I had seen it before. I knelt down and as I put my face close to hers I heard a faint bubbling — almost a rattling — in her breathing. I knew then.

'It's calcium deficiency,' I cried and began to gallop down the slope towards the car.

Rob trotted alongside me. 'But what the 'ell? They get that after lambin', don't they?'

'Yes, usually,' I puffed. 'But sudden exertion and stress can bring it on.'

'Well ah never knew that,' panted Rob. 'How does it happen?'

I saved my breath. I wasn't going to start an

18

exposition on the effects of sudden derangement of the parathyroid. I was more concerned with wondering if I had enough calcium in the boot for fifty ewes. It was reassuring to see the long row of round tin caps peeping from their cardboard box; I must have filled up recently.

I injected the first ewe in the vein just to check my diagnosis — calcium works as quickly as that in sheep — and felt a quiet elation as the unconscious animal began to blink and tremble, then tried to struggle on to its chest.

'We'll inject the others under the skin,' I said. 'It'll save time.'

I began to work my way up the field. Rob pulled forward the fore leg of each sheep so that I could insert the needle under the convenient patch of unwoolled skin just behind the elbow; and by the time I was halfway up the slope the ones at the bottom were walking about and getting their heads into the food troughs and hay racks.

It was one of the most satisfying experiences of my working life. Not clever, but a magical transfiguration; from despair to hope, from death to life within minutes.

I was throwing the empty bottles into the boot when Rob spoke. He was looking wonderingly up at the last of the ewes getting to its feet at the far end of the field.

'Well, Jim, I'll tell you. I've never seen owt like that afore. But there's one thing bothers me.' He turned to me and his weathered features screwed up in puzzlement. 'Ah can understand how gettin' chased by a dog could affect some of

them ewes, but why should the whole bloody lot
go down?'

'Rob,' I said. 'I don't know.'

And, thirty years later, I still wonder. I still
don't know why the whole bloody lot went
down.

★　★　★

I thought Rob had enough to worry about at the
time, so I didn't point out to him that other
complications could be expected after the
Alsatian episode. I wasn't surprised when I had a
call to the Benson farm within days.

I met him again on the hillside with the same
wind whipping over the straw bale pens. The
lambs had been arriving in a torrent and the
noise was louder than ever. He led me to my
patient.

'There's one with a bellyful of dead lambs, I
reckon,' he said, pointing to a ewe with her head
drooping, ribs heaving. She stood quite motionless and made no attempt to move away when I
went up to her; this one was really sick and as
the stink of decomposition came up to me I
knew the farmer's diagnosis was right.

'Well I suppose it had to happen to one at least
after that chasing round,' I said. 'Let's see what
we can do, anyway.'

This kind of lambing is without charm but it
has to be done to save the ewe. The lambs were
putrid and distended with gas and I used a sharp
scalpel to skin the legs to the shoulders so that I
could remove them and deliver the little bodies

with the least discomfort to the mother. When I had finished, the ewe's head was almost touching the ground, she was panting rapidly and grating her teeth. I had nothing to offer her — no wriggling new creature for her to lick and revive her interest in life. What she needed was an injection of penicillin, but this was 1939 and the antibiotics were still a little way round the corner.

'Well I wouldn't give much for her,' Rob grunted. 'Is there owt more you can do?'

'Oh, I'll put some pessaries in her and give her an injection, but what she needs most is a lamb to look after. You know as well as I do that ewes in this condition usually give up if they've nothing to occupy them. You haven't a spare lamb to put on her, have you?'

'Not right now, I haven't. And it's now she needs it. Tomorrow'll be too late.'

Just at that moment a familiar figure wandered into view. It was Herbert, the unwanted lamb, easily recognizable as he prowled from sheep to sheep in search of nourishment.

'Hey, do you think she'd take that little chap?' I asked the farmer.

He looked doubtful. 'Well I don't know — he's a bit old. Nearly a fortnight and they like 'em newly born.'

'But it's worth a try isn't it? Why not try the old trick on her?'

Rob grinned. 'OK, we'll do that. There's nowt to lose. Anyway the little youth isn't much bigger than a new-born 'un. He hasn't grown as fast as his mates.' He took out his penknife and quickly

21

skinned one of the dead lambs, then he tied the skin over Herbert's back and round his jutting ribs.

'Poor little bugger, there's nowt on 'im,' he muttered. 'If this doesn't work he's going in with the pet lambs.'

When he had finished he set Herbert on the grass and the lamb, resolute little character that he was, bored straight in under the sick ewe and began to suck. It seemed he wasn't having much success because he gave the udder a few peremptory thumps with his hard little head; then his tail began to wiggle.

'She's lettin' him have a drop, any road,' Rob laughed.

Herbert was a type you couldn't ignore and the big sheep, sick as she was, just had to turn her head for a look at him. She sniffed along the tied-on skin in a non-committal way, then after a few seconds she gave a few quick licks and the merest beginning of the familiar deep chuckle.

I began to gather up my gear. 'I hope he makes it,' I said. 'Those two need each other.' As I left the pen Herbert, in his new jacket, was still working away.

★　★　★

For the next week I hardly seemed to have my coat on. The flood of sheep work was at its peak and I spent hours of every day with my arms in and out of buckets of hot water in all corners of the district — in the pens, in dark nooks in farm buildings or very often in the open fields,

22

because the farmers of those days didn't find anything disturbing in the sight of a vet kneeling in his shirt sleeves for an hour in the rain.

I had one more visit to Rob Benson's place. To a ewe with a prolapsed uterus after lambing — a job whose chief delight was comparing it with the sweat of replacing a uterus in a cow.

It was so beautifully easy. Rob rolled the animal on to her side then held her more or less upside down by tying a length of rope to her hind legs and passing it round her neck. In that position she couldn't strain and I disinfected the organ and pushed it back with the minimum of effort, gently inserting an arm at the finish to work it properly into place.

Afterwards the ewe trotted away unperturbed with her family to join the rapidly growing flock whose din was all around us.

'Look!' Rob cried. 'There's that awd ewe with Herbert. Over there on t'right — in the middle of that bunch.' They all looked the same to me but to Rob, like all shepherds, they were as different as people and he picked out these two effortlessly.

They were near the top of the field and as I wanted to have a close look at them we manoeuvred them into a corner. The ewe, fiercely possessive, stamped her foot at us as we approached, and Herbert, who had discarded his woolly jacket, held close to the flank of his new mother. He was, I noticed, faintly obese in appearance.

'You couldn't call him a runt now, Rob,' I said.

The farmer laughed. 'Nay, t'awd lass has a bag

23

like a cow and Herbert's gettin' the lot. By gaw, he's in clover is that little youth and I reckon he saved the ewe's life — she'd have pegged out all right, but she never looked back once he came along.'

I looked away, over the noisy pens, over the hundreds of sheep moving across the fields. I turned to the farmer. 'I'm afraid you've seen a lot of me lately, Rob. I hope this is the last visit.'

'Aye well it could be. We're getting well through now . . . but it's a hell of a time, lambin' isn't it?'

'It is that. Well I must be off — I'll leave you to it.' I turned and made my way down the hillside, my arms raw and chafing in my sleeves, my cheeks whipped by the eternal wind gusting over the grass. At the gate I stopped and gazed back at the wide landscape, ribbed and streaked by the last of the winter's snow, and at the dark grey banks of cloud riding across on the wind followed by lakes of brightest blue; and in seconds the fields and walls and woods burst into vivid life and I had to close my eyes against the sun's glare. As I stood there the distant uproar came faintly down to me, the tumultuous harmony from deepest bass to highest treble; demanding, anxious, angry, loving.

The sound of the sheep, the sound of spring.

3

'Them masticks,' said Mr Pickersgill judicially, 'is a proper bugger.'

I nodded my head in agreement that his mastitis problem was indeed giving cause for concern; and reflected at the same time that while most farmers would have been content with the local word 'felon' it was typical that Mr Pickersgill should make a determined if somewhat inaccurate attempt at the scientific term.

Sometimes he got very wide of the mark as one time long after this when Artificial Insemination or AI was gaining a foothold in the Dales he made my day by telling me he had a cow in calf to the ICI.

However he usually did better than this — most of his efforts were near misses or bore obvious evidence of their derivation — but I could never really fathom where he got the masticks. I did know that once he fastened on to an expression it never changed; mastitis had always been 'them masticks' with him and it always would be. And I knew, too, that nothing would ever stop him doggedly trying to be right.

Because Mr Pickersgill had what he considered to be a scholastic background. He was a man of about sixty and when in his teens he had attended a two week course of instruction for agricultural workers at Leeds University. This brief glimpse of the academic life had left an indelible impression on his mind, and it was as if the intimation of something deep and true behind the facts of his everyday work had kindled a flame in him which had illumined his subsequent life.

No capped and gowned don ever looked back to his years among the spires of Oxford with more nostalgia than did Mr Pickersgill to his fortnight at Leeds and his conversation was usually laced with references to a godlike Professor Malleson who had apparently been in charge of the course.

'Ah don't know what to make of it,' he continued. 'In ma college days I was allus told that you got a big swollen bag and dirty milk with them masticks but this must be another kind. Just little bits of flakes in the milk off and on — neither nowt nor something, but I'm right fed up with it, I'll tell you.'

I took a sip from the cup of tea which Mrs Pickersgill had placed in front of me on the kitchen table. 'Yes, it's very worrying the way it keeps going on and on. I'm sure there's a definite factor behind it all — I wish I could put my finger on it.'

But in fact I had a good idea what was behind it. I had happened in at the little byre late one afternoon when Mr Pickersgill and his daughter Olive were milking their ten cows. I had watched the two at work as they crouched under the row of roan and red backs and one thing was immediately obvious; while Olive drew the milk by almost imperceptible movements of her fingers and with a motionless wrist, her father

26

hauled away at the teats as though he was trying to ring in the new year.

This insight coupled with the fact that it was always the cows Mr Pickersgill milked that gave trouble was enough to convince me that the chronic mastitis was of traumatic origin.

But how to tell the farmer that he wasn't doing his job right and that the only solution was to learn a more gentle technique or let Olive take over all the milking?

It wouldn't be easy because Mr Pickersgill was an impressive man. I don't suppose he had a spare penny in the world but even as he sat there in the kitchen in his tattered, collarless flannel shirt and braces he looked, as always, like an industrial tycoon. You could imagine that massive head with its fleshy cheeks, noble brow and serene eyes looking out from the financial pages of *The Times*. Put him in a bowler and striped trousers and you'd have the perfect chairman of the board.

I was very chary of affronting such natural dignity and anyway, Mr Pickersgill was fundamentally a fine stocksman. His few cows, like all the animals of that fast-dying breed of small farmer, were fat and sleek and clean. You had to look after your beasts when they were your only source of income and somehow Mr Pickersgill had brought up a family by milk production eked out by selling a few pigs and the eggs from his wife's fifty hens.

I could never quite work out how they did it but they lived, and they lived graciously. All the family but Olive had married and left home but there was still a rich decorum and harmony in that house. The present scene was typical. The farmer expounding gravely, Mrs Pickersgill bustling about in the background, listening to him with quiet pride. Olive too, was happy. Though in her late thirties, she had no fears of spinsterhood because she had been assiduously courted for fifteen years by Charlie Hudson from the Darrowby fish shop and though Charlie was not a tempestuous suitor there was nothing flighty about him and he was confidently expected to pop the question over the next ten years or so.

Mr Pickersgill offered me another buttered scone and when I declined he cleared his throat a few times as though trying to find words. 'Mr Herriot,' he said at last, 'I don't like to tell anybody his job, but we've tried all your remedies for them masticks and we've still got trouble. Now when I studied under Professor Malleson I noted down a lot of good cures and I'd like to try this 'un. Have a look at it.'

He put his hand in his hip pocket and produced a yellowed slip of paper almost falling apart at the folds. 'It's an udder salve. Maybe if we gave the bags a good rub with it it'd do t'trick.'

I read the prescription in the fine copperplate writing. Camphor, eucalyptus, zinc oxide — a long list of the old familiar names. I couldn't help feeling a kind of affection for them but it was tempered by a growing disillusion. I was about to say that I didn't think rubbing anything on the udder would make the slightest difference when the farmer groaned loudly.

The action of reaching into his hip pocket had brought on a twinge of his lumbago and he sat very upright, grimacing with pain.

'This bloody old back of mine! By gaw, it does give me some stick, and doctor can't do nowt about it. I've had enough pills to make me rattle but ah get no relief.'

I'm not brilliant but I do get the odd blinding flash and I had one now.

'Mr Pickersgill,' I said solemnly, 'You've suffered from that lumbago ever since I've known you and I've just thought of something. I believe I know how to cure it.'

The farmer's eyes widened and he stared at me with a childlike trust in which there was no trace of scepticism. This could be expected, because just as people place more reliance on the words of knacker men and meal travellers than their vets' when their animals are concerned it was natural that they would believe the vet rather than their doctor with their own ailments.

'You know how to put me right?' he said faintly.

'I think so, and it has nothing to do with medicine. You'll have to stop milking.'

'Stop milking! What the 'ell . . . ?'

'Of course. Don't you see, it's sitting crouched on that little stool night and morning every day of the week that's doing it. You're a big chap and you've got to bend to get down there — I'm sure it's bad for you.'

Mr Pickersgill gazed into space, as though he had seen a vision. 'You really think . . . '

'Yes, I do. You ought to give it a try, anyway. Olive can do the milking. She's always saying she ought to do it all.'

'That's right, Dad,' Olive chimed in. 'I like milking, you know I do, and it's time you gave it up — you've done it ever since you were a lad.'

'Dang it, young man, I believe you're right! I'll pack it in, now — I've made my decision!' Mr Pickersgill threw up his fine head, looked imperiously around him and crashed his fist on the table as though he had just concluded a merger between two oil companies.

I stood up. 'Fine, fine. I'll take this prescription with me and make up the udder salve. It'll be ready for you tonight and I should start using it immediately.'

It was about a month later that I saw Mr Pickersgill. He was on a bicycle, pedalling majestically across the market place and he dismounted when he saw me.

'Now then, Mr Herriot,' he said, puffing slightly. 'I'm glad I've met you. I've been meaning to come and tell you that we don't have no flakes in the milk now. Ever since we started with t'salve they began to disappear and milk's as clear as it can be now.'

'Oh, great. And how's your lumbago?'

'Well I'll tell you, you've really capped it and I'm grateful. Ah've never milked since that day and I hardly get a twinge now.' He paused and smiled indulgently. 'You gave me some good advice for me back, but we had to go back to awd Professor Malleson to cure them masticks, didn't we?'

30

My next encounter with Mr Pickersgill was on the telephone.

'I'm speaking from the cossack,' he said in a subdued shout.

'From the what?'

'The cossack, the telephone cossack in t'village.'

'Yes, indeed,' I said, 'and what can I do for you?'

'I want you to come out as soon as possible, to treat a calf for semolina.'

'I beg your pardon?'

'I 'ave a calf with semolina.'

'Semolina?'

'Aye, that's right. A feller was on about it on t'wireless the other morning.'

'Oh! Ah yes, I see.' I too had heard a bit of the farming talk on Salmonella infection in calves. 'What makes you think you've got this trouble?'

'Well it's just like that feller said. Me calf's bleeding from the rectrum.'

'From the . . . ? Yes, yes, of course. Well I'd better have a look at him — I won't be long.'

The calf was pretty ill when I saw him and he did have rectal bleeding, but it wasn't like Salmonella.

'There's no diarrhoea, you see, Mr Pickersgill,' I said. 'In fact, he seems to be constipated. This is almost pure blood coming away from him. And he hasn't got a very high temperature.'

The farmer seemed a little disappointed. 'Dang, I thowt it was just same as that feller was

31

talking about. He said you could send samples off to the labrador.'

'Eh? To the what?'

'The investigation labrador — you know.'

'Oh yes, quite, but I don't think the lab would be of any help in this case.'

'Aye well, what's wrong with him, then? Is something the matter with his rectrum?'

'No, no,' I said. 'But there seems to be some obstruction high up his bowel which is causing this haemorrhage.' I looked at the little animal standing motionless with his back up. He was totally preoccupied with some internal discomfort and now and then he strained and grunted softly.

And of course I should have known straight away — it was so obvious. But I suppose we all have blind spells when we can't see what is pushed in front of our eyes, and for a few days I played around with that calf in a haze of ignorance, giving it this and that medicine which I'd rather not talk about.

But I was lucky. He recovered in spite of my treatment. It wasn't until Mr Pickersgill showed me the little roll of necrotic tissue which the calf had passed that the thing dawned on me.

I turned, shame-faced, to the farmer. 'This is a bit of dead bowel all telescoped together — an intussusception. It's usually a fatal condition but fortunately in this case the obstruction has sloughed away and your calf should be all right now.'

'What was it you called it?'

'An intussusception.'

Mr Pickersgill's lips moved tentatively and for a moment I thought he was going to have a shot at it. But he apparently decided against it. 'Oh,' he said. 'That's what it was, was it?'

'Yes, and it's difficult to say just what caused it.'

The farmer sniffed. 'I'll bet I know what was behind it. I always said this one 'ud be a weakly calf. When he was born he bled a lot from his biblical cord.'

* * *

Mr Pickersgill hadn't finished with me yet. It was only a week later that I heard him on the phone again.

'Get out here, quick. There's one of me pigs going bezique.'

'Bezique?' With an effort I put away from me a mental picture of two porkers facing each other over a green baize table. 'I'm afraid I don't quite . . .'

'Aye, ah gave him a dose of worm medicine and he started jumpin' about and rollin' on his back. I tell you he's going proper bezique.'

'Ah! Yes, yes I see, right, I'll be with you in a few minutes.'

The pig had quietened down a bit when I arrived but was still in considerable pain, getting up, lying down, trotting in spurts round the pen. I gave him half a grain of morphine hydrochloride as a sedative and within a few minutes he began to relax and finally curled up in the straw.

'Looks as though he's going to be all right,' I

said. 'But what's this worm medicine you gave him?'

Mr Pickersgill produced the bottle sheepishly.

'Bloke was coming round sellin' them. Said it would shift any worms you cared to name.'

'It nearly shifted your pig, didn't it?' I sniffed at the mixture. 'And no wonder. It smells almost like pure turpentine.'

'Turpentine! Well by gaw is that all it is? And bloke said it was summat new. Charged me an absorbent price for it too.'

I gave him back the bottle. 'Well never mind, I don't think there's any harm done, but I think the dustbin's the best place for that.'

As I was getting into my car I looked up at the farmer. 'You must be about sick of the sight of me. First the mastitis, then the calf and now your pig. You've had a bad run.'

Mr Pickersgill squared his shoulders and gazed at me with massive composure. Again I was conscious of the sheer presence of the man.

'Young feller,' he said. 'That don't bother me. Where there's stock there's trouble and ah know from experience that trouble allus comes in cyclones.'

4

I knew I shouldn't do it, but the old Drovers'
Road beckoned to me irresistibly. I ought to be
hurrying back to the surgery after my morning
call but the broad green path wound beguilingly
over the moor top between its crumbling walls
and almost before I knew, I was out of the car
and treading the wiry grass.

The wall skirted the hill's edge and as I looked
across and away to where Darrowby huddled far
below between its folding green fells the wind
thundered in my ears; but when I squatted in the
shelter of the grey stones the wind was only a
whisper and the spring sunshine hot on my face.
The best kind of sunshine — not heavy or
cloying but clear and bright and clean as you
find it down behind a wall in Yorkshire with the
wind singing over the top.

I slid lower till I was stretched on the turf,
gazing with half-closed eyes into the bright sky,
luxuriating in the sensation of being detached
from the world and its problems.

This form of self-indulgence had become part
of my life and still is; a reluctance to come down
from the high country; a penchant for stepping
out of the stream of life and loitering on the
brink for a few minutes as an uninvolved
spectator.

And it was easy to escape, lying up there quite
alone with no sound but the wind sighing and

gusting over the empty miles and, far up in the wide blue, the endless brave trilling of the larks.

Not that there was anything unpleasant about going back down the hill to Darrowby. I had worked there for two years now and Skeldale House had become home and the two bright minds in it my friends. It didn't bother me that both the brothers were cleverer than I was. Siegfried — unpredictable, explosive, generous; I had been lucky to have him as a boss. As a city bred youth trying to tell expert stock farmers how to treat their animals I had needed all his skill and guidance behind me. And Tristan; a rum lad as they said, but very sound. His humour and zest for life had lightened my days.

And all the time I was adding practical experience to my theory. The mass of facts I had learned at college were all coming to life, and there was the growing realization, deep and warm, that this was for me. There was nothing else I'd rather do.

It must have been fifteen minutes later when I finally rose, stretched pleasurably, took a last deep gulp of the crisp air and pottered slowly back to the car for the six mile journey back down the hill to Darrowby.

When I drew up by the railings with Siegfried's brass plate hanging lopsidedly by the fine Georgian doorway I looked up at the tall old house with the ivy swarming untidily over the weathered brick. The white paint on windows and doors was flaking and that ivy needed trimming but the whole place had style, a serene, unchangeable grace.

But I had other things on my mind at the moment. I went inside, stepping quietly over the coloured tiles which covered the floor of the long passage till I reached the long offshoot at the back of the house. And I felt, as I always did, subdued excitement as I breathed the smell of our trade which always hung there; ether, carbolic and pulv aromat. The latter was the spicy powder which we mixed with the cattle medicines to make them more palatable and it had a distinctive bouquet which even now can take me back thirty years with a single sniff.

And today the thrill was stronger than usual because my visit was of a surreptitious nature. I almost tiptoed along the last stretch of passage, dodged quickly round the corner and into the dispensary. Gingerly I opened the cupboard door at one end and pulled out a little drawer. I was pretty sure Siegfried had a spare hoof knife hidden away within and I had to suppress a cackle of triumph when I saw it lying there; almost brand new with a nicely turned gleaming blade and a polished wooden handle.

My hand was outstretched to remove it when a cry of anger exploded in my right ear.

'Caught in the act! Bloody red-handed, by God!' Siegfried, who had apparently shot up through the floorboards was breathing fire into my face.

The shock was so tremendous that the instrument dropped from my trembling fingers and I cowered back against a row of bottles of formalin bloat mixture.

'Oh hello, Siegfried,' I said with a ghastly

attempt at nonchalance. 'Just on my way to that horse of Thompson's. You know — the one with the pus in the foot. I seem to have mislaid my knife so I thought I'd borrow this one.'

'Thought you'd nick it, you mean! My spare hoof knife! By heaven, is nothing sacred, James?'

I smiled sheepishly. 'Oh you're wrong. I'd have given it back to you straight away.'

'A likely story!' Siegfried said with a bitter smile. 'I'd never have seen it again and you know damn well I wouldn't. Anyway, where's your own knife? You've left it on some farm, haven't you?'

'Well as a matter of fact I laid it down at Willie Denholm's place after I'd finished trimming his cow's overgrown foot and I must have forgotten to pick it up.' I gave a light laugh.

'But God help us, James, you're always forgetting to pick things up. And you're always making up the deficiency by purloining my equipment.' He stuck his chin out. 'Have you any idea how much all this is costing me?'

'Oh but I'm sure Mr Denholm will drop the knife in at the surgery the first time he's in town.'

Siegfried nodded gravely. 'He may, I'll admit that, he may. But on the other hand he might think it is the ideal tool for cutting up his plug tobacco. Remember when you left your calving overall at old Fred Dobson's place? The next time I saw it was six months later and Fred was wearing it. He said it was the best thing he'd ever found for stooking corn in wet weather.'

'Yes, I remember. I'm sorry about it all.' I fell silent, breathing in the pungency of the pulv aromat. Somebody had let a bagful burst on the floor and the smell was stronger than ever.

My employer kept his fiery gaze fixed on me for a few moments more then he shrugged his shoulders. 'Ah well, there's none of us perfect, James. And I'm sorry I shouted at you. But you know I'm deeply attached to that knife and this business of leaving things around is getting under my skin.' He took down a Winchester of his favourite colic draught and polished it with his handkerchief before replacing it carefully on its shelf. 'I tell you what, let's go and sit down for a few minutes and talk about this problem.'

We went back along the passage and as I followed him into the big sitting-room Tristan got up from his favourite chair and yawned deeply. His face looked as boyish and innocent as ever but the lines of exhaustion round his eyes and mouth told an eloquent story. Last night he had travelled with the darts team from the Lord Nelson and had taken part in a gruelling match against the Dog and Gun at Drayton. The contest had been followed by a pie and peas supper and the consumption of something like twelve pints of bitter a man. Tristan had crawled into bed at 3 AM and was clearly in a delicate condition.

'Ah, Tristan,' Siegfried said. 'I'm glad you're here because what I have to say concerns you just as much as James. It's about leaving instruments on farms and you're as guilty as he is.' (It must be remembered that before the Veterinary Surgeons' act of 1948 it was quite legal for students to treat cases and they regularly did so. Tristan in fact had done much sterling work when called on and was very popular with the farmers.)

'Now I mean this very seriously,' my employer said, leaning his elbow on the mantelpiece and looking from one of us to the other. 'You two are bringing me to the brink of ruin by losing expensive equipment. Some of it is returned but a lot of it is never seen again. What's the use of sending you to visits when you come back without your artery forceps or scissors or something else? The profit's gone, you see?'

We nodded silently.

'After all, there's nothing difficult about bringing your instruments away, is there? You may wonder why I never leave anything behind — well I can tell you it's just a matter of concentration. When I lay a thing down I always impress on my mind that I've got to lift it up again. That's all there is to it.'

The lecture over, he became very brisk. 'Right, let's get on. There's nothing much doing, James, so I'd like you to come with me to Kendall's of Brookside. He's got a few jobs including a cow with a tumour to remove. I don't know the details but we may have to cast her. You can go on to Thompson's later.' He turned to his brother. 'And you'd better come too, Tristan. I don't know if we'll need you but an extra man might come in handy.'

We made quite a procession as we trooped into the farm yard and Mr Kendall met us with his customary ebullience.

'Hello, 'ello, we've got plenty of man power

40

today, I see. We'll be able to tackle owt with this regiment.'

Mr Kendall had the reputation in the district of being a 'bit clever' and the phrase has a different meaning in Yorkshire from elsewhere. It meant he was something of a know-all; and the fact that he considered himself a wag and leg-puller of the first degree didn't endear him to his fellow farmers either.

I always felt he was a good-hearted man, but his conviction that he knew everything and had seen it all before made him a difficult man to impress.

'Well what d'you want to see first, Mr Farnon?' he asked. He was a thick-set little man with a round, smooth-skinned face and mischievous eyes.

'I believe you have a cow with a bad eye,' Siegfried said. 'Better begin with that.'

'Right squire,' the farmer cried, then he put his hand in his pocket. 'But before we start, here's something for you.' He pulled forth a stethoscope. 'You left it last time you were 'ere.'

There was a silence, then Siegfried grunted a word of thanks and grabbed it hastily from his hand.

Mr Kendall continued. 'And the time afore that you left your bloodless castrators. We did a swop over, didn't we? I gave you back the nippers and you left me the earphones.' He burst into a peal of laughter.

'Yes, yes, quite,' Siegfried snapped, glancing uneasily round at us, 'but we must be getting on. Where is . . . ?'

41

'You know lads,' chuckled the farmer, turning to us. 'Ah don't think I've ever known 'im come here without leaving summat.'

'Really?' said Tristan interestedly.

'Aye, if I'd wanted to keep 'em all I'd have had a drawerful by now.'

'Is that so?' I said.

'Aye it is, young man. And it's the same with all me neighbours. One feller said to me t'other day, 'He's a kind man is Mr Farnon — never calls without leavin' a souvenir.'' He threw back his head and laughed again.

We were enjoying the conversation but my employer was stalking up the byre. 'Where's this damn cow, Mr Kendall? We haven't got all day.'

The patient wasn't hard to find; a nice light roan cow which looked round at us carefully, one eye almost closed. From between the lashes a trickle of tears made a dark stain down the hair of the face, and there was an eloquent story of pain in the cautious movements of the quivering lids.

'There's something in there,' murmured Siegfried.

'Aye, ah know!' Mr Kendall always knew. 'She's got a flippin' great lump of chaff stuck on her eyeball but I can't get to it. Look here.' He grabbed the cow's nose with one hand and tried to prise the eyelids apart with the fingers of the other, but the third eyelid came across and the whole orbit rolled effortlessly out of sight leaving only a blank expanse of white sclera.

'There!' he cried. 'Nowt to see. You can't make her keep her eye still.'

'I can, though.' Siegfried turned to his brother. 'Tristan, get the chloroform muzzle from the car. Look sharp!'

The young man was back in seconds and Siegfried quickly drew the canvas bag over the cow's face and buckled it behind the ears. From a bottle of spirit he produced a small pair of forceps of an unusual type with tiny jaws operated by a spring. He poised them just over the closed eye.

'James,' he said. 'Give her about an ounce.'

I dribbled the chloroform on to the sponge in the front of the muzzle. Nothing happened for a few moments while the animal took a few breaths then her eyes opened wide in surprise as the strange numbing vapour rolled into her lungs.

The whole area of the affected eye was displayed, with a broad golden piece of chaff splayed out across the dark cornea. I only had a glimpse of it before Siegfried's little forceps had seized it and whisked it away.

'Squeeze in some of that ointment, Tristan,' said my employer. 'And get the muzzle off, James, before she starts to rock.'

With the bag away from her face and the tormenting little object gone from her eye the cow looked around her, vastly relieved. The whole thing had taken only a minute or two and was as slick a little exhibition as you'd wish to see, but Mr Kendall didn't seem to think a great deal of it.

'Aye right,' he grunted. 'Let's get on with t'next job.'

As we went down the byre I looked out and saw a horse being led across the yard. Siegfried pointed to it.

'Is that the gelding I operated on for fistulous withers?' he asked.

'That's the one.' The farmer's voice was airy.

We went out and Siegfried ran his hand over the horse's shoulders. The broad fibrous scar over the withers was all that was left of the discharging, stinking sinus of a few weeks back. Healing was perfect. These cases were desperately difficult to treat and I remembered my boss cutting and chiselling at the mass of necrotic tissue, curetting deeply till only healthy flesh and bone remained. His efforts had been rewarded; it was a brilliant success.

Siegfried gave the gelding a final pat on the neck. 'That's done rather well.'

Mr Kendall shrugged and turned back towards the byre. 'Aye, not so bad, I suppose.' But he really wasn't impressed.

The cow with the tumour was standing just inside the door. The growth was in the perineal region, a smooth round object like an apple projecting from the animal's rear end, clearly visible an inch to the right of the tail.

Mr Kendall was in full cry again. 'Now we'll see what you're made of. How are you chaps going to get that thing off, eh? It's a big 'un — you'll need a carving knife or a hack saw for t'job. And are you goin' to put her to sleep or tie her up or what?' He grinned and his bright little eyes darted at each of us in turn.

Siegfried reached out and grasped the tumour,

feeling round the base with his fingers. 'Hmm
. . . yes . . . hmm . . . bring me some soap and
water and a towel, will you please?'

'I have it just outside t'door.' The farmer
scuttled into the yard and back again with the
bucket.

'Thank you very much,' Siegfried said. He
washed his hands and gave them a leisurely
towelling. 'Now I believe you have another case
to see. A scouring calf, wasn't it?'

The farmer's eyes widened. 'Yes, I 'ave. But
how about getting this big lump off the cow
first?'

Siegfried folded the towel and hung it over the
half door. 'Oh, I've removed the tumour,' he said
quietly.

'What's that?' Mr Kendall stared at the cow's
backside. We all stared at it. And there was no
doubt about it — the growth was gone. And
there was another funny thing — there wasn't
even a scar or mark remaining. I was standing
quite close to the animal and I could see exactly
to a fraction of an inch where that big ugly
projection had been; and there was nothing, not
a drop of blood, nothing.

'Aye,' Mr Kendall said irresolutely. 'You've er
. . . you've removed . . . you've removed it, aye,
that's right,' The smile had vanished from his
face and his entire personality seemed suddenly
deflated. Being a man who knew everything and
was surprised by nothing he was unable to say,
'When the devil did you do it? And how? And
what on earth have you done with it?' He had to
maintain face at all costs, but he was rattled. He

darted little glances around the byre, along the channel. The cow was standing in a clean-swept stall with no straw and there was nothing lying on the floor there or anywhere. Casually, as though by accident, he pushed a milking stool to one side with his foot — still nothing.

'Well now, perhaps we can see the calf.' Siegfried began to move away.

Mr Kendall nodded. 'Yes . . . yes . . . the calf. He's in t'corner there. I'll just lift bucket first.'

It was a blatant excuse. He went over to the bucket and as he passed behind the cow he whipped out his spectacles, jammed them on his nose and directed a piercing glare at the cow's bottom. He only took an instant because he didn't want to show undue concern, but when he turned back towards us his face registered utter despair and he put his spectacles away with a weary gesture of defeat.

As he approached I turned and brushed against my employer.

'Where the hell is it?' I hissed.

'Up my sleeve,' murmured Siegfried without moving his lips or changing expression.

'What . . . ?' I began, but Siegfried was climbing over a gate into the makeshift pen where the calf was cornered.

He was in expansive mood as he examined the little creature and injected it. He kept up a steady flow of light conversation and Mr Kendall, showing great character, managed to get his smile back on and answer back. But his preoccupied manner, the tortured eyes and the repeated incredulous glances back along the byre floor in the direction of the cow betrayed the fact that he was under immense strain.

Siegfried didn't hurry over the calf and when he had finished he lingered a while in the yard, chatting about the weather, the way the grass was springing, the price of fat bullocks.

Mr Kendall hung on grimly but by the time Siegfried finally waved farewell the farmer's eyes were popping and his face was an anguished mask. He bolted back into the byre and as the car backed round I could see him bent double with his glasses on again, peering into the corners.

'Poor fellow,' I said. 'He's still looking for that thing. And for God's sake where is it, anyway?'

'I told you, didn't I?' Siegfried removed one arm from the wheel and shook it. A round fleshy ball rolled down into his hand.

I stared at it in amazement. 'But . . . I never saw you take it off . . . what happened?'

'I'll tell you.' My employer smiled indulgently. 'I was fingering it over to see how deeply it was attached when I felt it begin to move. The back of it was merely encapsulated by the skin and when I gave another squeeze it just popped out and shot up my sleeve. And after it had gone the lips of the skin sprang back together again so that you couldn't see where it had been. Extraordinary thing.'

Tristan reached over from the back seat. 'Give it to me,' he said. 'I'll take it back to college with me and get it sectioned. We'll find out what kind of tumour it is.'

His brother smiled. 'Yes, I expect they'll give it

some fancy name, but I'll always remember it as the only thing that shook Mr Kendall.'

'That was an interesting session in there,' I said. 'And I must say I admired the way you dealt with that eye, Siegfried. Very smooth indeed.'

'You're very kind, James,' my boss murmured. 'That was just one of my little tricks — and of course the forceps helped a lot.'

I nodded. 'Yes, wonderful little things. I've never seen anything like them. Where did you get them?'

'I picked them up on an instrument stall at the last Veterinary Congress. They cost me a packet but they've been worth it. Here, let me show them to you.' He put his hand in his breast pocket, then his side pockets, and as he continued to rummage all over his person a look of sick dismay spread slowly across his face.

Finally he abandoned the search, cleared his throat and fixed his eyes on the road ahead.

'I'll er . . . I'll show you them some other time, James,' he said huskily.

I didn't say anything but I knew and Siegfried knew and Tristan knew.

He'd left them on the farm.

5

'Well, it's a good sign.' Tristan reluctantly expelled a lungful of Woodbine smoke and looked at me with wide, encouraging eyes.

'You think so?' I said doubtfully.

Tristan nodded. 'Sure of it. Helen just rang you up, did she?'

'Yes, out of the blue. I haven't seen her since I took her to the pictures that night and it's been hectic ever since with the lambing — and suddenly there she was asking me to tea on Sunday.'

'I like the sound of it,' Tristan said. 'But of course you don't want to get the idea you're home and dry or anything like that. You know there are others in the field?'

'Hell, yes, I suppose I'm one of a crowd.'

'Not exactly, but Helen Alderson is really something. Not just a looker but . . . mm-mm, very nice. There's a touch of class about that girl.'

'Oh I know, I know. There's bound to be a mob of blokes after her. Like young Richard Edmundson — I hear he's very well placed.'

'That's right,' Tristan said. 'Old friends of the family, big farmers, rolling in brass. I understand old man Alderson fancies Richard strongly as a son-in-law.'

I dug my hands into my pockets. 'Can't blame him. A ragged-arsed young vet isn't much competition.'

'Well, don't be gloomy, old lad, you've made a bit of progress, haven't you?'

'In a way,' I said with a wry smile. 'I've taken her out twice — to a dinner dance which wasn't on and to a cinema showing the wrong film. A dead loss the first time and not much better the second. I just don't seem to have any luck there — something goes wrong every time. Maybe this invitation is just a polite gesture — returning hospitality or something like that.'

'Nonsense!' Tristan laughed and patted me on the shoulder. 'This is the beginning of better things. You'll see — nothing will go wrong this time.'

★　★　★

And on Sunday afternoon as I got out of the car to open the gate to Heston Grange it did seem as if all was right with the world. The rough track snaked down from the gate through the fields to Helen's home slumbering in the sunshine by the curving river, and the grey-stoned old building was like a restful haven against the stark backcloth of the fells beyond.

I leaned on the gate for a moment, breathing in the sweet air. There had been a change during the last week; the harsh winds had dropped, everything had softened and greened and the warming land gave off its scents. On the lower slopes of the fell, in the shade of the pine woods, a pale mist of bluebells drifted among the dead bronze of the bracken and their fragrance came up to me on the breeze.

I drove down the track among the cows relishing the tender young grass after their long winter in the byres and as I knocked on the farmhouse door I felt a surge of optimism and well-being. Helen's younger sister answered and it wasn't until I walked into the big flagged kitchen that I experienced a qualm. Maybe it was because it was so like that first disastrous time I had called for Helen; Mr Alderson was there by the fireside, deep in the *Farmer and Stock-Breeder* as before, while above his head the cows in the vast oil painting still paddled in the lake of startling blue under the shattered peaks. On the whitewashed wall the clock still tick-tocked inexorably.

Helen's father looked up over his spectacles just as he had done before. 'Good afternoon, young man, come and sit down.' And as I dropped into the chair opposite to him he looked at me uncertainly for a few seconds. 'It's a better day,' he murmured, then his eyes were drawn back irresistibly to the pages on his knee. As he bent his head and started to read again I gained the strong impression that he hadn't the slightest idea who I was.

It came back to me forcibly that there was a big difference in coming to a farm as a vet and visiting socially. I was often in farm kitchens on my rounds, washing my hands in the sink after kicking my boots off in the porch, chatting effortlessly to the farmer's wife about the sick beast. But here I was in my good suit sitting stiffly across from a silent little man whose daughter I had come to court. It wasn't the same at all.

I was relieved when Helen came in carrying a cake which she placed on the big table. This wasn't easy as the table was already loaded; ham and egg pies rubbing shoulders with snowy scones, a pickled tongue, cheek by jowl with a bowl of mixed salad, luscious-looking custard tarts jockeying for position with sausage rolls, tomato sandwiches, fairy cakes. In a clearing near the centre a vast trifle reared its cream-topped head. It was a real Yorkshire tea.

Helen came over to me. 'Hello, Jim, it's nice to see you — you're quite a stranger.' She smiled her slow, friendly smile.

'Hello, Helen. Yes, you know what lambing time's like. I hope things will ease up a bit now.'

'Well I hope so too. Hard work's all right up to a point but you need a break some time. Anyway, come and have some tea. Are you hungry?'

'I am now,' I said, gazing at the packed foodstuffs. Helen laughed. 'Well come on, sit in. Dad, leave your precious *Farmer and Stock-Breeder* and come over here. We were going to sit you in the dining-room, Jim, but Dad won't have his tea anywhere but in here, so that's all about it.'

I took my place along with Helen, young Tommy and Mary, her brother and sister, and Auntie Lucy, Mr Alderson's widowed sister who had recently come to live with the family. Mr Alderson groaned his way over the flags, collapsed on to a high-backed wooden chair and began to saw phlegmatically at the tongue.

As I accepted my laden plate I can't say I felt entirely at ease. In the course of my work I had eaten many meals in the homes of the hospitable Dalesmen and I had discovered that light chatter was not welcomed at table. The accepted thing, particularly among the more old-fashioned types, was to put the food away in silence and get back on the job, but maybe this was different. Sunday tea might be a more social occasion; I looked round the table, waiting for somebody to lead the way.

Helen spoke up. 'Jim's had a busy time among the sheep since we saw him last.'

'Oh yes?' Auntie Lucy put her head on one side and smiled. She was a little bird-like woman, very like her brother and the way she looked at me made me feel she was on my side.

The young people regarded me fixedly with twitching mouths. The only other time I had met them they had found me an object of some amusement and things didn't seem to have changed. Mr Alderson sprinkled some salt on a radish, conveyed it to his mouth and crunched it impassively.

'Did you have much twin lamb disease this time, Jim?' Helen asked, trying again.

'Quite a bit,' I replied brightly. 'Haven't had much luck with treatment, though. I tried dosing the ewes with glucose this year and I think it did a bit of good.'

Mr Alderson swallowed the last of his radish. 'I think nowt to glucose,' he grunted. 'I've had a go with it and I think nowt to it.'

'Really?' I said. 'Well now that's interesting. Yes . . . yes . . . quite.'

I buried myself in my salad for a spell before

offering a further contribution.

'There's been a lot of sudden deaths in the lambs,' I said. 'Seems to be more Pulpy Kidney about.'

'Fancy that,' said Auntie Lucy, smiling encouragingly.

'Yes,' I went on, getting into my stride. 'It's a good job we've got a vaccine against it now.'

'Wonderful things, those vaccines,' Helen chipped in. 'You'll soon be able to prevent a lot of the sheep diseases that way.' The conversation was warming up.

Mr Alderson finished his tongue and pushed his plate away. 'I think nowt to the vaccines. And those sudden deaths you're on about — they're caused by wool ball on t'stomach. Nowt to do wi' the kidneys.'

'Ah yes, wool ball eh? I see, wool ball.' I subsided and decided to concentrate on the food.

And it was worth concentrating on. As I worked my way through I was aware of a growing sense of wonder that Helen had probably baked the entire spread. It was when my teeth were sinking into a poem of a curd tart that I really began to appreciate the miracle that somebody of Helen's radiant attractiveness should be capable of this.

I looked across at her. She was a big girl, nothing like her little wisp of a father. She must have taken after her mother. Mrs Alderson had been dead for many years and I wondered if she had had that same wide, generous mouth that smiled so easily, those same warm blue eyes

54

under the soft mass of black-brown hair.

A spluttering from Tommy and Mary showed that they had been appreciatively observing me gawping at their sister.

'That's enough, you two,' Auntie Lucy reproved. 'Anyway you can go now, we're going to clear the table.'

Helen and she began to move the dishes to the scullery beyond the door while Mr Alderson and I returned to our chairs by the fireside.

The little man ushered me to mine with a vague wave of the hand. 'Here . . . take a seat, er . . . young man.'

A clattering issued from the kitchen as the washing-up began. We were alone.

Mr Alderson's hand strayed automatically towards his *Farmer and Stock-Breeder*, but he withdrew it after a single hunted glance in my direction and began to drum his fingers on the arm of the chair, whistling softly under his breath.

I groped desperately for an opening gambit but came up with nothing. The ticking of the clock boomed out into the silence. I was beginning to break out into a sweat when the little man cleared his throat.

'Pigs were a good trade on Monday,' he vouchsafed.

'They were, eh? Well, that's fine — jolly good.'

Mr Alderson nodded, fixed his gaze somewhere above my left shoulder and started drumming his fingers again. Once more the heavy silence blanketed us and the clock continued to hammer out its message.

After several years Mr Alderson stirred in his seat and gave a little cough. I looked at him eagerly.

'Store cattle were down, though,' he said.

'Ah, too bad, what a pity,' I babbled. 'But that's how it goes, I suppose, eh?'

Helen's father shrugged and we settled down again. This time I knew it was hopeless. My mind was a void and my companion had the defeated look of a man who has shot his conversational bolt. I lay back and studied the hams and sides of bacon hanging from their hooks in the ceiling, then I worked my way along the row of plates on the big oak dresser to a gaudy calendar from a cattle cake firm which dangled from a nail on the wall. I took a chance then and stole a glance at Mr Alderson out of the corner of my eye and my toes curled as I saw he had chosen that precise moment to have a sideways peep at me. We both looked away hurriedly.

By shifting round in my seat and craning my neck I was able to get a view of the other side of the kitchen where there was an old-fashioned roll top desk surmounted by a wartime picture of Mr Alderson looking very stern in the uniform of the Yorkshire Yeomanry, and I was proceeding along the wall from there when Helen opened the door and came quickly into the room.

'Dad,' she said, a little breathlessly. 'Stan's here. He says one of the cows is down with staggers.'

Her father jumped up in obvious relief. I think he was delighted he had a sick cow and I, too, felt like a released prisoner as I hurried out with him.

Stan, one of the cowmen, was waiting in the yard.

'She's at t'top of t'field, boss,' he said. 'I just spotted 'er when I went to get them in for milkin'.'

Mr Alderson looked at me questioningly and I nodded at him as I opened the car door.

'I've got the stuff with me,' I said. 'We'd better drive straight up.'

The three of us piled in and I set course to where I could see the stretched-out form of a cow near the wall in the top corner. My bottles and instruments rattled and clattered as we bumped over the rig and furrow.

This was something every vet gets used to in early summer; the urgent call to milk cows which have collapsed suddenly a week or two after being turned out to grass. The farmers called it grass staggers and, as its scientific name of hypomagesaemia implied, it was associated with lowered magnesium level in the blood. An alarming and highly fatal condition but fortunately curable by injection of magnesium in most cases.

Despite the seriousness of the occasion I couldn't repress a twinge of satisfaction. It had got me out of the house and it gave me a chance to prove myself by doing something useful. Helen's father and I hadn't established anything like a rapport as yet, but maybe when I gave his unconscious cow my magic injection and it leaped to its feet and walked away he might look at me in a different light. And it often happened that way; some of the cures were really dramatic.

'She's still alive, any road,' Stan said as we roared over the grass. 'I saw her legs move then.'

He was right, but as I pulled up and jumped from the car I felt a tingle of apprehension. Those legs were moving too much.

This was the kind that often died; the convulsive type. The animal, prone on her side, was pedalling frantically at the air with all four feet, her head stretched backwards, eyes staring, foam bubbling from her mouth. As I hurriedly unscrewed the cap from the bottle of magnesium lactate she stopped and went into a long, shuddering spasm, legs stiffly extended, eyes screwed tightly shut; then she relaxed and lay inert for a frightening few seconds before recommencing the wild thrashing with her legs.

My mouth had gone dry. This was a bad one. The strain on the heart during these spasms was enormous and each one could be her last.

I crouched by her side, my needle poised over the milk vein. My usual practice was to inject straight into the blood-stream to achieve the quickest possible effect, but in this case I hesitated. Any interference with the heart's action could kill this cow; best to play safe — I reached over and pushed the needle under the skin of the neck.

As the fluid ran in, bulging the subcutaneous tissues and starting a widening swelling under the roan-coloured hide, the cow went into another spasm. For an agonizing few seconds she lay there, the quivering limbs reaching desperately out at nothing, the eyes disappearing deep down under tight-twisted lids. Helplessly I watched her, my heart thudding, and this time as she came out of the rigor and started to move again it wasn't with the purposeful pedalling of before; it was an aimless laboured pawing and as even this grew weaker her eyes slowly opened and gazed outwards with a vacant stare.

I bent and touched the cornea with my finger, there was no response.

The farmer and cowman looked at me in silence as the animal gave a final jerk then lay still.

'I'm afraid she's dead, Mr Alderson,' I said.

The farmer nodded and his eyes moved slowly over the still form, over the graceful limbs, the fine dark roan flanks, the big, turgid udder that would give no more milk.

'I'm sorry,' I said. 'I'm afraid her heart must have given out before the magnesium had a chance to work.'

'It's a bloody shame,' grunted Stan. 'She was a right good cow, that 'un.'

Mr Alderson turned quietly back to the car. 'Aye well, these things happen,' he muttered.

We drove down the field to the house.

Inside, the work was over and the family was collected in the parlour. I sat with them for a while but my overriding emotion was an urgent desire to be elsewhere. Helen's father had been silent before but now he sat hunched miserably in an armchair taking no part in the conversation. I wondered whether he thought I had actually killed his cow. It certainly hadn't looked very good, the vet walking up to the sick animal, the quick injection and hey presto, dead. No, I had been blameless but it hadn't looked good.

On an impulse I jumped to my feet.

'Thank you very much for the lovely tea,' I said, 'but I really must be off. I'm on duty this evening.'

Helen came with me to the door. 'Well it's been nice seeing you again, Jim.' She paused and looked at me doubtfully. 'I wish you'd stop worrying about that cow. It's a pity but you couldn't help it. There was nothing you could do.'

'Thanks, Helen, I know. But it's a nasty smack for your father isn't it?'

She shrugged and smiled her kind smile. Helen was always kind.

Driving back through the pastures up to the farm gate I could see the motionless body of my patient with her companions sniffing around her curiously in the gentle evening sunshine. Any time now the knacker man would be along to winch the carcase on to his wagon. It was the grim epilogue to every vet's failure.

I closed the gate behind me and looked back at Heston Grange. I had thought everything would be all right this time but it hadn't worked out that way.

The jinx was still on.

6

'Monday morning disease' they used to call it. The almost unbelievably gross thickening of the hind limb in cart horses which had stood in the stable over the weekend. It seemed that the sudden suspension of their normal work and exercise produced the massive lymphangitis and swelling which gave many a farmer a nasty jolt right at the beginning of the week.

But it was Wednesday evening now and Mr Crump's big Shire gelding was greatly improved.

'That leg's less than half the size it was,' I said, running my hand over the inside of the hock, feeling the remains of the oedema pitting under my fingers. 'I can see you've put in some hard work here.'

'Aye, ah did as you said.' Mr Crump's reply was typically laconic, but I knew he must have spent hours fomenting and massaging the limb and forcibly exercising the horse as I had told him when I gave the arecoline injection on Monday.

I began to fill the syringe for a repeat injection. 'He's having no corn, is he?'

'Nay, nowt but bran.'

'That's fine. I think he'll be back to normal in a day or two if you keep up the treatment.'

The farmer grunted and no sign of approval showed in the big, purple-red face with its perpetually surprised expression. But I knew he was pleased all right; he was fond of the horse and had been unable to hide his concern at the animal's pain and distress on my first visit.

I went into the house to wash my hands and Mr Crump led the way into the kitchen, his big frame lumbering clumsily ahead of me. He proffered soap and towel, in his slow-moving way and stood back in silence as I leaned over the long shallow sink of brown earthenware.

As I dried my hands he cleared his throat and spoke hesitantly. 'Would you like a drink of ma wine?'

Before I could answer, Mrs Crump came bustling through from an inner room. She was pulling on her hat and behind her her teenage son and daughter followed, dressed ready to go out.

'Oh Albert, stop it!' she snapped, looking up at her husband. 'Mr Herriot doesn't want your wine. I wish you wouldn't pester people so with it!'

The boy grinned. 'Dad and his wine, he's always looking for a victim.' His sister joined in the general laughter and I had an uncomfortable feeling that Mr Crump was the odd man out in his own home.

'We're going down t'village institute to see a school play, Mr Herriot,' the wife said briskly. 'We're late now so we must be off.' She hurried away with her children, leaving the big man looking after her sheepishly.

There was a silence while I finished drying my hands, then I turned to the farmer. 'Well, how about that drink, Mr Crump?'

He hesitated for a moment and the surprised look deepened. 'Would you . . . you'd really like to try some?'

'I'd love to. I haven't had my evening meal yet — I could just do with an aperitif.'

'Right, I'll be back in a minute.' He disappeared into the large pantry at the end of the kitchen and came back with a bottle of amber liquid and glasses.

'This is ma rhubarb,' he said, tipping out two good measures.

I took a sip and then a good swallow, and gasped as the liquid blazed a fiery trail down to my stomach.

'It's strong stuff,' I said a little breathlessly, 'but the taste is very pleasant. Very pleasant indeed.'

Mr Crump watched approvingly as I took another drink. 'Aye, it's just right. Nearly two years old.'

I drained the glass and this time the wine didn't burn so much on its way down but seemed to wash around the walls of my empty stomach and send glowing tendrils creeping along my limbs.

'Delicious,' I said. 'Absolutely delicious.'

The farmer expanded visibly. He refilled the glasses and watched with rapt attention as I drank. When we had finished the second glass he jumped to his feet.

'Now for a change I want you to try summat different.' He almost trotted to the pantry and produced another bottle, this time of colourless fluid. 'Elderflower,' he said, panting slightly.

When I tasted it I was amazed at the delicate flavour, the bubbles sparkling and dancing on my tongue.

'Gosh, this is terrific! It's just like champagne. You know, you really have a gift — I never thought home-made wines could taste like this.'

Mr Crump stared at me for a moment then one corner of his mouth began to twitch and incredibly a shy smile spread slowly over his face. 'You're about fust I've heard say that. You'd think I was trying to poison folks when I offer them ma wine — they always shy off but they can sup plenty of beer and whisky.'

'Well they don't know what they're missing, Mr Crump.' I watched while the farmer replenished my glass. 'I wouldn't have believed you could make stuff as good as this at home.' I sipped appreciatively at the elderflower. It still tasted like champagne.

I hadn't got more than halfway down the glass before Mr Crump was clattering and clinking inside the pantry again. He emerged with a bottle with contents of a deep blood red. 'Try that,' he gasped.

I was beginning to feel like a professional taster and rolled the first mouthful around my mouth with eyes half closed. 'Mm, mm, yes. Just like an excellent port, but there's something else here — a fruitiness in the background — something familiar about it — it's . . . it's . . . '

'Blackberry!' shouted Mr Crump triumphantly. 'One of t'best I've done. Made it two back-ends since — it were a right good year for it.'

Leaning back in the chair I took another drink of the rich, dark wine; it was round-flavoured, warming, and behind it there was always the elusive hint of the brambles. I could almost see the heavy-hanging clusters of berries glistening black and succulent in the autumn sunshine. The mellowness of the image matched my mood which was becoming more expansive by the minute and I looked round with leisurely appreciation at the rough comfort of the farmhouse kitchen; at the hams and sides of bacon hanging from their hooks in the ceiling, and at my host sitting across the table, watching me eagerly. He was, I noticed for the first time, still wearing his cap.

'You know,' I said, holding the glass high and studying its ruby depths against the light. 'I can't make up my mind which of your wines I like best. They're all excellent and yet so different.'

Mr Crump, too, had relaxed. He threw back his head and laughed delightedly before hurriedly refilling both of our tumblers. 'But you haven't started yet. Ah've got dozens of bottles in there — all different. You must try a few more.' He shambled again over to the pantry and this time when he reappeared he was weighed down by an armful of bottles of differing shapes and colours.

What a charming man he was, I thought. How wrong I had been in my previous assessment of him; it had been so easy to put him down as lumpish and unemotional but as I looked at him now his face was alight with friendship, hospitality, understanding. He had cast off his inhibitions and as he sat down surrounded by the latest batch he began to talk rapidly and fluently about wines and wine making.

Wide-eyed and impassioned he ranged at length over the niceties of fermentation and sedimentation, of flavour and bouquet. He dealt learnedly with the relative merits of Chambertin and Nuits St George, Montrachet and Chablis. Enthusiasts are appealing but a fanatic is irresistible and I sat spellbound while Mr Crump pushed endless samples of his craft in front of me, mixing and adjusting expertly.

'How did you find that 'un?'

'Very nice . . . '

'But sweet, maybe?'

'Well, perhaps . . . '

'Right, try some of this with it.' The meticulous addition of a few drops of nameless liquid from the packed rows of bottles. 'How's that?'

'Marvellous!'

'Now this 'un. Perhaps a bit sharpish, eh?'

'Possibly . . . yes . . . '

Again the tender trickling of a few mysterious droplets into my drink and again the anxious enquiry.

'Is that better?'

'Just right.'

The big man drank with me, glass by glass. We tried parsnip and dandelion, cowslip and parsley, clover, gooseberry, beetroot and crab apple. Incredibly, we had some stuff made from turnips which was so exquisite that I insisted on a refill.

Everything gradually slowed down as we sat there. Time slowed down till it was finally meaningless. Mr Crump and I slowed down and our speech and actions became more and more deliberate. The farmer's visits to the pantry developed into laboured, unsteady affairs; sometimes he took a round-about route to reach the door and on one occasion there was a tremendous crash from within and I feared he had fallen among his bottles. But I couldn't be bothered to get up to see and in due course he reappeared, apparently unharmed.

It was around nine o'clock that I heard the soft knocking on the outer door. I ignored it as I didn't want to interrupt Mr Crump who was in the middle of a deep exposition.

'Thish,' he was saying, leaning close to me, and tapping a bulbous flagon with his forefinger. 'Thish is, in my 'pinion, comp'rable to a fine Moselle. Made it lash year and would 'predate it if you'd tell me what you think.' He bent low over the glass, blinking, heavy-eyed as he poured.

'Now then, wha' d'you say? Ish it or ishn't it?'

I took a gulp and paused for a moment. It all tasted the same now and I had never drunk Moselle anyway, but I nodded and hiccuped solemnly in reply.

The farmer rested a friendly hand on my shoulder and was about to make a further speech when he, too, heard the knocking. He made his way across the floor with some difficulty and opened the door. A young lad was standing there and I heard a few muttered words.

'We 'ave a cow on calving and we phoned

surgery and they said vitnery might still be here.'

Mr Crump turned to face me. 'It's the Bamfords of Holly Bush. They wan' you to go there — jush a mile along t'road.'

'Right,' I heaved myself to my feet then gripped the table tightly as the familiar objects of the room began to whirl rapidly around me. When they came to rest Mr Crump appeared to be standing at the head of a fairly steep slope. The kitchen floor had seemed perfectly level when I had come in but now it was all I could do to fight my way up the gradient.

When I reached the door Mr Crump was staring owlishly into the darkness.

''Sraining,' he said! ''Sraining like 'ell.'

I peered out at the steady beat of the dark water on the cobbles of the yard, but my car was just a few yards away and I was about to set out when the farmer caught my arm.

'Jus' minute, can't go out like that.' He held up a finger then went over and groped about in a drawer. At length he produced a tweed cap which he offered me with great dignity.

I never wore anything on my head whatever the weather but I was deeply touched and wrung my companion's hand in silence. It was understandable that a man like Mr Crump who wore his cap at all times, indoors and out, would recoil in horror from the idea of anybody venturing uncovered into the rain.

The tweed cap which I now put on was the biggest I had ever seen; a great round flat pancake of a thing which even at that moment I felt would keep not only my head but my

68

shoulders and entire body dry in the heaviest downpour.

I took my leave of Mr Crump with reluctance and as I settled in the seat of the car trying to remember where first gear was situated I could see his bulky form silhouetted against the light from the kitchen; he was waving his hand with gentle benevolence and it struck me as I at length drove away what a deep and wonderful friendship had been forged that night.

Driving at walking pace along the dark narrow road, my nose almost touching the windscreen, I was conscious of some unusual sensations. My mouth and lips felt abnormally sticky as though I had been drinking liquid glue instead of wine, my breath seemed to be whistling in my nostrils like a strong wind blowing under a door, and I was having difficulty focusing my eyes. Fortunately I met only one car and as it approached and flashed past in the other direction I was muzzily surprised by the fact that it had two complete sets of headlights which kept merging into each other and drawing apart again.

In the yard at Holly Bush I got out of the car, nodded to the shadowy group of figures standing there, fumbled my bottle of antiseptic and calving ropes from the boot and marched determinedly into the byre. One of the men held an oil lamp over a cow lying on a deep bed of straw in one of the standings; from the vulva a calf's foot protruded a few inches and as the cow strained a little muzzle showed momentarily then disappeared as she relaxed.

Far away inside me a stone cold sober

veterinary surgeon murmured: 'Only a leg back and a big roomy cow. Shouldn't be much trouble.' I turned and looked at the Bamfords for the first time. I hadn't met them before but it was easy to classify them; simple, kindly, anxious-to-please people — two middle-aged men, probably brothers, and two young men who would be the sons of one or the other. They were all staring at me in the dim light, their eyes expectant, their mouths slightly open as though ready to smile or laugh if given half a chance.

I squared my shoulders, took a deep breath and said in a loud voice: 'Would you please bring me a bucket of hot water, some soap and a towel.' Or at least that's what I meant to say, because what actually issued from my lips was a torrent of something that sounded like Swahili. The Bamfords, poised, ready to spring into action to do my bidding, looked at me blankly. I cleared my throat, swallowed, took a few seconds' rest and tried again. I cleared my throat, swallowed, another volley of gibberish echoing uselessly round the cow house.

Clearly I had a problem. It was essential to communicate in some way, particularly since these people didn't know me and were waiting for some action. I suppose I must have appeared a strange and enigmatic figure standing there, straight and solemn, surmounted and dominated by a vast cap. But through the mists a flash of insight showed me where I was going wrong. It was over-confidence. It wasn't a bit of good trying to speak loudly like that. I tried again in the faintest of whispers.

70

'Could I have a bucket of hot water, some soap and a towel, please.' It came out beautifully though the oldest Mr Bamford didn't quite get it first time. He came close, cupped an ear with his hand and watched my lips intently. Then he nodded eagerly in comprehension, held up a forefinger at me, tiptoed across the floor like a tight-rope walker to one of the sons and whispered in his ear. The young man turned and crept out noiselessly, closing the door behind him with the utmost care; he was back in less than a minute, padding over the cobbles daintily in his heavy boots and placing the bucket gingerly in front of me.

I managed to remove my jacket, tie and shirt quite efficiently and they were taken from me in silence and hung upon nails by the Bamfords who were moving around as though in church. I thought I was doing fine till I started to wash my arms. The soap kept shooting from my arms, slithering into the dung channel, disappearing into the dark corners of the byre with the Bamfords in hot pursuit. It was worse still when I tried to work up to the top of my arms. The soap flew over my shoulders like a live thing, at times cannoning off the walls, at others gliding down my back. The farmers never knew where the next shot was going and they took on the appearance of a really sharp fielding side crouching around me with arms outstretched waiting for a catch.

However I did finally work up a lather and was ready to start, but the cow refused firmly to get to her feet, so I had to stretch out behind her, face down on the unyielding cobbles. It wasn't till I got down there that I felt the great cap dropping over my ears; I must have put it on again after removing my shirt though it was difficult to see what purpose it might serve.

Inserting a hand gently into the vagina I pushed along the calf's neck, hoping to come upon a flexed knee or even a foot, but I was disappointed; the leg really was right back, stretching from the shoulder away flat against the calf's side. Still, I would be all right — it just meant a longer reach.

And there was one reassuring feature; the calf was alive. As I lay, my face was almost touching the rear end of the cow and I had a close up of the nose which kept appearing every few seconds; it was good to see the little nostrils twitching as they sought the outside air. All I had to do was get that leg round.

But the snag was that as I reached forward the cow kept straining, squeezing my arm cruelly against her bony pelvis making me groan and roll about in agony for a few seconds till the pressure went off. Quite often in these crises my cap fell on to the floor and each time gentle hands replaced it immediately on my head.

At last the foot was in my hand — there would be no need for ropes this time — and I began to pull it round. It took me longer than I thought and it seemed to me that the calf was beginning to lose patience with me because when its head was forced out by the cow's contractions we were eye to eye and I fancied the little creature was giving me a disgusted 'For heaven's sake get on with it' look.

When the leg did come round it was with a rush and in an instant everything was laid as it should have been.

'Get hold of the feet,' I whispered to the Bamfords and after a hushed consultation they took up their places. In no time at all a fine heifer calf was wriggling on the cobbles shaking its head and snorting the placental fluid from its nostrils.

In response to my softly hissed instructions the farmers rubbed the little creature down with straw wisps and pulled it round for its mother to lick.

It was a happy ending to the most peaceful calving I have ever attended. Never a voice raised, everybody moving around on tiptoe. I got dressed in a cathedral silence, went out to the car, breathed a final goodnight and left with the Bamfords waving mutely.

★ ★ ★

To say I had a hangover next morning would be failing even to hint at the utter disintegration of my bodily economy and personality. Only somebody who had consumed two or three quarts of assorted home-made wines at a sitting could have an inkling of the quaking nausea, the raging inferno within, the jangling nerves, the black despairing outlook.

Tristan had seen me in the bathroom running the cold tap on my tongue and had intuitively administered a raw egg, aspirins and brandy which, as I came downstairs, lay in a cold, unmoving blob in my outraged stomach.

'What are you walking like that for, James?' asked Siegfried in what sounded like a bull's bellow as I came in on him at breakfast. 'You look as though you'd pee'd yourself.'

'Oh it's nothing much.' It was no good telling him I was treading warily across the carpet because I was convinced that if I let my heels down too suddenly it would jar my eyeballs from their sockets. 'I had a few glasses of Mr Crump's wine last night and it seems to have upset me.'

'A few glasses! You ought to be more careful — that stuff's dynamite. Could knock anybody over.' He crashed his cup into its saucer then began to clatter about with knife and fork as if trying to give a one man rendering of the Anvil Chorus. 'I hope you weren't any the worse to go to Bamford's.'

I listlessly crumbled some dry toast on my plate. 'Well I did the job all right, but I'd had a bit too much — no use denying it.'

Siegfried was in one of his encouraging moods. 'By God, James, those Bamfords are very strict Methodists. They're grand chaps but absolutely dead nuts against drink — if they thought you were under the influence of alcohol they'd never have you on the place again.' He ruthlessly bisected an egg yolk. 'I hope they didn't notice anything. Do you think they knew?'

'Oh maybe not. No, I shouldn't think so.' I closed my eyes and shivered as Siegfried pushed a forkful of sausage and fried bread into his

74

mouth and began to chew briskly. My mind went back to the gentle hands replacing the monstrous cap on my head and I groaned inwardly.

Those Bamfords knew all right. Oh yes, they knew.

7

The silvery-haired old gentleman with the pleasant face didn't look the type to be easily upset but his eyes glared at me angrily and his lips quivered with indignation.

'Mr Herriot,' he said. 'I have come to make a complaint. I strongly object to your callousness in subjecting my dog to unnecessary suffering.'

'Suffering? What suffering?' I was mystified.

'I think you know, Mr Herriot. I brought my dog in a few days ago. He was very lame and I am referring to your treatment on that occasion.'

I nodded. 'Yes, I remember it well . . . but where does the suffering come in?'

'Well, the poor animal is going around with his leg dangling and I have it on good authority that the bone is fractured and should have been put in plaster immediately.' The old gentleman stuck his chin out fiercely.

'All right, you can stop worrying,' I said. 'Your dog has a radial paralysis caused by a blow on the ribs and if you are patient and follow my treatment he'll gradually improve. In fact I think he'll recover completely.'

'But he trails his leg when he walks.'

'I know — that's typical, and to the layman it does give the appearance of a broken leg. But he shows no sign of pain, does he?'

'No, he seems quite happy, but this lady

76

seemed to be absolutely sure of her facts. She was adamant.'

'Lady?'

'Yes,' said the old gentleman. 'She is very clever with animals and she came round to see if she could help in my dog's convalescence. She brought some excellent condition powders with her.'

'Ah!' A blinding shaft pierced the fog in my mind. All was suddenly clear. 'It was Mrs Donovan, wasn't it?'

'Well . . . er, yes. That was her name.'

Old Mrs Donovan was a woman who really got around. No matter what was going on in Darrowby — Weddings, funerals, house-sales — you'd find the dumpy little figure and walnut face among the spectators, the darting, black-button eyes taking everything in. And always, on the end of its lead, her terrier dog.

When I say 'old', I'm only guessing, because she appeared ageless; she seemed to have been around a long time but she could have been anything between fifty-five and seventy-five. She certainly had the vitality of a young woman because she must have walked vast distances in her dedicated quest to keep abreast of events. Many people took an uncharitable view of her acute curiosity but whatever the motivation, her activities took her into almost every channel of life in the town. One of these channels was our veterinary practice.

Because Mrs Donovan, among her other widely ranging interests, was an animal doctor. In fact I think it would be safe to say that this

77

facet of her life transcended all the others.

She could talk at length on the ailments of small animals and she had a whole armoury of medicines and remedies at her command, her two specialities being her miracle-working condition powders and a dog shampoo,of unprecedented value for improving the coat. She had an uncanny ability to sniff out a sick animal and it was not uncommon when I was on my rounds to find Mrs Donovan's dark gipsy face poised intently over what I had thought was my patient while she administered calf's foot jelly or one of her own patent nostrums.

I suffered more than Siegfried because I took a more active part in the small animal side of our practice. I was anxious to develop this aspect and to improve my image in this field and Mrs Donovan didn't help at all. 'Young Mr Herriot,' she would confide to my clients, 'is all right with cattle and such like, but he don't know nothing about dogs and cats.'

And of course they believed her and had implicit faith in her. She had the irresistible mystic appeal of the amateur and on top of that there was her habit, particularly endearing in Darrowby, of never charging for her advice, her medicines, her long periods of diligent nursing.

Older folk in the town told how her husband, an Irish farm worker, had died many years ago and how he must have had a 'bit put away' because Mrs Donovan had apparently been able to indulge all her interests over the years without financial strain. Since she inhabited the streets of Darrowby all day and every day I often encountered her and she always smiled up at me sweetly and told me how she had been sitting up all night with Mrs So-and-so's dog that I'd been treating. She felt sure she'd be able to pull it through.

There was no smile on her face, however, on the day when she rushed into the surgery while Siegfried and I were having tea.

'Mr Herriot!' she gasped. 'Can you come? My little dog's been run over!'

I jumped up and ran out to the car with her. She sat in the passenger seat with her head bowed, her hands clasped tightly on her knees.

'He slipped his collar and ran in front of a car,' she murmured. 'He's lying in front of the school halfway up Cliffend Road. Please hurry.'

I was there within three minutes but as I bent over the dusty little body stretched on the pavement I knew there was nothing I could do. The fast-glazing eyes, the faint, gasping respirations, the ghastly pallor of the mucous membranes all told the same story.

'I'll take him back to the surgery and get some saline into him, Mrs Donovan,' I said. 'But I'm afraid he's had a massive internal haemorrhage. Did you see what happened exactly?'

She gulped. 'Yes, the wheel went right over him.'

Ruptured liver, for sure. I passed my hands under the little animal and began to lift him gently, but as I did so the breathing stopped and the eyes stared fixedly ahead.

Mrs Donovan sank to her knees and for a few moments she gently stroked the rough hair of the head and chest. 'He's dead, isn't he?' she whispered at last.

'I'm afraid he is,' I said.

She got slowly to her feet and stood bewilderedly among the little group of bystanders on the pavement. Her lips moved but she seemed unable to say any more.

I took her arm, led her over to the car and opened the door. 'Get in and sit down,' I said. 'I'll run you home. Leave everything to me.'

I wrapped the dog in my calving overall and laid him in the boot before driving away. It wasn't until we drew up outside Mrs Donovan's house that she began to weep silently. I sat there without speaking till she had finished. Then she wiped her eyes and turned to me.

'Do you think he suffered at all?'

'I'm certain he didn't. It was all so quick — he wouldn't know a thing about it.'

She tried to smile. 'Poor little Rex, I don't know what I'm going to do without him. We've travelled a few miles together, you know.'

'Yes, you have. He had a wonderful life, Mrs Donovan. And let me give you a bit of advice — you must get another dog. You'd be lost without one.'

She shook her head. 'No, I couldn't. That little dog meant too much to me. I couldn't let another take his place.'

'Well I know that's how you feel just now but I wish you'd think about it. I don't want to seem callous — I tell everybody this when they lose an animal and I know it's good advice.'

'Mr Herriot, I'll never have another one.' She

shook her head again, very decisively. 'Rex was my faithful friend for many years and I just want to remember him. He's the last dog I'll ever have.'

★ ★ ★

I often saw Mrs Donovan around the town after this and I was glad to see she was still as active as ever, though she looked strangely incomplete without the little dog on its lead. But it must have been over a month before I had the chance to speak to her.

It was on the afternoon that Inspector Halliday of the RSPCA rang me.

'Mr Herriot,' he said, 'I'd like you to come and see an animal with me. A cruelty case.'

'Right, what is it?'

'A dog, and it's pretty grim. A dreadful case of neglect.' He gave me the name of a row of old brick cottages down by the river and said he'd meet me there.

Halliday was waiting for me, smart and business-like in his dark uniform, as I pulled up in the back lane behind the houses. He was a big, blond man with cheerful blue eyes but he didn't smile as he came over to the car.

'He's in here,' he said, and led the way towards one of the doors in the long, crumbling wall. A few curious people were hanging around and with a feeling of inevitability I recognized a gnome-like brown face. Trust Mrs Donovan, I thought, to be among those present at a time like this.

We went through the door into the long garden. I had found that even the lowliest dwellings in Darrowby had long strips of land at the back as though the builders had taken it for granted that the country people who were going to live in them would want to occupy themselves with the pursuits of the soil; with vegetable and fruit growing, even stock-keeping in a small way. You usually found a pig there, a few hens, often pretty beds of flowers.

But this garden was a wilderness. A chilling air of desolation hung over the few gnarled apple and plum trees standing among a tangle of rank grass as though the place had been forsaken by all living creatures.

Halliday went over to a ramshackle wooden shed with peeling paint and a rusted corrugated iron roof. He produced a key, unlocked the padlock and dragged the door partly open. There was no window and it wasn't easy to identify the jumble inside; broken gardening tools, an ancient mangle, rows of flower pots and partly-used paint tins; And right at the back, a dog sitting quietly.

I didn't notice him immediately because of the gloom and because the smell in the shed started me coughing, but as I drew closer I saw that he was a big animal, sitting very upright, his collar secured by a chain to a ring in the wall. I had seen some thin dogs but this advanced emaciation reminded me of my text books on anatomy; nowhere else did the bones of pelvis, face and rib cage stand out with such horrifying clarity. A deep, smoothed out hollow in the earth floor showed where he had lain, moved about, in fact lived for a very long time.

The sight of the animal had a stupefying effect on me; I only half took in the rest of the scene — the filthy shreds of sacking scattered nearby, the bowl of scummy water.

'Look at his back end,' Halliday muttered.

I carefully raised the dog from his sitting position and realized that the stench in the place was not entirely due to the piles of excrement. The hindquarters were a welter of pressure sores which had turned gangrenous and strips of sloughing tissue hung down from them. There were similar sores along the sternum and ribs. The coat, which seemed to be a dull yellow, was matted and caked with dirt.

The Inspector spoke again. 'I don't think he's ever been out of here. He's only a young dog — about a year old — but I understand he's been in this shed since he was an eight-week-old pup. Somebody out in the lane heard a whimper or he'd never have been found.'

I felt a tightening of the throat and a sudden nausea which wasn't due to the smell. It was the thought of this patient animal sitting starved and forgotten in the darkness and filth for a year. I looked again at the dog and saw in his eyes only a calm trust. Some dogs would have barked their heads off and soon been discovered, some would have become terrified and vicious, but this was one of the totally undemanding kind, the kind which had complete faith in people and accepted all their actions without complaint. Just an occasional whimper perhaps as he sat interminably in the empty blackness which had been his world and at times wondered what it was all about.

'Well, Inspector, I hope you're going to throw the book at whoever's responsible,' I said.

Halliday grunted. 'Oh, there won't be much done. It's a case of diminished responsibility. The owner's definitely simple. Lives with an aged mother who hardly knows what's going on either. I've seen the fellow and it seems he threw in a bit of food when he felt like it and that's about all he did. They'll fine him and stop him keeping an animal in the future but nothing more than that.'

'I see.' I reached out and stroked the dog's head and he immediately responded by resting a paw on my wrist. There was a pathetic dignity about the way he held himself erect, the calm eyes regarding me, friendly and unafraid. 'Well, you'll let me know if you want me in court.'

'Of course, and thank you for coming along.' Halliday hesitated for a moment. 'And now I expect you'll want to put this poor thing out of his misery right away.'

I continued to run my hand over the head and ears while I thought for a moment. 'Yes . . . yes, I suppose so. We'd never find a home for him in this state. It's the kindest thing to do. Anyway, push the door wide open will you so that I can get a proper look at him.'

In the improved light I examined him more thoroughly. Perfect teeth, well-proportioned. limbs with a fringe of yellow hair. I put my stethoscope on his chest and as I listened to the slow, strong thudding of the heart the dog again put his paw on my hand.

I turned to Halliday, 'You know, Inspector, inside this bag of bones there's a lovely healthy Golden Retriever. I wish there was some way of letting him out.'

As I spoke I noticed there was more than one figure in the door opening. A pair of black pebble eyes were peering intently at the big dog from behind the Inspector's broad back. The other spectators had remained in the lane but Mrs Donovan's curiosity had been too much for her. I continued conversationally as though I hadn't seen her.

'You know, what this dog needs first of all is a good shampoo to clean up his matted coat.'

'Huh?' said Halliday.

'Yes. And then he wants a long course of some really strong condition powders.'

'What's that?' The Inspector looked startled.

'There's no doubt about it,' I said. 'It's the only hope for him, but where are you going to find such things? Really powerful enough, I mean.' I sighed and straightened up. 'Ah well, I suppose there's nothing else for it. I'd better put him to sleep right away. I'll get the things from my car.'

When I got back to the shed Mrs Donovan was already inside examining the dog despite the feeble remonstrances of the big man.

'Look!' she said excitedly, pointing to a name roughly scratched on the collar. 'His name's Roy.' She smiled up at me. 'It's a bit like Rex, isn't it, that name?'

'You know, Mrs Donovan, now you mention it, it is. It's very like Rex, the way it comes off your tongue.' I nodded seriously.

She stood silent for a few moments, obviously in the grip of a deep emotion, then she burst out.

'Can I have 'im? I can make him better, I know I can. Please, please let me have 'im!'

'Well I don't know,' I said. 'It's really up to the Inspector. You'll have to get his permission.'

Halliday looked at her in bewilderment, then he said: 'Excuse me, Madam,' and drew me to one side. We walked a few yards through the long grass and stopped under a tree.

'Mr Herriot,' he whispered, 'I don't know what's going on here, but I can't just pass over an animal in this condition to anybody who has a casual whim. The poor beggar's had one bad break already — I think it's enough. This woman doesn't look a suitable person . . .'

I held up a hand. 'Believe me, Inspector, you've nothing to worry about. She's a funny old stick but she's been sent from heaven today. If anybody in Darrowby can give this dog a new life it's her.'

Halliday still looked very doubtful. 'But I still don't get it. What was all that stuff about him needing shampoos and condition powders?'

'Oh never mind about that. I'll tell you some other time. What he needs is lots of good grub, care and affection and that's just what he'll get. You can take my word for it.'

'All right, you seem very sure.' Halliday looked at me for a second or two then turned and walked over to the eager little figure by the shed.

86

I had never before been deliberately on the look
out for Mrs Donovan: she had just cropped up
wherever I happened to be, but now I scanned
the streets of Darrowby anxiously day by day
without sighting her. I didn't like it when
Gobber Newhouse got drunk and drove his
bicycle determinedly through a barrier into a ten
foot hole where they were laying the new sewer
and Mrs Donovan was not in evidence among
the happy crowd who watched the council
workmen and two policemen trying to get him
out; and when she was nowhere to be seen when
they had to fetch the fire engine to the fish and
chip shop the night the fat burst, into flames I
became seriously worried.

Maybe I should have called round to see how
she was getting on with that dog. Certainly I had
trimmed off the necrotic tissue and dressed the
sores before she took him away, but perhaps he
needed something more than that. And yet at the
time I had felt a strong conviction that the main
thing was to get him out of there and clean him
and feed him and nature would do the rest. And
I had a lot of faith in Mrs Donovan — far more
than she had in me — when it came to animal
doctoring; it was hard to believe I'd been
completely wrong.

It must have been nearly three weeks and I
was on the point of calling at her home when I
noticed her stumping briskly along the far side of
the market place, peering closely into every shop
window exactly as before. The only difference

was that she had a big yellow dog on the end of the lead.

I turned the wheel and sent my car bumping over the cobbles till I was abreast of her. When she saw me getting out she stopped and smiled impishly but she didn't speak as I bent over Roy and examined him. He was still a skinny dog but he looked bright and happy, his wounds were healthy and granulating and there was not a speck of dirt in his coat or on his skin. I knew then what Mrs Donovan had been doing all this time; she had been washing and combing and teasing at that filthy tangle till she had finally conquered it.

As I straightened up she seized my wrist in a grip of surprising strength and looked up into my eyes.

'Now, Mr Herriot,' she said. 'Haven't I made a difference to this dog!'

'You've done wonders, Mrs Donovan,' I said. 'And you've been at him with that marvellous shampoo of yours, haven't you?'

She giggled and walked away and from that day I saw the two of them frequently, but at a distance, and something like two months went by before I had a chance to talk to her again. She was passing by the surgery as I was coming down the steps and again she grabbed my wrist.

'Mr Herriot,' she said, just as she had done before. 'Haven't I made a difference to this dog!'

I looked down at Roy with something akin to awe. He had grown and filled out and his coat, no longer yellow but a rich gold, lay in luxuriant shining swathes over the well-fleshed ribs and back. A new, brightly-studded collar glittered on his neck and his tail, beautifully fringed, fanned the air gently. He was now a Golden Retriever in full magnificence. As I stared at him he reared up, plunked his fore paws on my chest and looked into my face, and in his eyes I read plainly the same calm affection and trust I had seen back in that black, noisome shed.

'Mrs Donovan,' I said softly, 'he's the most beautiful dog in Yorkshire.' Then, because I knew she was waiting for it. 'It's those wonderful condition powders. Whatever do you put in them?'

'Ah, wouldn't you like to know!' She bridled and smiled up at me coquettishly and indeed she was nearer being kissed at that moment than for many years.

★　★　★

I suppose you could say that that was the start of Roy's second life. And as the years passed I often pondered on the beneficent providence which had decreed that an animal which had spent his first twelve months abandoned and unwanted, staring uncomprehendingly into that unchanging, stinking darkness, should be whisked in a moment into an existence of light and movement and love. Because I don't think any dog had it quite so good as Roy from then on.

His diet changed dramatically from odd bread crusts to best stewing steak and biscuit, meaty bones and a bowl of warm milk every evening. And he never missed a thing. Garden fêtes, school sports, evictions, gymkhanas — he'd be there. I was pleased to note that as time went on Mrs Donovan seemed to be clocking up an even greater daily mileage. Her expenditure on shoe leather must have been phenomenal, but of course it was absolute pie for Roy — a busy round in the morning, home for a meal then straight out again; it was all go.

Mrs Donovan didn't confine her activities to the town centre; there was a big stretch of common land down by the river where there were seats, and people used to take their dogs for a gallop and she liked to get down there fairly regularly to check on the latest developments on the domestic scene. I often saw Roy loping majestically over the grass among a pack of assorted canines, and when he wasn't doing that he was submitting to being stroked or patted or generally fussed over. He was handsome and he just liked people; it made him irresistible.

It was common knowledge that his mistress had bought a whole selection of brushes and combs of various sizes with which she laboured over his coat. Some people said she had a little brush for his teeth, too, and it might have been true, but he certainly wouldn't need his nails clipped — his life on the roads would keep them down.

Mrs Donovan, too, had her reward; she had a faithful companion by her side every hour of the day and night. But there was more to it than that; she had always had the compulsion to help and heal animals and the salvation of Roy was the high point of her life — a blazing triumph which never dimmed.

I know the memory of it was always fresh because many years later I was sitting on the sidelines at a cricket match and I saw the two of them; the old lady glancing keenly around her, Roy gazing placidly out at the field of play, apparently enjoying every ball. At the end of the match I watched them move away with the dispersing crowd; Roy would be about twelve then and heaven only knows how old Mrs Donovan must have been, but the big golden animal was trotting along effortlessly and his mistress, a little more bent perhaps and her head rather nearer the ground, was going very well.

When she saw me she came over and I felt the familiar tight grip on my wrist.

'Mr Herriot,' she said, and in the dark probing eyes the pride was still as warm, the triumph still as bursting new as if it had all happened yesterday.

'Mr Herriot, haven't I made a difference to this dog!'

8

'How would you like to officiate at Darrowby Show, James?' Siegfried threw the letter he had been reading on to the desk and turned to me.

'I don't mind, but I thought you always did it.'

'I do, but it says in that letter that they've changed the date this year and it happens I'm going to be away that weekend.'

'Oh well, fine. What do I have to do?'

Siegfried ran his eye down his list of calls. 'It's a sinecure, really. More a pleasant day out than anything else. You have to measure the ponies and be on call in case any animals are injured. That's about all. Oh and they want you to judge the Family Pets.'

'Family Pets?'

'Yes, they run a proper dog show but they have an expert judge for that. This is just a bit of fun — all kinds of pets. You've got to find a first, second and third.'

'Right,' I said. 'I think I should just about be able to manage that.'

'Splendid.' Siegfried tipped up the envelope in which the letter had come. 'Here are your car park and luncheon tickets for self and friend if you want to take somebody with you. Also your vet's badge. OK?'

* * *

The Saturday of the show brought the kind of weather that must have had the organizers purring with pleasure; a sky of wide, unsullied blue, hardly a whiff of wind and the kind of torrid, brazen sunshine you don't often find in North Yorkshire.

As I drove down towards the show ground I felt I was looking at a living breathing piece of old England; the group of tents and marquees vivid against the green of the riverside field, the women and children in their bright summer dresses, the cattle with their smocked attendants, a line of massive Shire horses parading in the ring.

I parked the car and made for the stewards' tent with its flag hanging limply from the mast. Tristan parted from me there. With the impecunious student's unerring eye for a little free food and entertainment he had taken up my spare tickets. He headed purposefully for the beer tent as I went in to report to the show secretary.

Leaving my measuring stick there I looked around for a while.

A country show is a lot of different things to a lot of different people. Riding horses of all kinds from small ponies to hunters were being galloped up and down and in one ring the judges hovered around a group of mares and their beautiful little foals.

In a corner four men armed with buckets and brushes were washing and grooming a row of young bulls with great concentration, twiddling and crimping the fuzz over the rumps like society hairdressers.

Wandering through the marquees I examined the bewildering variety of produce from stalks of rhubarb to bunches of onions, the flower displays, embroidery, jams, cakes, pies. And the children's section; a painting of 'The Beach at Scarborough' by Annie Heseltine, aged nine; rows of wobbling copperplate handwriting — 'A thing of beauty is a joy for ever', Bernard Peacock, aged twelve.

Drawn by the occasional gusts of melody I strolled across the grass to where the Darrowby and Houlton Silver Band was rendering *Poet and Peasant*. The bandsmen were of all ages from seventies down to one or two boys of about fourteen and most of them had doffed their uniform tunics as they sweated in the hot sun. Pint pots reposed under many of the chairs and the musicians refreshed themselves frequently with leisurely swigs.

I was particularly fascinated by the conductor, a tiny frail man who looked about eighty. He alone had retained his full uniform, cap and all, and he stood apparently motionless in front of the crescent of bandsmen, chin sunk on chest, arms hanging limply by his sides. It wasn't until I came right up to him that I realized his fingers were twitching in time with the music and that he was, in fact, conducting. And the more I watched him the more fitting it seemed that he should do it like that. The Yorkshireman's loathing of exhibitionism or indeed any outward show of emotion made it unthinkable that he should throw his arms about in the orthodox manner; no doubt he had spent weary hours rehearsing and coaching his players but here, when the results of his labours were displayed to the public he wasn't going to swank about it. Even the almost imperceptible twitching of the finger-ends had something guilty about it as if the old man felt he was being caught out in something shameful.

But my attention was jerked away as a group of people walked across on the far side of the band. It was Helen with Richard Edmundson and behind them Mr Alderson and Richard's father deep in conversation. The young man walked very close to Helen, his shining, plastered-down fair hair hovering possessively over her dark head, his face animated as he talked and laughed.

There were no clouds in the sky but it was as if a dark hand had reached across and smudged away the brightness of the sunshine. I turned quickly and went in search of Tristan.

I soon picked out my colleague as I hurried into the marquee with 'Refreshments' over the entrance. He was leaning with an elbow on the makeshift counter of boards and trestles chatting contentedly with a knot of cloth-capped locals, a Woodbine in one hand, a pint glass in the other. There was a general air of earthy bonhomie. Drinking of a more decorous kind would be taking place at the president's bar behind the stewards' headquarters with pink gins or sherry as the main tipple but here it was beer, bottled and draught, and the stout ladies behind the counter were working with the fierce

95

concentration of people who knew they were in for a hard day.

'Yes, I saw her,' Tristan said when I gave him my news. 'In fact there she is now.' He nodded in the direction of the family group as they strolled past the entrance. 'I've had my eye on them for some time — I don't miss much from in here you know, Jim.'

'Ah well.' I accepted a half of bitter from him. 'It all looks pretty cosy. The two dads like blood brothers and Helen hanging on to that bloke's arm.'

Tristan squinted over the top of his pint at the scene outside and shook his head. 'Not exactly. He's hanging on to HER arm.' He looked at me judicially. 'There's a difference, you know.'

'I don't suppose it makes much difference to me either way,' I grunted.

'Well don't look so bloody mournful.' He took an effortless swallow which lowered the level in his glass by about six inches. 'What do you expect an attractive girl to do? Sit at home waiting for you to call? If you've been pounding on her door every night you haven't told me about it.'

'It's all right you talking. I think old man Alderson would set his dogs on me if I showed up there. I know he doesn't like me hanging around Helen and on top of that I've got the feeling he thinks I killed his cow on my last visit.'

'And did you?'

'No, I didn't. But I walked up to a living animal, gave it an injection and it promptly died, so I can't blame him.'

96

I took a sip at my beer and watched the Alderson party who had changed direction and were heading away from our retreat. Helen was wearing a pale blue dress and I was thinking how well the colour went with the deep brown of her hair and how I liked the way she walked with her legs swinging easily and her shoulders high and straight when the loudspeaker boomed across the show ground.

'Will Mr Herriot, Veterinary Surgeon, please report to the stewards immediately.'

It made me jump but at the same time I felt a quick stab of pride. It was the first time I had heard myself and my profession publicly proclaimed. I turned to Tristan. He was supposed to be seeing practice and this could be something interesting. But he was immersed in a story which he was trying to tell to a little stocky man with a fat, shiny face, and he was having difficulty because the little man, determined to get his full measure of enjoyment, kept throwing himself into helpless convulsions at the end of every sentence, and the finish was a long way away. Tristan took his stories very seriously; I decided not to interrupt him.

A glow of importance filled me as I hurried over the grass, my official badge with 'Veterinary Surgeon' in gold letters dangling from my lapel. A steward met me on the way.

'It's one of the cattle. Had an accident, I think.' He, pointed to a row of pens along the edge of the field.

A curious crowd had collected around my patient which had been entered in the in-calf

97

heifers class. The owner, a stranger from outside the Darrowby practice came up to me, his face glum.

'She tripped coming off the cattle wagon and went 'ead first into the wall. Knocked one of 'er horns clean off.'

The heifer, a bonny little light roan, was a pathetic sight. She had been washed, combed, powdered and primped for the big day and there she was with one horn dangling drunkenly down the side of her face and an ornamental fountain of bright arterial blood climbing gracefully in three jets from the broken surface high into the air.

I opened my bag. I had brought a selection of the things I might need and I fished out some artery forceps and suture material. The rational way to stop haemorrhage of this type is to grasp the bleeding vessel and ligate it, but it wasn't always as easy as that. Especially when the patient won't cooperate.

The broken horn was connected to the head only by a band of skin and I quickly snipped it away with scissors; then, with the farmer holding the heifer's nose I began to probe with my forceps for the severed vessels. In the bright sunshine it was surprisingly difficult to see the spurting blood and as the little animal threw her head about I repeatedly felt the warm spray across my face and heard it spatter on my collar.

It was when I was beginning to lose heart with my ineffectual groping that I looked up and saw Helen and her boy friend watching me from the crowd. Young Edmundson looked mildly amused as he watched my unavailing efforts but Helen smiled encouragingly as she caught my eye. I did my best to smile back at her through my bloody mask but I don't suppose it showed.

I gave it up when the heifer gave a particularly brisk toss which sent my forceps flying on to the grass. I did what I should probably have done at the beginning — clapped a pad of cotton wool and antiseptic powder on to the stump and secured it with a figure of eight bandage round the other horn.

'That's it, then,' I said to the farmer as I tried to blink the blood out of my eyes. 'The bleeding's stopped, anyway, I'd advise you to have her properly de-horned soon or she's going to look a bit odd.'

Just then Tristan appeared from among the spectators.

'What's got you out of the beer tent?' I enquired with a touch of bitterness.

'It's lunch time, old lad,' Tristan replied equably. 'But we'll have to get you cleaned up a bit first. I can't be seen with you in that condition. Hang on, I'll get a bucket of water.'

The show luncheon was so excellent that it greatly restored me. Although it was taken in a marquee the committee men's wives had somehow managed to conjure up a memorable cold spread. There was fresh salmon and home fed ham and slices of prime beef with mixed salads and apple pie and the big brimming jugs of cream you only see at farming functions. One of the ladies was a noted cheese maker and we finished with some delicious goat cheese and coffee. The liquid side was catered for too with a bottle of Magnet Pale Ale and a glass at every place.

I didn't have the pleasure of Tristan's company at lunch because he had strategically placed himself well down the table between two strict Methodists so that his intake of Magnet was trebled.

I had hardly emerged into the sunshine when a man touched me on the shoulder.

'One of the dog show judges wants you to examine a dog. He doesn't like the look of it.'

He led me to where a thin man of about forty with a small dark moustache was standing by his car. He held a wire-haired fox terrier on a leash and he met me with an ingratiating smile.

'There's nothing whatever the matter with my dog,' he declared, 'but the chap in there seems very fussy.'

I looked down at the terrier. 'I see he has some matter in the corner of his eyes.'

The man shook his head vigorously. 'Oh no, that's not matter. I've been using some white powder on him and a bit's got into his eyes, that's all.'

'Hmm, well let's see what his temperature says, shall we?'

The little animal stood uncomplaining as I inserted the thermometer. When I took the reading my eyebrows went up.

'It's a hundred and four. I'm afraid he's not fit to go into the show.'

'Wait a minute.' The man thrust out his jaw. 'You're talking like that chap in there. I've come

100

a long way to show this dog and I'm going to show him.'

'I'm sorry but you can't show him with a temperature of a hundred and four.'

'But he's had a car journey. That could put up his temperature.'

I shook my head. 'Not as high as that it couldn't. Anyway he looks sick to me. Do you see how he's half closing his eyes as though he's frightened of the light? It's possible he could have distemper.'

'What? That's rubbish and you know it. He's never been fitter!' The man's mouth trembled with anger.

I looked down at the little dog. He was crouching on the grass miserably. Occasionally he shivered, he had a definite photophobia and there was that creamy blob of pus in the corner of each eye. 'Has he been inoculated against distemper?'

'Well no, he hasn't, but why do you keep on about it?'

'Because I think he's got it now and for his sake and for the sake of the other dogs here you ought to take him straight home and see your own vet.'

He glared at me. 'So you won't let me take him into the show tent?'

'That's right. I'm very sorry, but it's out of the question.' I turned and walked away.

I had gone only a few yards when the loudspeaker boomed again. 'Will Mr Herriot please go to the measuring stand where the ponies are ready for him.'

I collected my stick and trotted over to a corner of the field where a group of ponies had assembled; Welsh, Dales, Exmoor, Dartmoor — all kinds of breeds were represented.

For the uninitiated, horses are measured in hands which consist of four inches and a graduated stick is used with a cross piece and a spirit level which rests on the withers, the highest point of the shoulders. I had done a fair bit of it in individual animals but this was the first time I had done the job at a show. With my stick at the ready I stood by the two wide boards which had been placed on the turf to give the animals a reasonably level standing surface.

A smiling young woman led the first pony, a smart chestnut, on to the boards.

'Which class?' I asked.

'Thirteen hands.'

I tried the stick on him. He was well under.

'Fine, next please.'

A few more came through without incident then there was a lull before the next group came up. The ponies were arriving on the field all the time in their boxes and being led over to me, some by their young riders, others by the parents. It looked as though I could be here quite a long time.

During one of the lulls a little man who had been standing near me spoke up.

'No trouble yet?' he asked.

'No, everything's in order,' I replied.

He nodded expressionlessly and as I took a closer look at him his slight body, dark, leathery features and high shoulders seemed to give him the appearance of a little brown gnome. At the same time there was something undeniably horsy about him.

'You'll 'ave some awkward 'uns,' he grunted. 'And they allus say the same thing. They allus tell you the vet at some other show passed their pony.' His swarthy cheeks crinkled in a wry smile.

'Is that so?'

'Aye, you'll see.'

Another candidate, led by a beautiful blonde, was led on to the platform. She gave me the full blast of two big greenish eyes and flashed a mouthful of sparkling teeth at me.

'Twelve two,' she murmured seductively.

I tried the stick on the pony and worked it around, but try as I might I couldn't get it down to that.

'I'm afraid he's a bit big,' I said.

The blonde's smile vanished. 'Have you allowed half an inch for his shoes?'

'I have indeed, but you can see for yourself, he's well over.'

'But he passed the vet without any trouble at Hickley,' she snapped and out of the corner of my eye I saw the gnome nodding sagely.

'I can't help that,' I said. 'I'm afraid you'll have to put him into the next class.'

For a moment two green pebbles from the cold sea bed fixed me with a frigid glare then the blonde was gone taking her pony with her.

Next, a little bay animal was led on to the stand by a hard-faced gentleman in a check suit and I must say I was baffled by its behaviour.

Whenever the stick touched the withers it sank at the knees so that I couldn't be sure whether I was getting the right reading or not. Finally I gave up and passed him through.

The gnome coughed. 'I know that feller.'

'You do?'

'Aye, he's pricked that pony's withers with a pin so many times that it drops down whenever you try to measure 'im.'

'Sure as I'm standing here.'

I was staggered, but the arrival of another batch took up my attention for a few minutes. Some I passed, others I had to banish to another class and the owners took it in different ways — some philosophically, a few with obvious annoyance. One or two of the ponies just didn't like the look of the stick at all and I had to dance around them as they backed away and reared.

The last pony in this group was a nice grey led by a bouncy man wearing a great big matey smile.

'How are you, all right?' he inquired courteously. 'This 'un's thirteen two.'

The animal went under the stick without trouble but after he had trotted away the gnome spoke up again.

'I know that feller, too.'

'Really?'

'Not 'alf. Weighs down 'is ponies before they're measured. That grey's been standing in 'is box for the last hour with a twelve stone sack of corn oh 'is back. Knocks an inch off.'

'Good God! Are you sure?'

'Don't worry, I've seen 'im at it.'

My mind was beginning to reel just a little. Was the man making it all up or were there really these malign forces at work behind all this innocent fun?

'That same feller,' continued the gnome. 'I've seen 'im bring a pony to a show and get half an inch knocked off for shoes when it never 'ad no shoes on.'

I wished he'd stop. And just then there was an interruption. It was the man with the moustache. He sidled up to me and whispered confidentially in my ear.

'Now I've just been thinking. My dog must have got over his journey by now and I expect his temperature will be normal. I wonder if you'd just try him again. I've still got time to show him.'

I turned wearily. 'Honestly, it'll be a waste of time. I've told you, he's ill.'

'Please! Just as a favour.' He had a desperate look and a fanatical light flickered in his eye.

'All right.' I went over to the car with him and produced my thermometer. The temperature was still a hundred and four.

'Now I wish you'd take this poor little dog home,' I said. 'He shouldn't be here.'

For a moment I thought the man was going to strike me. 'There's nothing wrong with him!' he hissed, his whole face working with emotion.

'I'm sorry,' I said, and went back to the measuring stand.

A boy of about fifteen was waiting for me with his pony. It was supposed to be in the thirteen two class but was nearly one and a half inches over.

'Much too big, I'm afraid,' I said. 'He can't go in that class.'

The boy didn't answer. He put his hand inside his jacket and produced a sheet of paper. 'This is a veterinary certificate to say he's under thirteen two.'

'No good, I'm sorry,' I replied. 'The stewards have told me not to accept any certificates. I've turned down two others today. Everything has to go under the stick. It's a pity, but there it is.'

His manner changed abruptly. 'But you've GOT to accept it!' he shouted in my face. 'There doesn't have to be any measurements when you have a certificate.'

'You'd better see the stewards. Those are my instructions.'

'I'll see my father about this, that's what!' he shouted and led the animal away.

Father was quickly on the scene. Big, fat, prosperous-looking, confident. He obviously wasn't going to stand any nonsense from me.

'Now look here, I don't know what this is all about but you have no option in this matter. You have to accept the certificate.'

'I don't, I assure you,' I answered. 'And anyway, it's not as though your pony was slightly over the mark. He's miles over — nowhere near the height.'

Father flushed dark red. 'Well let me tell you he was passed through by the vet at . . . '

'I know, I know,' I said, and I heard the gnome

give a short laugh. 'But he's not going through here.'

There was a brief silence then both father and son began to scream at me. And as they continued to hurl abuse I felt a hand on my arm. It was the man with the moustache again.

'I'm going to ask you just once more to take my dog's temperature,' he whispered with a ghastly attempt at a smile. 'I'm sure he'll be all right this time. Will you try him again?'

I'd had enough. 'No, I bloody well won't!' I barked. 'Will you kindly stop bothering me and take that poor animal home.'

It's funny how the most unlikely things motivate certain people. It didn't seem a life and death matter whether a dog got into a show or not but it was to the man with the moustache. He started to rave at me.

'You don't know your job, that's the trouble with you! I've come all this way and you've played a dirty trick on me. I've got a friend who's a vet, a proper vet, and I'm going to tell him about you, yes I am. I'm going to tell him about you!'

At the same time the father and son were still in full cry, snarling and mouthing at me and I became suddenly aware that I was in the centre of a hostile circle. The blonde was there too, and some of the others whose ponies I had outed and they were all staring at me belligerently, making angry gestures.

I felt very much alone because the gnome, who had seemed an ally, was nowhere to be seen. I was disappointed in the gnome; he was a big talker but had vanished at the first whiff of danger. As I surveyed the threatening crowd I moved my measuring stick round in front of me; it wasn't much of a weapon but it might serve to fend them off if they rushed me.

And just at that moment, as the unkind words were thick upon the air, I saw Helen and Richard Edmundson on the fringe of the circle, taking it all in. I wasn't worried about him but again it struck me as strange that it should be my destiny always to be looking a bit of a clown when Helen was around.

Anyway, the measuring was over and I felt in need of sustenance. I retreated and went to find Tristan.

9

The atmosphere in the beer tent was just what I needed. The hot weather had made the place even more popular than usual and it was crowded; many of the inhabitants had been there since early morning and the air was thick with earthy witticisms, immoderate laughter, cries of joy; and the nice thing was that nobody in there cared a damn about the heights of ponies or the temperatures of dogs.

I had to fight my way through the crush to reach Tristan who was leaning across the counter in earnest conversation with a comely young barmaid. The other serving ladies were middle-aged but his practised eye had picked this one out; glossy red hair, a puckish face and an inviting smile. I had been hoping for a soothing chat with him but he was unable to give me his undivided attention, so after juggling with a glass among the throng for a few minutes I left.

Out on the field the sun still blazed, the scent of the trampled grass rose into the warm air, the band was playing a selection from *Rose Marie* and peace began to steal into my soul. Maybe I could begin to enjoy the show now the pinpricks were over; there was only the Family Pets to judge and I was looking forward to that.

For about an hour I wandered among the pens of mountainous pigs and haughty sheep; the rows of Shorthorn cows with their classical wedge-shaped grace, their level udders and dainty feet.

I watched in fascination a contest which was new to me; shirt-sleeved young men sticking a fork into a a straw bale and hurling it high over a bar with a jerk of their thick brown arms.

Old Steve Bramley, a local farmer, was judging the heavy horses and I envied him his massive authority as he stumped, bowler-hatted and glowering around each animal, leaning occasion-ally on his stick as he took stock of the points. I couldn't imagine anyone daring to argue with him.

It was late in the afternoon when the loudspeaker called me to my final duty. The Family Pets contestants were arranged on wooden chairs drawn up in a wide circle on the turf. They were mainly children but behind them an interested ring of parents and friends watched me warily as I arrived.

The fashion for exotic pets was still in its infancy but I experienced a mild shock of surprise when I saw the variety of creatures on show. I suppose I must have had a vague mental picture of a few dogs and cats but I walked round the circle in growing bewilderment looking down at rabbits — innumerable rabbits of all sizes and colours — guinea pigs, white mice, several budgerigars, two tortoises, a canary, a kitten, a parrot, a mynah bird, a box of puppies, a few dogs and cats and a goldfish in a bowl. The smaller pets rested on their owners' knees, the others squatted on the ground.

How, I asked myself, was I going to come to a

decision here? How did you choose between a parrot and a puppy, a budgie and a bulldog, a mouse and a mynah? Then as I circled it came to me; it couldn't be done. The only way was to question the children in charge and find which ones looked after their pets best, which of them knew most about their feeding and general husbandry. I rubbed my hands together and repressed a chuckle of satisfaction; I had something to work on now.

I don't like to boast, but I think I can say in all honesty that I carried out an exhaustive scientific survey of that varied group. From the outset I adopted an attitude of cold detachment, mercilessly banishing any ideas of personal preference. If I had been pleasing only myself I would have given first prize to a gleaming black Labrador sitting by a chair with massive composure and offering me a gracious paw every time I came near. And my second would have been a benevolent tabby — I have always had a thing about tabby cats — which rubbed its cheek against my hand as I talked to its owner. The pups, crawling over each other and grunting obesely, would probably have come third. But I put away these unworthy thoughts and pursued my chosen course.

I was distracted to some extent by the parrot which kept saying 'Hellow' in a voice of devastating refinement like a butler answering a telephone and the mynah which repeatedly adjured me to 'Shut door as you go out', in a booming Yorkshire baritone.

The only adult in the ring was a bosomy lady

111

with glacial pop eyes and a white poodle on her knee. As I approached she gave me a challenging stare as though defying me to place her pet anywhere but first.

'Hello, little chap,' I said, extending my hand. The poodle responded by drawing its lips soundlessly back from its teeth and giving me much the same kind of look as its owner. I withdrew my hand hastily.

'Oh you needn't be afraid of him,' the lady said frigidly. 'He won't hurt you.'

I gave a light laugh. 'I'm sure he won't.' I held out my hand again. 'You're a nice little dog, aren't you?' Once more the poodle bared his teeth and when I persevered by trying to stroke his ears he snapped noiselessly, his teeth clicking together an inch from my fingers.

'He doesn't like you, I can see that. Do you, darling?' The lady put her cheek against the dog's head and stared at me distastefully as though she knew just how he felt.

'Shut door as you go out,' commanded the mynah gruffly from somewhere behind me.

I gave the lady my questionnaire and moved on.

And among the throng there was one who stood out; the little boy with the goldfish. In reply to my promptings he discoursed knowledgeably about his fish, its feeding, life history and habits. He even had a fair idea of the common diseases. The bowl, too, was beautifully clean and the water fresh; I was impressed.

When I had completed the circuit I swept the ring for the last time with a probing eye. Yes, there was no doubt about it; I had the three prize winners fixed in my mind beyond any question and in an order based on strictly scientific selection. I stepped out into the middle.

'Ladies and gentlemen,' I said, scanning the company with an affable smile.

'Hellow,' responded the parrot fruitily,

I ignored him and continued. 'These are the successful entrants. First, number six, the goldfish. Second, number fifteen, the guinea pig. And third, number ten, the white kitten.'

I half expected a little ripple of applause but there was none. In fact my announcement was greeted by a tight-lipped silence. I had noticed an immediate change in the atmosphere when I mentioned the goldfish. It was striking — a sudden cold wave which swept away the expectant smiles and replaced them with discontented muttering.

I had done something wrong, but what? I looked around helplessly as the hum of voices increased. 'What do you think of that, then?' 'Not fair, is it?' 'Wouldn't have thought it of him?' 'All them lovely rabbits and he hardly looked at them.'

I couldn't make it out, but my job was done, anyway. I pushed between the chairs and escaped to the open field.

'Shut door as you go out,' the mynah requested in deepest bass as I departed.

I sought out Tristan again. The atmosphere in the beer tent had changed, too. The drinkers were long since past their peak and the hilarious babel which had met me on my last visit had died to an exhausted murmur. There was a

113

general air of satiation. Tristan, pint in hand, was being addressed with great solemnity by a man in a flat cap and braces. The man swayed slightly as he grasped Tristan's free hand and gazed into his eyes. Occasionally he patted him on the shoulder with the utmost affection. Obviously my colleague had been forging deep and lasting friendships in here while I was making enemies outside.

I sidled up to him and spoke into his ear. 'Ready to go soon, Triss?'

He turned slowly and looked at me. 'No, old lad,' he said, articulating carefully. 'I'm afraid I shan't be coming with you. They're having a dance here on the showfield later and Doreen has consented to accompany me.' He cast a loving glance across the counter at the redhead who crinkled her nose at him.

I was about to leave when a snatch of conversation from behind made me pause.

'A bloody goldfish!' a voice saying disgustedly.

'Aye, it's a rum 'un, George,' a second voice replied.

There was a slurping sound of beer being downed.

'But tha knows, Fred,' the first voice said. 'That vet feller had to do it. Didn't 'ave no choice. He couldn't pass over t'squire's son.'

'Reckon you're right, but it's a bugger when you get graft and corruption in t'Family Pets.'

A heavy sigh, then 'It's the way things are nowadays, Fred. Everything's hulterior.'

'You're right there, George. It's hulterior, that's what it is.'

I fought down a rising panic. The Pelhams had been Lords of the Manor of Darrowby for generations and the present squire was Major Pelham. I knew him as a friendly farmer client, but that was all. I'd never heard of his son.

I clutched at Tristan's arm. 'Who is that little boy over there?'

Tristan peered out glassily across the sward. 'The one with the goldfish bowl, you mean?'

'That's right.'

'It's young Nigel Pelham, the squire's son.'

'Oh Gawd,' I moaned. 'But I've never seen him before. Where's he been?'

'Boarding school down south, I believe. On holiday just now.'

I stared at the boy again. Tousled fair hair, grey open-necked shirt, sunburned legs. Just like all the others.

George was at it again. 'Lovely dogs and cats there was, but squire's lad won it with a bloody goldfish.'

'Well, let's be right,' his companion put in. 'If that lad 'ad brought along a bloody stuffed monkey he'd still 'ave got fust prize with it.'

'No doubt about it, Fred. T'other kids might as well 'ave stopped at 'ome.'

'Aye, it's not like it used to be, George. Nobody does owt for nowt these days.'

'True, Fred, very true.' There was a gloomy silence punctuated by noisy gulpings. Then, in weary tones: 'Well you and me can't alter it. It's the kind of world we're living in today.'

I reeled out into the fresh air and the sunshine. Looking round at the tranquil scene,

115

the long stretch of grass, the loop of pebbly river with the green hills rising behind, I had a sense of unreality. Was there any part of this peaceful cameo of rural England without its sinister undertones? As if by instinct I made my way into the long marquee which housed the produce section. Surely among those quiet rows of vegetables I would find repose.

The place was almost empty but as I made my way down the long lines of tables I came upon the solitary figure of old John William Enderby who had a little grocer's shop in the town.

'Well how are things?' I inquired.

'Nobbut middlin' lad,' the old man replied morosely.

'Why, what's wrong?'

'Well, ah got a second with me broad beans but only a highly commended for me shallots. Look at 'em.'

I looked. 'Yes, they're beautiful shallots, Mr Enderby.'

'Aye, they are, and nobbut a highly commended. It's a insult, that's what it is a insult.'

'But Mr Enderby . . . highly commended . . . I mean, that's pretty good isn't it?'

'No it isn't, it's a insult!'

'Oh bad luck.'

John William stared at me wide-eyed for a moment. 'It's not bad luck, lad, it's nowt but a twist.'

'Oh surely not!'

'Ah'm tellin' you. Jim Houlston got first with 'is shallots and judge is his wife's cousin.'

'Never!'

'It's true,' grunted John William, nodding solemnly. 'It's nowt but a twist.'

'Well I've never heard of such a thing!'

'You don't know what goes on, young man. Ah wasn't even placed with me taties. Frank Thompson got first wi' that lot.' He pointed to a tray of noble tubers.

I studied them. 'I must admit they look splendid potatoes.'

'Aye, they are, but Frank pinched 'em.'

'What?'

'Aye, they took first prize at Brisby show last Thursday and Frank pinched 'em off t'stand.'

I clutched at the nearby table. The foundations of my world were crumbling. 'That can't be true, Mr Enderby.'

'Ah'm not jokin' nor jestin',' declared John William. 'Them's self and same taties, ah'd know them anywhere. It's nowt but a . . . '

I could take no more. I fled.

Outside the evening sunshine was still warm and the whole field was awash with the soft light which, in the Dales, seems to stream down in a golden flood from the high tops. But it was as if the forces of darkness were pressing on me; all I wanted was to get home.

I hurried to the stewards' tent and collected my measuring stick, running a gauntlet of hostile stares from the pony people I had outed earlier in the day. They were still waving their certificates and arguing.

On the way to the car I had to pass several of the ladies who had watched me judge the pets and though they didn't exactly draw their skirts

117

aside they managed to convey their message. Among the rows of vehicles I spotted the man with the moustache. He still hadn't taken his terrier away and his eyes, full of wounded resentment, followed my every step.

I was opening my door when Helen and her party, also apparently on the way home, passed about fifty yards away. Helen waved, I waved back, and Richard Edmundson gave me a nod before helping her into the front seat of a gleaming, silver Daimler. The two fathers got into the back.

As I settled into the seat of my little Austin, braced my feet against the broken floor boards and squinted through the cracked windscreen I prayed that just this once the thing would go on the starter. Holding my breath I pulled at the knob but the engine gave a couple of lazy turns then fell silent.

Fishing the starting handle from under the seat I crept out and inserted it in its hole under the radiator; and as I began the old familiar winding the silver monster purred contemptuously past me and away.

Dropping into the driver's seat again I caught sight of my face in the mirror and could see the streaks and flecks of blood still caked on my cheek and around the roots of my hair. Tristan hadn't done a very good job with his bucket of cold water.

I looked back at the emptying field and at the Daimler disappearing round a distant bend. It seemed to me that in more ways than one the show was over.

10

Ben Ashby the cattle dealer looked over the gate with his habitual deadpan expression. It always seemed to me that after a lifetime of buying cows from farmers he had developed a terror of showing any emotion which might be construed as enthusiasm. When he looked at a beast his face registered nothing beyond, occasionally, a gentle sorrow.

This was how it was this morning as he leaned on the top spar and directed a gloomy stare at Harry Sumner's heifer. After a few moments he turned to the farmer.

'I wish you'd had her in for me, Harry. She's too far away. I'm going to have to get over the top.' He began to climb stiffly upwards and it was then that he spotted Monty. The bull hadn't been so easy to see before as he cropped the grass among the group of heifers but suddenly the great head rose high about the others, the nose ring gleamed, and an ominous, strangled bellow sounded across the grass. And as he gazed at us he pulled absently at the turf with a fore foot.

Ben Ashby stopped climbing, hesitated for a second then returned to ground level.

'Aye well,' he muttered, still without changing expression. 'It's not that far away. I reckon I can see all right from here.'

Monty had changed a lot since the first day I

saw him about two years ago. He had been a fortnight old then, a skinny, knock-kneed little creature, his head deep in a calf bucket.

'Well, what do you think of me new bull?' Harry Sumner had asked, laughing. 'Not much for a hundred quid is he?'

I whistled. 'As much as that?'

'Aye, it's a lot for a new-dropped calf, isn't it? But I can't think of any other way of getting into the Newton strain. I haven't the brass to buy a big 'un.'

Not all the farmers of those days were as farseeing as Harry and some of them would use any type of male bovine to get their cows in calf.

One such man produced a gaunt animal for Siegfried's inspection and asked him what he thought of his bull. Seigfried's reply of 'All horns and balls' didn't please the owner but I still treasure it as the most graphic description of the typical scrub bull of that period.

Harry was a bright boy. He had inherited a little place of about a hundred acres on his father's death and with his young wife had set about making it go. He was in his early twenties and when I first saw him I had been deceived by his almost delicate appearance into thinking that he wouldn't be up to the job; the pallid face, the large, sensitive eyes and slender frame didn't seem fitted for the seven days a week milking, feeding, mucking-out slog that was dairy farming. But I had been wrong.

The fearless way he plunged in and grabbed at the hind feet of kicking cows for me to examine and his clenched-teeth determination as he hung

120

on to the noses of the big loose beasts at testing time made me change my mind in a hurry. He worked endlessly and tirelessly and it was natural that his drive should have taken him to the south of Scotland to find a bull.

Harry's was an Ayrshire herd — unusual among the almost universal shorthorns in the Dales — and there was no doubt an injection of the famous Newton blood would be a sure way of improving his stock.

'He's got prize winners on both his sire and dam's side,' the young farmer said. 'And a grand pedigree name, too. Newton Montmorency the Sixth — Monty for short.'

As though recognizing his name, the calf raised his head from the bucket and looked at us. It was a comic little face — wet-muzzled, milk slobbered halfway up his cheeks and dribbling freely from his mouth. I bent over into the pen and scratched the top of the hard little head, feeling the tiny horn buds no bigger than peas under my fingers. Limpid-eyed and unafraid, Monty submitted calmly to the caress for a few moments then sank his head again in the bucket.

I saw quite a bit of Harry Sumner over the next few weeks and usually had a look at his expensive purchase. And as the calf grew you could see why he had cost £100. He was in a pen with three of Harry's own calves and his superiority was evident at a glance; the broad forehead and wide-set eyes; the deep chest and short straight legs; the beautifully even line of the back from shoulder to tail head. Monty had class; and small as he was he was all bull.

He was about three months old when Harry rang to say he thought the calf had pneumonia. I was surprised because the weather was fine and warm and I knew Monty was in a draught-free building. But when I saw him I thought immediately that his owner's diagnosis was right. The heaving of the rib cage, the temperature of 105 degrees — it looked fairly straightforward. But when I got my stethoscope on his chest and listened for the pneumonic sounds I heard nothing. His lungs were perfectly clear. I went over him several times but there was not a squeak, not a râle, not the slightest sign of consolidation.

This was a facer. I turned to the farmer. 'It's a funny one, Harry. He's sick, all right, but his symptoms don't add up to anything recognizable.'

I was going against my early training because the first vet I ever saw practice with in my student days told me once: 'If you don't know what's wrong with an animal for God's sake don't admit it Give it a name — call it McLuskie's Disease or Galloping Dandruff — anything you like, but give it a name.' But no inspiration came to me as I looked at the panting, anxious-eyed little creature.

Treat the symptoms. That was the thing to do. He had a temperature so I'd try to get that down for a start. I brought out my pathetic armoury of febrifuges; the injection of non-specific anti-serum, the 'fever drink' of sweet spirit of nitre; but over the next two days it was obvious that the time-honoured remedies were having no effect.

122

On the fourth morning, Harry Sumner met me as I got out of my car. 'He's walking funny, this morning, Mr Herriot — and he seems to be blind.'

Blind! An unusual form of lead-poisoning — could that be it? I hurried into the calf pen and began to look round the walls, but there wasn't a scrap of paint anywhere and Monty had spent his entire life in there.

And anyway, as I looked at him I realized that he wasn't really blind; his eyes were staring and slightly upturned and he blundered unseeingly around the pen, but he blinked as I passed my hand in front of his face. To complete my bewilderment he walked with a wooden, stiff-legged gait almost like a mechanical toy and my mind began to snatch at diagnostic straws — tetanus, no — meningitis — no, no; I always tried to maintain the calm, professional exterior but I had to fight an impulse to scratch my head and stand gaping.

I got off the place as quickly as possible and settled down to serious thought as I drove away. My lack of experience didn't help, but I did have a knowledge of pathology and physiology and when stumped for a diagnosis I could usually work something out on rational grounds. But this thing didn't make sense.

That night I got out my books, notes from college, back numbers of the Veterinary Record and anything else I could find on the subject of calf diseases. Somewhere here there would surely be a clue. But the volumes on medicine and surgery were barren of inspiration and I had

123

about given up hope when I came upon the passage in a little pamphlet on calf diseases. 'Peculiar, stilted gait, staring eyes with a tendency to gaze upwards, occasionally respiratory symptoms with high temperature.' The words seemed to leap out at me from the printed page and it was as though the unknown author was patting me on the shoulder and murmuring reassuringly: 'This is it, you see. It's all perfectly clear.'

I grabbed the phone and rang Harry Sumner. 'Harry, have you ever noticed Monty and those other calves in the pen licking each other?'

'Aye, they're allus at it, the little beggars. It's like a hobby with them. Why?'

'Well I know what's wrong with your bull. He's got a hair ball.'

'A hair ball? Where?'

'In the abomasum — the fourth stomach. That's what's setting up all those strange symptoms.'

'Well I'll go to hell. What do we do about it, then?'

'It'll probably mean an operation, but I'd like to try dosing him with liquid paraffin first. I'll put a pint bottle on the step for you if you'll come and collect it. Give him half a pint now and the same first thing in the morning. It might just grease the thing through. I'll see you tomorrow.'

I hadn't a lot of faith in the liquid paraffin. I suppose I suggested it for the sake of doing something while I played nervously with the idea of operating. And next morning the picture was

124

as I expected; Monty was still rigid-limbed, still staring sightlessly ahead of him, and an oiliness round his rectum and down his tail showed that the paraffin had by-passed the obstruction.

'He hasn't had a bite now for three days,' Harry said. 'I doubt he won't stick it much longer.'

I looked from his worried face to the little animal trembling in the pen. 'You're right. We'll have to open him up straight away to have any hope of saving him. Are you willing to let me have a go?'

'Oh, aye, let's be at t'job — sooner the better.' He smiled at me. It was a confident smile and my stomach gave a lurch. His confidence could be badly misplaced because in those days abdominal surgery in the bovine was in a primitive state. There were a few jobs we had begun to tackle fairly regularly but removal of a hairball wasn't one of them and my knowledge of the procedure was confined to some rather small-print reading in the text books.

But this young farmer had faith in me. He thought I could do the job so it was no good letting him see my doubts. It was at times like this that I envied our colleagues in human medicine. When a surgical case came up they packed their patient off to a hospital but the vet just had to get his jacket off on the spot and make an operating theatre out of the farm buildings.

Harry and I busied ourselves in boiling up the instruments, setting out buckets of hot water and laying a clean bed of straw in an empty pen.

125

Despite his weakness the calf took nearly sixty cc's of Nembutal into his vein before he was fully anaesthetized but finally he was asleep, propped on his back between two straw bales, his little hooves dangling above him. I was ready to start.

It's never the same as it is in the books. The pictures and diagrams look so simple and straightforward but it is a different thing when you are cutting into a living, breathing creature with the abdomen rising and falling gently and the blood oozing beneath your knife. The abomasum, I knew, was just down there, slightly to the right of the sternum but as I cut through the peritoneum there was this slippery mass of fat-streaked omentum obscuring everything; and as I pushed it aside one of the bales moved and Monty tilted to his left causing a sudden gush of intestines into the wound. I put the flat of my hand against the shining pink loops — it would be just great if my patient's insides started spilling out on to the straw before I had started.

'Pull him upright, Harry, and shove that bale back into place,' I gasped. The farmer quickly complied but the intestines weren't at all anxious to return to their place and kept intruding coyly as I groped for the abomasum. Frankly I was beginning to feel just a bit lost and my heart was thudding when I came upon something hard. It was sliding about beyond the wall of one of the stomachs — at the moment I wasn't sure which. I gripped it and lifted it into the wound. I had hold of the abomasum and that hard thing inside must be the hairball.

Repelling the intestines which had made

126

another determined attempt to push their way into the act, I incised the stomach and had my first look at the cause of the trouble. It wasn't a ball at all, rather a flat plaque of densely-matted hair, mixed freely with strands of hay, sour curd and a shining covering of my liquid paraffin. The whole thing was jammed against the pyloric opening.

Gingerly I drew it out through the incision and dropped it in the straw. It wasn't till I had closed the stomach wound with gut, stitched up the muscle layer and had started on the skin that I realized that the sweat was running down my face. As I blew away a droplet from my nose end Harry broke the silence.

'It's a hell of a tricky job, isn't it?' he said. Then he laughed and thumped my shoulder. 'I bet you felt a bit queer the first time you did one of these!'

I pulled another strand of suture silk through and knotted it. 'You're right, Harry,' I said. 'How right you are.'

When I had finished we covered Monty with a horse rug and piled straw on top of that, leaving only his head sticking out. I bent over and touched a corner of the eye. Not a vestige of corneal reflex. God, he was deep — had I given him too much anaesthetic? And of course there'd be surgical shock, too. As I left I glanced back at the motionless little animal. He looked smaller than ever and very vulnerable under the bare walls of the pen.

I was busy for the rest of the day but that evening my thoughts kept coming back to

Monty. Had he come out of it yet? Maybe he was dead. I hadn't the experience of previous cases to guide me and I simply had no idea of how a calf reacted to an operation like that. And I couldn't rid myself of the nagging consciousness of how much it all meant to Harry Sumner. The bull is half the herd, they say, and half of Harry's future herd was lying there under the straw — he wouldn't be able to find that much money again.

I jumped suddenly from my chair. It was no good, I had to find out what was happening. Part of me rebelled at the idea of looking amateurish and unsure of myself by going fussing back, but, I thought, I could always say I had returned to look for an instrument.

The farm was in darkness as I crept into the pen. I shone my torch on the mound of straw and saw with a quick thump of the heart that the calf had not moved. I dropped to my knees and pushed a hand under the rug; he was breathing anyway. But there was still no eye reflex — either he was dying or he was taking a hell of a time to come out.

In the shadows of the yard I looked across at the soft glow from the farmhouse kitchen. Nobody had heard me. I slunk over to the car and drove off with the sick knowledge that I was no further forward. I still didn't know how the job was going to turn out.

Next morning I had to go through the same thing again and as I walked stiffly across to the calf pen I knew for sure I'd see something this time. Either he'd be dead or better. I opened the outer door and almost ran down the passage. It was the third pen along and I stared hungrily into it.

Monty was sitting up on his chest. He was still under the rug and straw and he looked sorry for himself but when a bovine animal is on its chest I always feel hopeful. The tensions flowed from me in a great wave. He had survived the operation — the first stage was over; and as I knelt, rubbing the top of his head, I had the feeling that we were going to win.

And, in fact, he did get better, though I have always found it difficult to explain to myself scientifically why the removal of that pad of tangled fibres could cause such a dramatic improvement in so many directions. But there it was. His temperature did drop and his breathing returned to normal, his eyes did stop staring and the weird stiffness disappeared from his limbs.

But though I couldn't understand it, I was none the less delighted. Like a teacher with his favourite pupil I developed a warm proprietary affection for the calf and when I happened to be on the farm I found my feet straying unbidden to his pen. He always walked up to me and regarded me with friendly interest; it was as if he had a fellow feeling for me, too.

He was rather more than a year old when I noticed the change. The friendly interest gradually disappeared from his eyes and was replaced by a thoughtful, speculative look; and he developed a habit of shaking his head at me at the same time.

'I'd stop going in there, Mr Herriot, if I were you,' Harry said one day. 'He's getting big and I reckon he's going to be a cheeky bugger before he's finished.'

But cheeky was the wrong word. Harry had a long, trouble-free spell and Monty was nearly two years old when I saw him again. It wasn't a case of illness this time. One or two of Harry's cows had been calving before their time and it was typical of him that he should ask me to blood test his entire herd for Brucellosis.

We worked our way easily through the cows and I had a long row of glass tubes filled with blood in just over an hour.

'Well, that's the lot in here,' the farmer said. 'We only have bull to do and we're finished.' He led the way across the yard through the door into the calf pens and along a passage to the bull box at the end. He opened the half door and as I looked inside I felt a sudden sense of shock.

Monty was enormous. The neck with its jutting humps of muscle supported a head so huge that the eyes looked tiny. And there was nothing friendly in those eyes now; no expression at all, in fact, only a cold black glitter. He was standing sideways to me, facing the wall, but I knew he was watching me as he pushed his head against the stones, his great horns scoring the whitewash with slow, menacing deliberation. Occasionally he snorted from deep in his chest but apart from that he remained ominously still. Monty wasn't just a bull — he was a vast, brooding presence.

Harry grinned as he saw me staring over the door. 'Well, do you fancy popping inside to scratch his head? That's what you allus used to do.'

'No thanks.' I dragged my eyes away from the animal. 'But I wonder what my expectation of life would be if I did go in.'

'I reckon you'd last about a minute,' Harry said thoughtfully. 'He's a grand bull — all I ever expected — but by God he's a mean 'un. I never trust him an inch.'

'And how,' I asked without enthusiasm, 'am I supposed to get a sample of blood from him?'

'Oh I'll trap his head in yon corner.' Harry pointed to a metal yoke above a trough in an opening into the yard at the far side of the box. 'I'll give him some meal to 'tice him in.' He went back down the passage and soon I could see him out in the yard scooping meal into the trough.

The bull at first took no notice and continued to prod at the wall with his horns, then he turned with awesome slowness, took a few unhurried steps across the box and put his nose down to the trough. Harry, out of sight in the yard, pulled the lever and the yoke crashed shut on the great neck.

'All right,' the farmer cried, hanging on to the lever, 'I have 'im. You can go in now.'

I opened the door and entered the box and though the bull was held fast by the head there was still the uneasy awareness that he and I were alone in that small space together. And as I passed along the massive body and put my hand on the neck I sensed a quivering emanation of pent up power and rage. Digging my fingers into the jugular furrow I watched the vein rise up and poised my needle. It would take a good hard thrust to pierce that leathery skin.

The bull stiffened but did not move as I plunged the needle in and with relief I saw the blood flowing darkly into the syringe. Thank God I had hit the vein first time and didn't have to start poking around. I was withdrawing the needle and thinking that the job had been so simple after all when everything started to happen. The bull gave a tremendous bellow and whipped round at me with no trace of his former lethargy. I saw that he had got one horn out of the yoke and though he couldn't reach me with his head, his shoulder knocked me on my back with a terrifying revelation of unbelievable strength. I heard Harry shouting from outside and as I scrambled up and headed for the box door I saw that the madly plunging creature had almost got his second horn clear and when I reached the passage I heard the clang of the yoke as he finally freed himself.

Anybody who has travelled a narrow passage a few feet ahead of about a ton of snorting, pounding death will appreciate that I didn't dawdle. I was spurred on by the certain knowledge that if Monty caught me he would plaster me against the wall as effortlessly as I would squash a ripe plum, and though I was clad in a long oilskin coat and wellingtons I doubt whether an olympic sprinter in full running kit would have bettered my time.

I made the door at the end with a foot to spare, dived through and crashed it shut. The first thing I saw was Harry Sumner running round from the outside of the box. He was very pale. I couldn't see my face but it felt pale; even my lips were cold and numb.

'God, I'm sorry!' Harry said hoarsely. 'The yoke couldn't have closed properly — that bloody great neck of his. The lever just jerked out of my hand. Damn, I'm glad to see you — I thought you were a goner!'

I looked down at my hand. The blood-filled syringe was still tightly clutched there. 'Well I've got my sample anyway, Harry. And it's just as well, because it would take some fast talking to get me in there to try for another. I'm afraid you've just seen the end of a beautiful friendship.'

'Aye, the big sod!' Harry listened for a few moments to the thudding of Monty's horns against the door. 'And after all you did for him. That's gratitude for you.'

11

I suppose if it hadn't been for the Tuberculin Testing Scheme I'd never have come to know Ewan and Ginny Ross.

Siegfried broached the matter to me one morning as I was making up some colic mixture in the dispensary.

'All this extra testing work is a bit much for a one-man practice, especially when it's an older man. Ewan Ross has been on the phone asking me if I could help him and we've thrashed out a plan which could benefit us both. But it depends on you.'

'What do you mean?'

'Well, would you be willing to go up to Scarburn and do his testing say three days a week? Ewan and I would split the proceeds and you'd get a little cut too.'

I screwed a cork into the last bottle. 'It's all right with me. I'd enjoy a bit of fresh country. It's real wild up there — about twenty-five miles away isn't it?'

'Just about. It is a bit bleak, but it's beautiful in fine weather. And I'm sure you'll get on with Ewan.'

'I've heard quite a lot about him.' I laughed. 'They say he'd rather settle down with a bottle than work.'

Siegfried turned a level gaze on me. 'They say a lot of things but he's a good friend of mine and just about the best veterinary surgeon I've ever seen.' He paused for a moment then went on. 'I want you to go up there tomorrow to meet him, then you can judge for yourself.'

As I drove out next morning I reflected on the snippets which had come through to me about Ewan Ross. I didn't know all that much about him; twenty-five miles was enough to make him remote from my own working area and in any case hard drinking and wild behaviour were the norm among the older members of the profession. The more recent graduates were a different type altogether; more scientifically orientated, more conscious of professional standards; but the men who had been on the go for twenty years or more, many of them ex-servicemen, were a hard-bitten, rugged lot of characters. Most of them had had a hell of a life, working single-handed through the years when times were hard, money short and the work at its roughest and I suppose they just had to erupt now and then.

Ewan Ross, it was said, would incarcerate himself in some village pub and go on a bender lasting days on end until his wife finally managed to winkle him out and entice him back to his practice. People said, too, that he liked to challenge big farm men in bars to 'take a hold' — to shake hands with him and have a test of grip which usually finished with the big man on the floor. There were tales, too, of brushes with the police — he'd lost his licence for a while for being drunk in charge of a car — and other things.

The scene beyond my car windows was changing all the time as I drove. The Dales country around Darrowby was softened by the trees which lined the valley floors and by the lush, level pastures by the rivers where they wandered among leisurely shallows. But this was the high Pennines, the harsh, wind-blown roof of England, almost treeless with only the endless miles of dry stone walls climbing and criss-crossing over the bald heights.

And driving into Scarburn, it occurred to me that this was just the sort of place some seedy character would want to hole up. It was only too easy to picture the broken-down vet and his harassed, blowsy wife. I had always thought Darrowby was quiet and a bit rough-hewn but it was a sophisticated metropolis compared to Scarburn.

On this windy, sunless day the grey horse-shoe of buildings grouped around the steeply sloping market place seemed in danger of sliding down the high fell on which it was perched. I drove past the ironmonger's, the Methodist Chapel, a draper's with a few dowdy clothes in the window, the Temperance Hotel; there was no attempt at adornment or softness anywhere and apart from a few muffled women battling against the wind the streets were empty.

I found the veterinary surgeon's plate on a small modern house about two hundred yards beyond the market place and knocked at the door. I had a fairly clear mental image by now of my colleague within; needing a shave, running to fat, the smell of whisky about him, and as the

136

door opened I drew in my breath in anticipation.

A tallish, heavy-shouldered man stood there. The face, ruddy and handsome with pale blue friendly eyes, could have been that of a young man but for the swathes of silver in the sandy hair above it. The suit of soft brown tweed hung gracefully on his lean frame. He held out his hand.

'You'll be James Herriot. Come away in.' The voice had the lilt of the Scottish Highlands with something else in it.

He led the way into the kitchen where a woman was standing by the stove. 'Ginny,' he called. 'Come and meet Siegfried's right hand man, young Mr Herriot.'

Virginia Ross turned her head and looked at me.

'Hello,' she said. 'You're just in time for coffee.' And she gave me a crooked smile with one eyebrow slightly raised which had an extraordinary effect. Over the years I knew her she always looked at me like that — as though I was a quite pleasant but amusing object — and it always did the same thing to me. It's difficult to put into words but perhaps I can best describe it by saying that if I had been a little dog I'd have gone leaping and gambolling around the room wagging my tail furiously.

She would be about ten years younger than Ewan — somewhere in her early forties — but she had the kind of attractiveness that was ageless. She filled three mugs with coffee and I sat down at the table with the feeling that I was with friends. I couldn't count the times I have sat

137

in that kitchen since that first day, drinking tea or coffee or if I happened in around lunch time, eating Ginny's delectable food. She was a cook with the magic touch; in fact as time went on I found she could do just about anything. She spoke several languages, had read everything, she painted and embroidered and as I said, she could cook. How she could cook! She must have had to work on a very tight budget but she managed to make a poem out of the simplest materials.

Ewan pushed away his mug and stood up. 'I've got to operate on a colt for umbilical hernia. Would you care to come along?'

'Yes,' I said. 'I'd like that very much.'

We went out to a small building alongside the house which was the surgery and dispensary. There is a fascination in seeing another man's set-up and I browsed happily along the shelves and tables. There isn't nearly so much fun in doing this nowadays because vets all use the same drugs — a narrow variation in the range of antibiotics, sulphonamides and steroids — but back there in 1939 we were still using the countless mystical remedies of the dark ages.

And Ewan's selection was even more primitive than ours at Darrowby, Physic balls, electuaries, red blister, stimulant draught, ammonia powders, cooling lotions, alterative mixture, Donovan's solution; and a lot of Ewan's own pet ideas with a whiff of black magic about them; like his paste of arsenic and soft soap which you smeared on a length of twine and tied around the necks of tumours where it was supposed to eat its way through.

As I wandered round I watched him preparing for the operation. He didn't seem to have a sterilizer but he was methodically boiling the instruments in a saucepan on a gas ring. Then he took them out with forceps and carefully wrapped them one by one in sheets of clean brown paper. He was a picture of unhurried calm.

It was the same when we got to the farm. Ewan paced about the field till he found a perfectly level spot where the grass was long and soft, then he pottered along, peering closely at the ground, throwing aside a few small stones which were lurking there. When he was satisfied he made a table out of a couple of straw bales, covered it with a clean sheet and laid out his instruments on it meticulously. Next to the bales he stationed a bucket of hot water, soap and towel and finally produced a beautiful soft white rope tied in a neat coil. Only then did he allow the colt to be led out.

I must have looked a bit open-mouthed because he grinned and said, 'I never start anything till I've set my stall out properly.'

What struck me was the difference from my boss in Darrowby. Siegfried would never have had the patience to go through all this procedure; his system was based on Napoleon's dictum of '*On s'engage et puis on voit*' and it usually involved a lot of yelling and rushing about. I had to admit that this was more peaceful.

But I really saw what Ewan was made of when he started to do the job. He was using the old-fashioned method of casting the horse by sidelines and trussing him up before administering the chloroform but he did it as I'd never seen it done before.

The patient was a shaggy little animal with the beginnings of feathers round his hooves; he was typical of the hundreds of cart colts we had to deal with every year and he trembled nervously as he looked around him.

Ewan seemed to pacify him immediately with a few soft words as he placed the rope around his neck then between the hind legs and back through the neck loop; and when the farm men pulled on the rope he stood by the head still talking so that the colt collapsed easily on to his grassy bed.

It was an education for me to watch him then, deftly tugging and knotting till the animal was positioned on his back with his legs tied together fore and hind and the operation area exposed. Once more Ewan had set his stall out properly.

He gave me the job of looking after the chloroform muzzle while he incised the skin, tucked away the hernia and neatly sutured the wound. He did it all with the firm, almost rough movements of the expert surgeon and as I watched the strong fingers at work I was reminded again, of the tales of 'take a hold'.

Even when he was finished and had thoroughly cleared away the last drop of blood and debris from the operation site he still was in no hurry. He washed and dried his instruments with great deliberation, wrapped them up again in the sheets of brown paper then sat down on

140

the straw bales to wait for the colt to come round from the anaesthetic. As he sat there, perfectly relaxed, he pulled a cigarette paper from his pocket, tipped a stream of dark brown dusty tobacco into it from a little pouch, rolled the paper effortlessly with one hand, licked it, screwed up one end and thrust it into his mouth.

As the smoke curled round his ears he gave a few instructions in his soft Highland voice.

'Now just pull him on to his chest will you. That's right, put your knee behind his shoulder and let him rest there for a while. Don't hurry him, now, he'll get up when he's ready.'

He didn't leave for another twenty minutes when the colt gave a final effort and heaved himself to his feet where he stood shakily, looking around him in some bewilderment.

'Let him stand there awhile till he's steady on his legs,' Ewan said. 'Then you can walk him back to his box.'

He turned to me. 'Well now, there's not a bad little pub in this village. How about a beer before lunch?'

There was nobody but ourselves in the bar. Ewan took a contented sip of his half pint then pulled the small pouch again from his pocket. I watched him again as he rolled another cigarette with one hand.

I laughed. 'You know, I've only seen that done by cowboys on the pictures. Where did you learn the art?'

'Oh that?' Ewan gave his shy smile, 'In Canada, a long time ago. It was the only way I had of getting a smoke for years and I've never got out of the way of it.'

He obviously found difficulty in talking about himself but as we sat I was able to build a picture of his history. He was a farmer's son from West Sutherland and even as a small boy he had worked with horses and been fascinated by them. On leaving school he had, like many other restless Highlanders, sailed away to seek his fortune. First he tried Australia where he took a job riding the rabbit fences, then he moved to Canada and worked on a ranch for years, more or less living in the saddle. He came to England with the Canadian Expeditionary Force at the beginning of the war and served till 1918 in the cavalry. I suppose he must have recognized then that his life seemed to be inevitably bound up with horses so he enrolled with a lot of other ex-servicemen in the London Veterinary College. That was where he met Ginny.

He didn't go into details of how he had finally landed in Scarburn and I didn't press him. But it seemed such a waste. You don't often find a top class horseman and a veterinary surgeon combined. Siegfried was such a one and I never thought I'd see a better. But Ewan Ross could beat them all. The extraordinary thing was that he had settled in a cattle and sheep district where his equine skills were seldom exploited. Certainly there were numbers of racing stables in the Pennines but Ewan made not the slightest attempt to gain a footing there; a 'horse specialist' in a big Bentley used to travel around doing most of the racing work and making a packet of money in the process. He wasn't a bad

142

chap, either. But Ewan had forgotten more about horses than he'd ever know.

I suppose the simple explanation was that Ewan was devoid of ambition. He didn't want a big successful practice, he wasn't interested in being rich or famous. Even this morning when I talked to him about our plans in Darrowby I could see he was listening with polite attention, but it didn't mean a thing to him. No, Ewan would do enough work to keep going and beyond that he just didn't give a damn.

We stayed for something like half an hour in the bar and we'd drunk three glasses of beer apiece. I looked at my watch.

'I'd better be getting back down the hill to Darrowby,' I said. 'I've got a few things fixed for this afternoon.'

Ewan smiled. 'Oh, there's no hurry. We'll just have one for the road.' His voice was soft as usual but it had a sleepy quality now and I was surprised to see a slight glassiness in the pale blue eyes. There was no doubt about it — that small amount of drink had affected him.

'No thanks,' I said. 'I've really got to go.'

And as I drove back along the narrow dry-walled road that crawled its slow way among the fells I pondered on the strange fact; Ewan Ross couldn't drink. Or he had a certain proportion of alcohol in his bloodstream so that he was easily topped up. But I didn't think it was that; he just had a low threshold for the stuff. I had a conviction that he would have stayed in that pub if I had been agreeable; and who knows when he might have come out? Ewan's famous benders could all have started as simply.

Anyway, I was only guessing and I never did find out, because I always said 'No thanks' when he said 'We'll just have one for the road.' All the years I knew him I never saw him drunk or anything like it so I can't say anything about that other side of his life.

Strangely enough, circumstances took me through Scarburn just a few days afterwards. It was Sunday and the church was turning out and from my car I saw Ewan and Ginny, dressed in their best, walking down the street ahead of me. I didn't catch them up — just watching them till the straight-backed easy-striding man and the elegant woman turned the corner out of sight, and I thought as I was to think so often what marvellous-looking people were my two new friends.

12

'You know, there's maybe something in this Raynes ghost business after all.' Tristan pushed his chair back from the breakfast table, stretched out his legs more comfortably and resumed his study of the *Darrowby and Houlton Times*. 'It says here they've got a historian looking into it and this man has unearthed some interesting facts.'

Siegfried didn't say anything, but his eyes narrowed as his brother took out a Woodbine and lit it. Siegfried had given up smoking a week ago and he didn't want to watch anybody light up; particularly somebody like Tristan who invested even the smallest action with quiet delight, rich fulfilment. My boss's mouth tightened to a grim line as the young man unhurriedly selected a cigarette, nicked his lighter and dragged the smoke deep with a kind of ecstatic gasp.

'Yes,' Tristan continued, thin outgoing wisps mingling with his words. 'This chap points out that several of the monks were murdered at Raynes Abbey in the fourteenth century.'

'Well, so what?' snapped Siegfried.

Tristan raised his eyebrows. 'This cowled figure that's been seen so often lately near the abbey — why shouldn't it be the spirit of one of those monks?'

'Whaat? What's that you say?'

'Well, after all it makes you think, doesn't it? Who knows what fell deeds might! have been . . . ?'

'What the hell are you talking about?' Siegfried barked.

Tristan looked hurt. 'That's all very well and you may laugh, but remember what Shakespeare said.' He raised a solemn finger. ' "There are more things in heaven and earth, Horatio, than are dreamt of in your . . . " '

'Oh balls!' said Siegfried, bringing the discussion effectively to a close.

I took a last thankful swallow of coffee and put down my cup, I was pleased that the topic had petered out fairly peacefully because Siegfried was in an edgy condition. Up to last week he had been a dedicated puffer of pipe and cigarettes but he had also developed a classical smoker's cough and had suffered increasingly from violent stomach ache. At times his long thin face had assumed the appearance of a skull, the cheeks deeply sunken, the eyes smouldering far down in their sockets. And the doctor had said he must give up smoking.

Siegfried had obeyed, felt immediately better and was instantly seized with the evangelical zeal of the convert. But he didn't just advise people to give up tobacco; I have seen him several times strike a cigarette from the trembling fingers of farm workers, push his face to within inches of theirs and grind out menacingly, 'Now don't ever let me see you with one of those bloody things in your mouth again, do you hear?'

Even now there are grizzled men who tell me

146

with a shudder, 'Nay, ah've never had a fag sin'
Mr Farnon told me to stop, thirty years back.
Nay, bugger it, the way 'e looked at me I durstn't
do it!'

However the uncomfortable fact remained
that his crusade hadn't the slightest effect on his
brother. Tristan smoked almost continually but
he never coughed and his digestion was
excellent.

Siegfried looked at him now as he contentedly
tapped off a little ash and took another blissful
suck. 'You smoke too many of those bloody
cigarettes!'

'So do you.'

'No I don't!' Siegfried retorted. 'I'm a
non-smoker and it's time you were too! It's a
filthy habit and you'll kill yourself the way you're
going!'

Tristan gave him a benign look and again his
words were floated out on the fine Woodbine
mist. 'Oh I'm sure you're wrong. Do you know, I
think it rather agrees with me.'

Siegfried got up and left the room. I
sympathized with him for he was in a difficult
position. Being *in loco parentis* he was in a sense
providing his brother with the noxious weeds
and his innate sense of propriety prevented him
from abusing this position by dashing the things
from Tristan's hands as he did with others. He
had to fall back on exhortation and it was getting
him nowhere. And there was another thing — he
probably wanted to avoid a row this morning as
Tristan was leaving on one of his mysterious
trips back to the Veterinary College; in fact my

147

first job was to take him down to the Great North Road where he was going to hitch a lift.

After I had left him there I set off on my rounds and, as I drove, my thoughts kept going back to the conversation at breakfast. A fair number of people were prepared to swear that they had seen the Raynes ghost and though it was easy to dismiss some of them as sensation mongers or drunkards the fact remained that others were very solid citizens indeed.

The story was always the same. There was a hill beyond Raynes village and at the top a wood came right up to the roadside. Beyond lay the abbey. People driving up the hill late at night said they had seen the monk in their headlights — a monk in a brown habit just disappearing into the wood. They believed the figure had been walking across the road but they weren't sure because it was always a little too far away. But they were adamant about the other part; they had seen a cowled figure, head bowed, go into that wood. There must have been something uninviting about the apparition because nobody ever said they had gone into the wood after it.

It was strange that after my thoughts had been on Raynes during the day I should be called to the village at one o'clock the following morning. Crawling from bed and climbing wearily into my clothes I couldn't help thinking of Tristan curled up peacefully in his Edinburgh lodgings far away from the troubles of practice. But I didn't feel too bad about getting up; Raynes was only three miles away and the job held no prospect of hard labour — a colic in a little boy's Shetland pony.

And it was a fine night — very cold with the first chill of autumn but with a glorious full moon to light my way along the road.

They were walking the pony round the yard when I got there. The owner was the accountant at my bank and he gave me a rueful smile.

'I'm very sorry to get you out of bed, Mr Herriot, but I was hoping this bit of bellyache would go off. We've been parading round here for two hours. When we stop he tries to roll.'

'You've done the right thing,' I said. 'Rolling can cause a twist in the bowel.' I examined the little animal and was reassured. He had a normal temperature, good strong pulse, and listening at his flank I could hear the typical abdominal sounds of spasmodic colic.

What he needed was a good evacuation of the bowel, but I had to think carefully when computing the dose of arecoline for this minute member of the equine species. I finally settled on an eighth of a grain and injected it into the neck muscles. The pony stood for a few moments in the typical colic position, knuckling over and sinking down on one hind leg then the other and occasionally trying to lie down.

'Walk him on again slowly will you?' I was watching for the next stage and I didn't have long to wait; the pony's jaws began to champ and his lips to slobber and soon long dribbles of saliva hung down from his mouth. All right so far but I had to wait another fifteen minutes before he finally cocked his tail and deposited a heap of faeces on the concrete of the yard.

'I think he'll be OK now,' I said. 'So I'll leave

you to it. Give me another ring if he's still in pain.'

Beyond the village the road curved suddenly out of sight of the houses then began the long straight climb to the abbey. Just up there at the limits of my headlights would be where the ghost was always seen — walking across the road and into the black belt of trees. At the top of the hill, on an impulse, I drew in to the side of the road and got out of the car. This was the very place. At the edge of the wood, under the brilliant moon, the smooth boles of the beeches shone with an eerie radiance and, high above, the branches creaked as they swayed in the wind.

I walked into the wood, feeling my way carefully with an arm held before me till I came out on the other side. Raynes Abbey lay before me.

I had always associated the beautiful ruin with summer days with the sun warming the old stones of the graceful arches, the chatter of voices, children playing on the cropped turf; but this was 2.30 AM in an empty world and the cold breath of the coming winter on my face. I felt suddenly alone.

In the cold glare everything was uncannily distinct. But there was a look of unreality about the silent rows of columns reaching into the dark sky and throwing their long pale shadows over the grass. Away at the far end I could see the monks' cells — gloomy black caverns deep in shadow — and as I looked an owl hooted, accentuating the heavy, blanketing silence.

A prickling apprehension began to creep over me, a feeling that my living person had no place here among these brooding relics of dead centuries. I turned quickly and began to hurry through the wood, bumping into the trees, tripping over roots and bushes, and when I reached my car I was trembling and more out of breath than I should have been. It was good to slam the door, turn the ignition and hear the familiar roar of the engine.

I was home within ten minutes and trotted up the stairs, looking forward to catching up on my lost sleep. Opening my bedroom door I flicked on the switch and felt a momentary surprise when the room remained in darkness. Then I stood frozen in the doorway.

By the window, where the moonlight flooded in, making a pool of silver in the gloom, a monk was standing. A monk in a brown habit, motionless, arms folded, head bowed. His face was turned from the light towards me but I could see nothing under the drooping cowl but a horrid abyss of darkness.

I thought I would choke. My mouth opened but no sound came. And in my racing mind one thought pounded above the others — there were such things as ghosts after all.

Again my mouth opened and a hoarse shriek emerged.

'Who in the name of God is that?'

The reply came back immediately in a sepulchral bass.

'Tristaan.'

I don't think I actually swooned, but I did

collapse limply across my bed and lay there gasping, the blood thundering in my ears. I was dimly aware of the monk standing on a chair and screwing in the light bulb, giggling helplessly the while. Then he flicked on the switch and sat on my bed. With his cowl pushed back on his shoulders he lit a Woodbine and looked down at me, still shaking with laughter.

'Oh God, Jim, that was marvellous — even better than I expected.'

I stared up at him and managed a whisper. 'But you're in Edinburgh . . . '

'Not me, old lad. There wasn't much doing so I concluded my business and hitched straight back, I'd just got in when I saw you coming up the garden. Barely had time to get the bulb out and climb into my outfit — I couldn't miss the opportunity.'

'Feel my heart,' I murmured.

Tristan rested his hand on my ribs for a moment and as he felt the fierce hammering a fleeting concern crossed his face.

'Hell, I'm sorry, Jim.' Then he patted my shoulder reassuringly. 'But don't worry. If it was going to be fatal you'd have dropped down dead on the spot. And anyway, a good fright is very beneficial — acts like a tonic. You won't need a holiday this year.'

'Thanks,' I said. 'Thanks very much.'

'I wish you could have heard yourself.' He began to laugh again. 'That scream of terror . . . oh dear, oh dear!'

I hoisted myself slowly into a sitting position, pulled out the pillow, propped it against the bed head and leaned back against it. I still felt very weak.

I eyed him coldly. 'So you're the Raynes ghost.'

Tristan grinned in reply but didn't speak.

'You young devil! I should have known. But tell me, why do you do it? What do you get out of it?'

'Oh I don't know.' The young man gazed dreamily at the ceiling through the cigarette smoke. 'I suppose it's just getting the timing right so that the drivers aren't quite sure whether they've seen me or not. And then I get a hell of a kick out of hearing them revving up like mad and roaring off for home. None of them ever slows down.'

'Well, somebody once told me your sense of humour was overdeveloped,' I said. 'And I'm telling you it'll land you in the cart one of these days.'

'Not a chance. I keep my bike behind a hedge about a hundred yards down the road so that I can make a quick getaway if necessary. There's no problem.'

'Well, please yourself.' I got off the bed and made shakily for the door. 'I'm going downstairs for a tot of whisky, and just remember this.' I turned and glared at him. 'If you try that trick on me again I'll strangle you.'

★   ★   ★

A few days later at about eight o'clock in the evening I was sitting reading by the fireside in

153

the big room at Skeldale House when the door burst open and Siegfried burst into the room.

'James,' he rapped out. 'Old Horace Dawson's cow has split its teat. Sounds like a stitching job. The old chap won't be able to hold the cow and he has no near neighbours to help him so I wonder if you'd come and give me a hand.'

'Sure, glad to.' I marked the place in my book, stretched and yawned then got up from the chair. I noticed Siegfried's foot tapping on the carpet and it occurred to me, not for the first time, that the only thing that would satisfy him would be some kind of ejector seat on my chair which would hurl me straight through the door and into action on the word of command. I was being as quick as I could but I had the feeling as always — when I was writing something for him or operating under his eyes — that I wasn't going nearly fast enough. There were elements of tension in the knowledge that the mere fact of watching me rise from the chair and replace my book in the fireside alcove was an almost unbearable strain for him.

By the time I was halfway across the carpet he had disappeared into the passage. I followed at a trot and just made it into the street as he was starting the car. Grabbing the door I made a dive for the interior and felt the road whip away from under my foot as we took off into the darkness.

Fifteen minutes later we screeched to a halt in the yard behind a little smallholding standing on its own across a couple of fields. The engine had barely stopped before my colleague was out of the car and striding briskly towards the cow house. He called to me over his shoulder as he went.

'Bring the suture materials, James, will you . . . and the local and syringe . . . and that bottle of wound lotion . . . '

I heard the brief murmur of conversation from within then Siegfried's voice again, raised this time in an impatient shout.

'James! What are you doing out there? Can't you find those things?'

I had hardly got the boot open and I rummaged frantically among the rows of tins and bottles. I found what he required, galloped across the yard and almost collided with him as he came out of the building.

He was in mid shout. 'James! What the hell's keeping you . . . oh, you're there. Right, let's have the stuff . . . what have you been doing all this time?'

He had been right about Horace Dawson, a tiny frail man of about eighty who couldn't be expected to do any strong-arm stuff. Despite his age he had stubbornly refused to give up milking the two fat shorthorn cows which stood in the little cobbled byre.

Our patient had badly damaged a teat; either she or her neighbour must have stood on it because there was a long tear running almost full length with the milk running from it.

'It's a bad one, Horace,' Siegfried said. 'You can see it goes right into the milk channel. But we'll do what we can for her — it'll need a good few stitches in there.'

He bathed and disinfected the teat then filled

155

a syringe with local anaesthetic.

'Grab her nose, James,' he said, then spoke gently to the farmer. 'Horace, will you please hold her tail for me. Just catch it by the very end, that's the way . . . lovely.'

The little man squared his shoulders. 'Aye, ah can do that fine, Mr Farnon.'

'Good lad, Horace, that's splendid, thank you. Now stand well clear.' He bent over and as I gripped the animal's nose he inserted the needle above the top extremity of the wound.

There was an instant smacking sound as the cow registered her disapproval by kicking Siegfried briskly halfway up his Wellington boot. He made no sound but breathed deeply and flexed his knee a couple of times before crouching down again.

'Gush pet,' he murmured soothingly as he stuck the needle in again.

This time the cloven foot landed on his forearm, sending the syringe winging gracefully through the air till it came to rest, by a piece of good fortune, in the hay-rack. Siegfried straightened up, rubbed his arm thoughtfully, retrieved his syringe and approached the patient again.

For a few moments he scratched around the root of her tail and addressed her in the friendliest manner. 'All right, old lady, it isn't very nice, is it?'

When he got down again he adopted a new stance, burrowing with his head into the cow's flank and stretching his long arms high he managed despite a few more near misses to infiltrate the tissues round the wound with local.

Then he proceeded to thread a needle unhurriedly, whistling tunelessly under his breath.

Mr Dawson watched him admiringly. 'Ah know why you're such a good feller wi' animals, Mr Farnon. It's because you're so patient — I reckon you're t'patientest man ah've ever seen.'

Siegfried inclined his head modestly and recommenced work. And it was more peaceful now. The cow couldn't feel a thing as my colleague put in a long, even row of stitches, pulling the lips of the wound firmly together.

When he had finished he put an arm round the old man's shoulders.

'Now, Horace, if that heals well the teat will be as good as new. But it won't heal if you pull at it, so I want you to use this tube to milk her.' He held up a bottle of spirit in which a teat syphon gleamed.

'Very good,' said Mr Dawson firmly. 'Ah'll use it.'

Siegfried wagged a playful finger in his face. 'But you've got to be careful, you know. You must boil the tube every time before use and keep it always in the bottle or you'll finish up with mastitis. Will you do that?'

'Mr Farnon,' the little man said, holding himself very erect. 'Ah'll do exactly as you say.'

'That's my boy, Horace.' Siegfried gave him a final pat on the back before starting to pick up his instruments. 'I'll pop back in about two weeks to take the stitches out.'

As we were leaving, the vast form of Claude Blenkiron loomed suddenly in the byre door. He

157

was the village policeman, though obviously off duty judging by the smart check jacket and slacks.

'I saw you had summat on, Horace, and I wondered if you wanted a hand.'

'Nay, thank ye, Mr Blenkiron. It's good of ye but you're ower late. We've done t'job,' the old man replied.

Siegfried laughed. 'Wish you'd arrived half an hour ago, Claude. You could have tucked this cow under your arm while I stitched her.'

The big man nodded and a slow smile spread over his face. He looked the soul of geniality but I felt, as always, that there was a lot of iron behind that smile. Claude was a well-loved character in the district, a magnificent athlete who bestowed lavish help and friendship on all who needed it on his beat. But though he was a sturdy prop to the weak and the elderly he was also a merciless scourge of the ungodly.

I had no first hand knowledge but there were rumours that Claude preferred not to trouble the magistrates with trivialities but dispensed his own form of instant justice. It was said that he kept a stout stick handy and acts of hooliganism and vandalism were rapidly followed by a shrill yowling down some dark alley. Second offenders were almost unknown and in fact his whole district was remarkably law-abiding. I looked again at the smiling face. He really was the most pleasant-looking man but as I say there was something else there and nothing would ever have induced me to pick a fight with him.

'Right, then,' he said. 'I was just on me way into Darrowby so I'll say goodnight, gentlemen.'

Siegfried put a hand on his arm. 'Just a moment, Claude, I want to go on to see another of my cases. I wonder if you'd give Mr Herriot a lift into the town.'

'I'll do that with pleasure, Mr Farnon,' the policeman replied and beckoned me to follow him.

In the darkness outside I got into the passenger seat of a little Morris Eight and waited for a few moments while Claude squeezed his bulk behind the wheel. As we set off he began to talk about his recent visit to Bradford where he had been taking part in a wrestling match.

We had to go through Raynes village on the way back and as we left the houses behind and began the ascent to the abbey he suddenly stopped talking. Then he startled me as he snapped upright in his seat and pointed ahead.

'Look, look there, it's that bloody monk!'

'Where? Where?' I feigned ignorance but I had seen it all right — the cowled, slow-pacing figure heading for the wood.

Claude's foot was on the boards and the car was screaming up the hill. At the top he swung savagely on to the roadside grass so that the headlights blazed into the depth of the wood and as he leapt from the car there was a fleeting moment when his quarry was in full view; a monk, skirts hitched high, legging it with desperate speed among the trees.

The big man reached into the back of the car and pulled out what looked like a heavy walking stick. 'After the bugger!' he shouted, plunging eagerly forward.

I panted after him. 'Wait a minute, what are you going to do if you catch him?'

'I'm goin' to come across his arse with me ash plant,' Claude said with chilling conviction and galloped ahead of me till he disappeared from the circle of light. He was making a tremendous noise, beating against the tree trunks and emitting a series of intimidating shouts.

My heart bled for the hapless spectre blundering in the darkness with the policeman's cries dinning in his ears. I waited with tingling horror for the final confrontation and the tension increased as time passed and I could still hear Claude in full cry; 'Come out of there, you can't get away! Come on, show yourself!' while his splintering blows echoed among the trees.

I did my own bit of searching but found nothing. The monk did indeed seem to have disappeared and when I finally returned to the car I found the big man already there.

'Well that's a rum 'un, Mr Herriot,' he said. 'I can't find 'im and I can't think where he's got to. I was hard on his heels when I first spotted him and he didn't get out of the wood because I can see over the fields in the moonlight. I've 'ad a scout round the abbey too, but he isn't there. He's just bloody vanished.'

I was going to say something like, 'Well, what else would you expect from a ghost?' but the huge hand was still swinging that stick and I decided against it.

'Well I reckon we'd better get on to

Darrowby,' the policeman grunted, stamping his feet on the frosty turf. I shivered. It was bitterly cold with an east wind getting up and I was glad to climb back into the car.

In Darrowby I had a few companionable beers with Claude at his favourite haunt, the Black Bull, and it was ten thirty when I got into Skeldale House. There was no sign of Tristan and I felt a twinge of anxiety.

It must have been after midnight when I was awakened by a faint scuffling from the next room. Tristan occupied what had been the long, narrow 'dressing room' in the grand days when the house was young. I jumped out of bed and opened the communicating door.

Tristan was in pyjamas and he cuddled two hot water bottles to his bosom. He turned his head and gave me a single haggard glance before pushing one of the bottles well down the bed. Then he crawled between the sheets and lay on his back with the second bottle clasped across his chest and his eyes fixed on the ceiling. I went over and looked down at him in some concern. He was shaking so much that the whole bed vibrated with him.

'How are you, Triss?' I whispered.

After a few moments a faint croak came up. 'Frozen to the bloody marrow, Jim.'

'But where the heck have you been?'

Again the croak. 'In a drainpipe.'

'A drainpipe!' I stared at him. 'Where?'

The head rolled feebly from side to side on the pillow. 'Up at the wood. Didn't you see the pipes by the roadside?'

A great light flashed. 'Of course, yes! They're going to put a new sewer into the village, aren't they?'

'That's right,' Tristan whispered. 'When I saw that big bloke pounding into the wood I cut straight back and dived into one of the pipes. God only knows how long I was in there.'

'But why didn't you come out after we left?'

A violent shudder shook the young man's frame and he closed his eyes briefly. 'I couldn't hear a thing in there. I was jammed tight with my cowl over my ears and there was a ninety mile an hour wind screaming down the pipe. I didn't hear the car start and I daren't come out in case that chap was still standing there with his bloody great shillelagh.' He took hold of the quilt with one hand and picked at it fitfully.

'Well never mind, Triss,' I said. 'You'll soon get warmed up and you'll be all right after a night's sleep.'

Tristan didn't appear to have heard. 'They're horrible things, drainpipes, Jim.' He looked up at me with hunted eyes. 'They're full of muck and they stink of cats' pee.'

'I know, I know.' I put his hand back inside the quilt and pulled the sheets up round his chin. 'You'll be fine in the morning.' I switched off the light and tiptoed from the room. As I closed the door I could still hear his teeth chattering.

Clearly it wasn't only the cold that was bothering him; he was still in a state of shock. And no wonder. The poor fellow had been enjoying a little session of peaceful haunting with never a care in the world when without warning there was a scream of brakes a blaze of light and that giant bounding into the middle of it like the demon king. It had all been too much.

Next morning at the breakfast table Tristan was in poor shape. He looked very pale, he ate little and at intervals his body was racked by deep coughing spasms.

Siegfried looked at him quizzically. 'I know what's done this to you. I know why you're sitting there like a zombie, coughing your lungs up.'

His brother stiffened in his chair and a tremor crossed his face. 'You do?'

'Yes, I hate to say I told you so, but I did warn you, didn't I? It's all those bloody cigarettes!'

★　★　★

Tristan never did give up smoking but the Raynes ghost was seen no more and remains an unsolved mystery to this day.

13

The arrangement with Ewan Ross had worked out very well. It meant a lot of driving for me; twenty-five miles to Scarburn, then a full day round the farms in that area followed by the run back to Darrowby at night, but I enjoyed working up there on the airy summit of Yorkshire and meeting a fresh community of farmers who, like all hillmen, seemed to vie with each other in hospitality. In their rough, flagged kitchens I ate superb meals which belied their modest description of 'a bit o' dinner' and it was almost routine for me to bring home a parcel of butter, a few eggs, sometimes an exquisite piece of spare rib.

Of course I realize I was lucky. At the commencement of the Tuberculin Testing Scheme there was a nice incentive bonus on the milk or on the numbers of cattle and I appeared on the farms almost as a bringer of bounty. In later years when attestation became universal the stock owners came to regard the tests as a necessary nuisance, but, as I say, I was lucky — I was in on the honeymoon period.

The arrangement suited Siegfried, too. Certainly he had to work hard on the days when I was away but it brought in some welcome revenue to the practice.

And best of all it suited Ewan, because without doing a single thing or even thinking about it he had a Ministry cheque on his breakfast table every quarter. This was absolutely tailored to his personality because nothing would ever have induced him to spend hours in routine work, then go home and fill in forms with long columns of descriptions and ages and measurements.

When he had to do a job he did it magnificently. And he did it with such care — always boiling up before he left the house and wrapping syringes and instruments in his strips of clean brown paper of which he must have had an endless supply. But if he could get away with it he stayed at home. In fact, after lunch every day he took off his shoes, put on his slippers and got down by the fireside. Once he was there it took something spectacular to shift him.

I have seen him sitting there smoking while Ginny answered the phone to farmers who wanted his services.

'Och, it'll do tomorrow,' he would say.

Not for him the sweat of fighting the clock, the panic of urgent calls coming in from opposite directions, the tightening ball of tension in the stomach when the work began to pile up. No, no, he put on his slippers, rolled cigarettes and let it all flow past him.

He had only a mild interest in the work we did in Darrowby but he was fascinated by the funny things that happened to us. He dearly loved to listen to my accounts of the various contretemps at Skeldale House and, strangely, he wanted to hear them again and again almost as a child would. Often, as he lay back in his chair with the smoke rising from his twisted little cigarette he would say suddenly in his soft Highland-Canadian voice.

'Tell me about the rubber suit.'

I must have told him that tale twenty times before but it made no difference. He would gaze fixedly at me as I went through the story again and though his expression hardly changed his shoulders would begin to shake silently and the pale blue eyes to brim with tears.

Looking back I often wonder who was right — Ewan or all the successful vets who gave themselves ulcers dashing round in circles. I do know that he enjoyed a deference from his clients which I never encountered elsewhere. Perhaps there is a lesson somewhere in the fact that he received grateful thanks if he went to an animal the same day he was called, whereas Siegfried and I who tried to get to a case within twenty minutes were greeted with 'what kept you?' if we took half an hour.

There was another advantage to Ewan in having me to do his testing; he was able to pass on occasional private jobs to me while I was on the farms and as the weeks passed he began to use me more and more as a general assistant. It became commonplace for the farmers to say, 'Oh, and Mr Ross said would you take some nan-berries off a stirk's belly while you're here,' or 'Will you inject some calves for scour? Mr Ross rang and said you were coming.' One morning I was startled to find a couple of strapping two-year-old horses waiting for me to castrate standing before I commenced the day's work.

If the farmers had any objection to a young stranger doing their work they never voiced it. Whatever Ewan did or arranged was right with them; in fact there didn't seem to be much they wouldn't do for him.

This was brought home to me forcibly one night. I had had a particularly rough day in the Scarburn district. Herds which I thought had about twenty animals turned out to have fifty or sixty and these were scattered around in little buildings miles apart on the fell-sides. There was only one way to get to them — you walked; and while this might have been enjoyable in good weather it had been a lowering late autumn day with a gusting wind scouring the flattened grass and almost piercing my bones like the first quick gleam of winter's teeth. It had almost stupefied me.

And on top of that I had had a wider than usual selection of Ewan's private jobs; a couple of cleansings, a farrowing, a few pregnancy diagnoses; all jacket-off jobs which left my arms raw and painful. I must have tested about four hundred unyielding bovines, elbowing and squeezing between their craggy bodies, and it seemed almost too much that just when I was turning away from the very last cow of the day she should kick me resoundingly just behind the knee. This farewell gesture dropped me in a moaning heap on the byre floor and it was some minutes before I was able to hobble away.

The journey back to Darrowby had seemed

interminable and it didn't help at all when I got home and found that Siegfried was out and there were a few more calls left for me in our own practice. When I finally crawled into bed I had nothing left to offer.

It was just after midnight when the bedside phone rang. With a feeling of disbelief I recognized Ewan's voice — what the devil could he possibly want with me at this hour?

'Hello, Jim, sorry to disturb you.' The words seemed to reach out and caress me.

'That's all right, Ewan, what can I do for you?' I said trying to sound casual but gripping the sheets tightly with my free hand.

Ewan paused for a moment. 'Well now I'm in a wee bit of bother here. It's a calving.'

The window rattled as the wind buffeted the glass. 'A calving?' I quavered.

'Yes, a big cow with a great long pelvis and the calf's head is back. I've been trying for an hour but I'm damned if I can reach it — my arm's not long enough.'

'Ah yes, I've a very short arm myself,' I babbled. 'I know just how you feel. I'm no good when it comes to jobs like that.'

A soft chuckle came over the line. 'Oh, I don't want your arm, Jim, it's that embryotome I want.'

'Embryotome?'

'That's right. Remember you were telling me what a wonderful instrument it was.'

Why couldn't I keep my big mouth shut? My mind began to hunt round desperately for a way of escape.

168

'But Ewan, you'd kill the calf. An embryotome isn't indicated in a case like this.'

'This calf's dead and stinking, Jim. All I want is to get its head off to save the cow.'

I was trapped. I didn't say anything more but lay quivering, waiting for the terrible words which I knew were coming.

They came all right. 'Just slip out here and do it for me will you, Jim?'

As I tottered from my bed I became aware immediately that the knee where I had been kicked had stiffened up and I could hardly bend it. In the darkness of the garden the dead leaves crunched softly under my feet and when I reached the yard the wind roared in the elms, tearing the last leaves from the branches and hurling them past my face like driven snow flakes.

Huddled over the wheel, my head nodding with weariness, I drove out of the town. My destination was Hutton House, a farm about five miles on the other side of Scarburn, and I muttered feebly to myself as I peered through the windscreen.

'Just slip out here!' he says. 'Just slip out thirty bloody miles over narrow twisting roads and get down on your belly and knock your guts out!' Damn Ewan Ross, and damn his Highland charm and his Highland indolence. I was like a bloody little shuttlecock — back and forth, back and forth. And I was absolutely whacked and my arms were sore and my knee ached. Almost whimpering with self pity I bemoaned my lot. This country vetting was a mug's game. I should have been a doctor, my mother always wanted me to be a doctor, and I wouldn't have to drive thirty miles to a cold cow house but just pop round the corner into a nice warm bedroom and pat the hand of some sweet old lady and dole out a few pills then back within minutes to my bed — my deep, deep, soft, soft bed . . .

I lurched suddenly into wakefulness as the car careered straight for the roadside wall. Gripping the wheel tightly, feeling the wind pulling against the steering, I decided that the main thing was not to fall asleep. It wasn't easy; there was a numbing sameness about the miles of walls, the endless strip of road rolling out before me, but finally, after about an hour, I chugged into Scarburn and for a few moments my headlights swept across the unheeding tight-shut face of the little town. Then the last five miles with the engine fighting against the rising ground before I drew up outside the gate of Hutton House.

I should say the first gate because there were four along the track leading to the pin point of light high on the fell-side. And at each gate the wind, whipping straight from the north, tugged fiercely at the car door as I got out and each time as I turned away from the headlights the fields were lost in the blackness and there was only the cold glitter of stars in a clean-swept sky.

At last the huddle of farm buildings lay before me and I drove up to the chink of brightness which came from the byre door. Even here in the yard the wind tore at me as I wrestled with the boot. Gasping, I lifted out my wellingtons, bottle of antiseptic and the accursed embryotome and

170

hurried over to the low building.

Inside, all was peace; a delicious warmth rising from the low row of somnolent cows, my patient propped on her chest between two bales, Mr Hugill, the stooping, wrinkled farmer and Ewan sitting comfortably cross-legged, smoking one of his funny cigarettes. He was sitting in a chair, too — they had even brought a chair out here for him — and in the light of the big oil lamp he looked across at me without speaking for a moment then he gave me his shy smile.

'Jim, it's good of you to come. I've had a damn hard try but I know when I'm beat. I can tell you you're a sight for sore eyes walking in that door.'

Mr Hugill chuckled. 'Aye, we're badly in need of a bit o'young blood on t'job.'

Suddenly I stopped feeling sorry for myself. I didn't care about the long journey, about being winkled from my delectable bed. But I didn't feel much like young blood as I stripped off, knelt down gingerly on my stiff knee and thrust an arm, chafed red and tingling from the antiseptic, into the cow.

I realized straight away what Ewan meant. This cow did have a hell of a long pelvis. The calf's feet were in the passage and the head was tucked away back along the ribs somewhere. I had to surmise this because at full stretch I could just reach the cleft made by the flexion of the neck. There was no chance of straightening it out, so my task was clear; I had to get an embryotomy wire down that cleft and round the neck so that I could cut off the head.

This was one of those calvings without the

171

true savour; without the rewarding sight of a new living creature at the finish. But sometimes it happened like this. The calf I was feeling had been dead for about twenty-four hours judging by the sweetish smell and the emphysematous crackling under the skin, and had to be regarded simply as a piece of inanimate tissue which had to be removed or the mother would surely die of septicaemia or have to be slaughtered. As though divining my thoughts the cow laid her head along her side, looked at me and moaned softly. She had the bonny white face of the Hereford Cross and she looked sick; she wanted rid of that thing inside her more than anybody.

The usual procedure is to pass a cord round the part to be cut off and then pull the wire through; but it isn't as easy as that. It is one thing pushing it into a tight space but quite another thing finding it at the other side. Fortunately some intelligent chap who clearly knew what calving was all about had come up with a simple invention — a heavy lead weight with a small hole at one end for the cord and a bigger one at the other end for your finger.

I fished my weight out now and again pushed an arm alongside the dry legs and up to the cleft in the neck. By straining to the limit I managed to force the weight forward and felt it fall down into the cleft. I came out of the cow now and carefully soaped my arm. This was the moment of truth. If I could get hold of the weight on the underside of the neck and pull it through with the cord attached the rest was easy. The job was over in fact. If I couldn't reach it all was lost.

Again down on the cobbles and again the long reach between the calf's legs and the clinging vaginal wall right forward beneath the twisted neck where my lead weight just had to be. It wasn't there. Digging my toes between the stones on the floor I fought for another inch and managed to pass my fingers up into the cleft. Still nothing. The weight hadn't fallen through — it was stuck up there, probably a fraction above my groping fingers; and my hopes were stuck with it.

I went back to the bucket and soaped the other arm. Sometimes that worked. But the result was the same; a desperate fumbling at nothing. Not for the first time I cursed the accident of anatomy which had given me a short arm. Siegfried with his slender build and long reach would have been putting his jacket on by now, all ready to go home.

But there was nothing else for it but to fight on — and I wasn't in shape for fighting. Even a man in peak condition can't spend much time inside a cow without having the blood squeezed relentlessly from his arm by the uterine contractions, but when he starts as I did from a point of maximum fragility it is really no contest. It took only about a minute for my arm to be reduced to something like a stalk of asparagus with useless twitching fingers on the end. I had to keep changing round faster and faster till I was flopping on the cobbles like a stranded fish. And all the time it was getting worse in there; drier, more clinging, everything closing down till I could hardly move, never mind get my hand on that precious lead weight.

I must have gone on like this for the best part of an hour before the futility of it became plain. I had to try something else. Hoisting myself on to my knees I turned round.

'Mr Hugill, would you please bring me some warm water in another bucket.'

As the farmer hurried from the byre I turned to Ewan.

'It's that bloody weight,' I said. 'I expected it to fall straight down but it hasn't. The bend in the neck must be so tight the thing can't get through. I'm going to pump some water in to see if it'll open things up a bit.'

Ewan looked with compassion at my sweating face and sagging jaw, at the caked dirt and slime and bits of straw sticking to my chest. 'Right, Jim,' he said. 'That sounds like a good idea.'

I didn't enjoy my visit out to the car. Standing stripped to the waist in total darkness in the teeth of a north wind is an overrated pastime but it made a change from the cobbles. I fumbled a pump and rubber tube from the boot and returned to the byre at a trot.

Ewan operated the pump as I pushed the tube forward over the dried-out legs, playing the water from side to side and especially into that bend in the neck.

When I had finished I came out of the cow quickly, dropped the tube and, slightly breathless, soaped my arm again. This was really it this time. That water would give me more room, but only for a few seconds.

Lying down again I inserted my arm and it

was like a different world — lots of space, everything moist and moveable. My fingers trembled as they inched forward under that neck and, hallelujah, the weight was there, the smooth, metallic, beautiful edge of the thing just projecting from among the hair. I could twiddle it with the end of my fingers and I felt it gradually coming down till the hole was within reach and I thrust my finger through it with savage relief and lay like that for a few moments smiling stupidly down at the wet stones and knowing I had won.

The rest was routine. Joining the cord to the wire and pulling it round the neck; threading the wire through the shining steel tubes of the embryotome which protected the vaginal wall from the cutting edge; the few minutes of steady sawing till the sudden lack of resistance told that the head was off and the obstruction removed.

After that, Ewan and I took a leg apiece and delivered the calf without difficulty, the head followed and the job was done. Swilling myself down with the last of the water I looked at the cow; she had had a long tussle but nothing to do her any harm; no hard pulling, no internal damage. She should be all right. And as though trying to reassure me she hunched her hind legs under her, gave a heave and got to her feet.

'By Gaw, that's a good sign,' Mr Hugill said.

The cow turned her fine white face towards me for a moment, straddled her legs, strained a couple of times, and the placenta welled in multi-coloured entirety from her vulva and plopped into the channel.

'And that's a better sign,' Ewan murmured. He looked at his watch. 'Nearly three o'clock.' Then he turned to the farmer. 'Is your missus up, Mr Hugill?'

The old man didn't seem surprised at the question, in fact he seemed to be expecting it. 'Aye, she's up, right enough, Mr Ross?'

'And is the fire on?'

'Aye, there's a real good fire, Mr Ross,' he replied eagerly.

'Splendid!' Ewan said, rubbing his hands. 'Well, I think we'll have some boiled eggs.' He looked over at me. 'Boiled eggs all right for you, Jim?'

'Boiled eggs?' The concept was difficult to grasp at this hour.

'Yes, just the thing for you after your hard work.'

'Oh well, right, just as you say.'

Ewan became very brisk. 'Fine, we'll have boiled eggs, Mr Hugill, and some tea of course, and maybe a little toast.' He rubbed his chin thoughtfully like a diner at his favourite restaurant pondering over the menu. 'Oh and a few scones would be very nice.'

'Very good, Mr Ross, I'll go in and tell t'missus.' The farmer nodded happily and scuttled away.

Ten minutes later, walking into the farmhouse kitchen, I felt strangely disembodied. Maybe it was because my physical state had progressed from mere exhaustion to something like coma, but the whole thing seemed unreal. The brasses of hearth and mantelpiece glinting in the flames from a crackling wood fire, the table under a hissing tilly lamp laden with its burden of scones, crusty bread, ham and egg pie, curd tarts, fruit cake; it all looked like something from a dream. And it was funny, but the most incredible objects of all were the boiled eggs, brown and massive, top heavy in their china cradles, two for Ewan at the top of the table and two for me down the side.

Mrs Hugill, stout and beaming, poured our tea, then she and her husband sat down on either side of the fire and waited with evident interest for us to go into action. Ewan with total lack of self consciousness began busily to knock the tops off his eggs and slap butter on the toast. I followed mechanically, noting even through the mists that the eggs had a creamy savour which you maybe only found when the hens spent their lives pecking around a 1,500 foot high farmyard, and that the tang of yeast was strong in the homemade bread even though I mumbled it with a dry mouth and numb lips. The tea, too, would have been excellent but for the fact that I added salt to it instead of sugar; just sat and watched myself pouring salt from the little spoon first on to my egg plate then into my tea. It tasted different, but I don't recommend it.

All the time the call of home and bed was getting stronger but Ewan was in no hurry. Speaking through a mouthful of ham and egg pie he addressed his hostess.

'Mrs Hugill, now I know why you always win the prizes at Scarburn show with your baking.'

As the good lady giggled with pleasure I

177

struggled to my feet. 'I second that, Mrs Hugill, I've really enjoyed it, but it's time I was away. I've a long way to go.

Ewan swallowed, wiped his lips and smiled across the table. 'Well I can't thank you enough, Jim. You've saved the situation. I couldn't have done what you've done tonight even if I'd had your magic embryotome.'

'Oh that's all right, it's been a pleasure.' I made my way to the door and took a last look back at the scene which I still could scarcely believe; the farmer and his wife nodding and waving from the bright fireside, Ewan, in lordly state at the head of the table, hacking vigorously at a large Wensleydale cheese.

I hardly noticed the run back. In a comfortable state of suspended animation I sat with half-closed eyes fixed on the road ahead. There was none of the apprehension of the journey out, none of the moaning and griping, just the warm satisfaction that a good cow would be pulling hay from its rack tomorrow instead of hanging from the butcher's hook. Only a little thing, nothing world-shaking about it, but good.

When I drove into the yard at Skeldale House the gale had blown itself out leaving a deep litter of leaves shining brilliant gold in the headlights and I scuffed my way through them, ankle deep, feeling the still air cool on my face in the darkness. Bed was an unbelievable haven and as I floated away my last emotion was a feeling of wonder at the things the farmers would do for Ewan Ross.

My clients had shown me many kindnesses in

the past and I had a lot of future still ahead of me, but I doubted whether anybody would ever give me boiled eggs at three o'clock in the morning.

14

It was the chance to start my public speaking career; a definite opportunity which I knew I should grasp, yet I shrank from it.

'Oh I don't know,' I said to the curate, 'I've never done anything of the sort before. Maybe you'd better look for somebody else.'

The curate beamed on me. He was in his thirties and had always struck me as being a saintly man since he obviously saw no evil in anything or anybody.

'Oh come now, Mr Herriot. I'm sure you'd manage splendidly and the youth club are longing to hear you. A lot of my young people are from farming families and they'd be quite fascinated to have a vet speak to them.'

'Well it's very nice of you to say so, Mr Blenkinsopp.' But I had a mental image of the packed church hall, the rows of faces looking up at me, and I began to sweat at the very thought. 'I tell you what — if they want to hear a vet I'll get Mr Farnon to give them a talk. He's very good.'

The curate squeezed my arm. 'But Mr Herriot, it's you I want. You are very young and the boys and girls would have something in common with you from the start. And you'd only have to speak for about half an hour and then there would be questions and a lively discussion.'

'Oh I don't think I'd better,' I muttered

though inwardly I writhed at the shame of being scared to get up in front of an audience. 'Maybe some other time, but I really don't feel I could do it just at present.'

Mr Blenkinsopp sighed. 'Ah well, just as you wish, but I know the club members will be disappointed. And Miss Alderson, too.'

'Miss Alderson?'

'Yes, Helen helps me run the club. In fact it was she who suggested you as a speaker.'

'She did?'

'Yes, indeed.'

'She attends all the meetings, I suppose?' I said.

'Oh of course. I'm sure she was looking forward to seeing you at our next get-together.'

'Mm . . . well . . . I wonder. Maybe I'd better have a bash at it.'

'Splendid!' The curate's face shone with pleasure. 'You have plenty of time — it's not till three weeks on Tuesday.'

★ ★ ★

'Well done, James.' Siegfried said at lunch. 'I'm glad you've grasped the nettle. All professional men have to get used to public speaking and the sooner you begin the better. And it helps our image — one has to wave the flag a little now and then.'

'I suppose so.' I fiddled with my napkin for a moment. 'But I haven't much idea about what to say. Have you any suggestions?'

'Thank you, Mrs Hall, that looks wonderful.'

181

Siegfried said to our housekeeper as she impassively placed a large steak and kidney pie in front of him. Then he turned to me again. 'Well, James, you've been asked to speak as a vet so you've got to deal with veterinary matters. If they're farmers' sons and daughters they'll lap it up.'

'Yes, but that's a big subject. What exactly do you mean?'

My employer attacked the pie resolutely and a heavenly steam escaped as his knife pierced the crust. 'Pass your plate, James.' He mounded on meat and pastry then pushed a tureen of mashed potatoes towards me. 'I know it's a big subject so you've got to pick out some attractive and interesting aspects.'

'I don't think I'd know where to start,' I said. 'I wish you'd sort of sketch something out for me.'

Siegfried chewed thoughtfully for a few moments. 'Everybody has their own ideas about these things, of course, but if I were you I'd start off with something to catch their attention — some provocative remark or question — then I'd paint a broad tapestry of the profession, including its history, and in between I'd shove in some practical things, maybe about first aid in animals.'

'First aid, eh?'

'Yes, that's right.' My employer was warming to his subject. 'How to stop haemorrhage, how to deal with emergencies when the vet isn't available. How about puncturing the rumen in a bloated cow? That would make them sit up.'

'It would, wouldn't it? Yes, I think I'll do that.'
I made a few mental notes. 'But how about the opening remark you mentioned? Any ideas about that?'

Siegfried carefully transported an extra boiled leek from its bed of white sauce on to his plate. For perhaps a minute he stared ahead of him in silence then without warning he crashed his fist down on the table, making me bite my tongue painfully.

'I've got it, James! Not a shadow of a doubt about it.' He held up a finger and intoned, 'WHAT DOES MRCVS MEAN TO YOU? There's your opening line — how about that?'

'Gosh, it's good!' I gazed at him admiringly. 'What does MRCVS mean to you? I really like that.'

'There you are, then,' he said, chewing smugly, 'and you must deliver it in loud, ringing tones. You'll have them on the edge of their seats right from the start, and gasping to hear more. A good beginning is vital.'

'Well thanks, Siegfried, you've been a big help. I think I can get the material together now but the only thing is, can I put it over? I've never spoken in public — what if I dry up as soon as I get on my feet? What if I can't remember a thing?'

'Oh there's no possibility of that, but I know how you feel and I'll give you one more piece of advice.' He pointed solemnly at me with his fork. 'Since it's your first time you ought to get the whole thing word perfect. Practise it day by day till you can recite it like poetry,

183

then you'll be all right.'

'OK,' I said. 'I'll do that, too.'

Siegfried leaned back and laughed. 'Good lad! And in the meantime, stop worrying. You're going to knock 'em cold, James, I just know you are.'

★ ★ ★

I took his advice literally and over the next three weeks as I drove along the frost-bound roads my lips were continually moving as I harangued my imaginary audience. Several times I saw roadside workers look up in surprise as my declamations boomed out at them through the open windows, and I got to the stage where every syllable, every inflection tripped effortlessly off my tongue in perfect order.

In fact, it all began to sound so good to me that in a fearful sort of way I began to look forward to the big night. How many would be there to hear me? Fifty? Sixty? Maybe even a hundred? Well, let 'em all come. And Helen would be there. Maybe my stock wasn't so high in that direction but it wouldn't do any harm if she were to see me hold the mass of young people in my thrall, the youthful faces upturned eagerly to me, drinking in my every word.

My confidence grew steadily as the days passed and when the fateful Tuesday evening finally arrived I was in a state of pallid resolution. No panic. A certain tension and dryness of the mouth, but above all a cold determination to make good.

Before I left for the church hall I bathed, put on my best suit and inspected my face carefully in the mirror. It wouldn't do if I had a piece of cow muck sticking on an eyebrow in front of all that throng.

I was glad I didn't have far to walk because there had been a fall of snow that morning followed by a few hours of icy rain and the streets were deep in slush. As I opened the hall door and stepped inside, the curate met me with a radiant smile.

'Ah, Mr Herriot, here you are! So kind of you to come. Our young people can hardly wait to hear you.'

We were in a narrow lobby with doors on either side and from somewhere I could hear music and laughter. But I didn't pay much attention because Helen was coming down the stairs at the far end.

She laughed and for a moment her eyes held mine with that warm, interested, kind look which was part of her. It was a funny thing but whenever I met Helen she looked at me like that. I hadn't had a lot of luck in my contacts with her but afterwards there was no difference; it was always the same calm, friendly smile.

Of course she was a kind girl, Helen, that was it. This was probably the way she looked at everybody — with that soft flame kindling in her eyes' blue depths and the full lips parted over the white teeth. And there was the way her mouth went into little upturned folds in the corners . . . and how her dark hair fell softly across the white of her cheek . . .

But Mr Blenkinsopp was giving a series of little coughs. I dragged my attention back to him.

'Come in and see our club room before you start,' he said, opening one of the doors. 'I think you'll agree that it's a pleasant place for them to come on these wintry evenings.'

We went inside. A gramophone was playing and some pretty teenage girls were fox-trotting together to the music. A few lads lounged about while two others were playing billiards on a miniature table in the corner. The curate gazed fondly at the scene, the music stopped, the record was changed for a waltz and the dancing began again. It struck me as strange that it didn't seem to occur to any of the boys to dance with those attractive girls.

I looked at the two billiard players. They would be about fifteen or sixteen and were obviously devotees of the cinema. There was something of the Bowery pool room in their scowling attitude, the cigarettes dangling from their lips, the way they squinted through the smoke as they bent to play a shot, the tough, deadpan chalking of the cues, the contemptuous gangsterish disregard of the other occupants of the room.

The curate clapped his hands. 'Come now, boys and girls, it's time you joined the others in the hall. Mr Herriot is ready to talk to you now.'

The room emptied rapidly as the young people went through a door in the far corner. Soon there only remained the gangsters at the billiard table; they didn't appear to have heard.

186

The curate called on them several times more but they took no notice. Finally Helen went over and whispered tensely at them and at length they threw down their cues and with a single malevolent glance in my direction they slouched from the room.

This then was the moment of truth when I would face my audience after the weeks of preparation. I took a deep breath and followed the others into the hall and on to the platform. Perched on a shaky chair between Helen and Mr Blenkinsopp I surveyed the scene.

It wasn't a big hall — it would probably have held a hundred if it had been full. But it wasn't full tonight, in fact the main feature about it was space. I made a quick count of the audience; there were twelve. They were disposed in little knots among the empty chairs. Halfway up clustered the six teenage girls, then a few rows behind, a very fat boy holding a bag of potato crisps and near him a thin, dispirited-looking youth with sleepy eyes. Right on the back row, against the wall, the two gangsters lounged in attitudes of studied boredom. What surprised me most, however, was the sight of two tiny girls, mere tots of about four, right in the middle of the front row, a long way from anybody else. One sported a big pink bow in her hair while the other wore pigtails. Their little legs swinging, they looked up at me incuriously.

I turned to Helen. 'Who are those two?'

'Oh, they like to come with their big sisters now and again,' she replied. 'They love it and they're very good. They won't be any trouble.'

I nodded stupidly, still trying to adjust my mind to the fact that these were the people who were going to receive my searching exposition on veterinary science. None of them seemed to be showing the slightest interest in me except for one very pretty little thing in the centre of the teenage group who gazed up at me with shining eyes as though she couldn't wait for me to begin.

Mr Blenkinsopp stood up and made a charming introductory speech. As he spoke, the gangsters at the back giggled, wrestled and dug at each other's ribs; the girls, with the exception of the little darling in the centre peeped back at the fighting pair in admiration.

At last I heard the curate's final words. 'And now I have great pleasure in asking Mr Herriot to address you.'

I got slowly to my feet and gazed over the twelve. The gangsters were still wrestling, the fat boy put a crisp in his mouth and began to crunch it loudly, down in the front, tot number one was sucking her thumb while the other, rocking her head from side to side, appeared to be singing to herself.

I felt a moment of wild panic. Should I change the entire plan and just talk casually about a few trivial points? But I couldn't. I had the whole thing off parrot-like and I'd have to deliver it as I had learned it. There was no way out.

With an effort I steadied myself and cleared my throat. 'What does MRCVS mean to you?' I cried.

It seemed to startle Mr Blenkinsopp because he jumped slightly in his chair, but the audience remained totally unmoved. MRCVS appeared to mean not a thing to them. I ploughed ahead, sketching out the history of the Royal College, painstakingly illustrating its development from the early days of farriery. Nobody was listening except the little pet in the centre but I was in the groove and couldn't stop.

'A supplemental Royal Charter was granted in 1932,' I pronounced after about ten minutes' hard going and just then the thin boy yawned. I had labelled him as an ineffectual sort of lad but he certainly could yawn; it was a stretching, groaning, voluptuous paroxysm which drowned my words and it went on and on till he finally lay back, bleary and exhausted by the effort. His companion munched his crisps stolidly.

By the time I had been holding forth for twenty minutes I seemed to be standing listening to myself with a kind of wonder. 'After qualification,' I was saying, 'the main avenues open to the new graduate are general practice and work under the Ministry of Agriculture and Fisheries. The latter is mainly concerned with preventive medicine and with the implementation of the laws governing the notifiable diseases.'

The gangsters punched each other fiercely with stifled laughter, the fat boy had another crisp, tot one drew ecstatically on her thumb while her other hand fondled a lock of her hair. Tot two stuck her legs straight out and admired her little white socks and red shoes. Only the dear girl in the middle paid any attention.

I began to break out in a light perspiration.

189

The thing was taking a lot longer than I had thought to get through, and I had the growing conviction that I must be looking more and more of a chump in Helen's eyes as time went on.

I had rehearsed a few light sallies designed to send my audience into convulsions of laughter as a contrast to the absorbing, serious stuff, but even those who were listening failed to change expression at my shafts of wit. Except, of course, for the little treasure in the middle who pealed back at me sweetly every time.

But I stuck to it grimly. Surely I'd get through to them when I came to the practical bit about first aid.

'All right,' I said, 'you've got a calf with a nasty cut on its leg. The blood is pouring out and you can't get hold of a vet. If you just leave it the blood will all run out and the calf will die. What are you going to do?'

Nobody seemed to care much either way except for tot two. She obviously didn't like the turn things were taking and she stared up at me, her lower lip protruding and trembling.

I went on to explain about tourniquets and pressure pads and then moved on to a discussion of bloat.

'This cow is blown up ready to burst,' I proceeded. 'You've got to do something or she could drop down dead any second.'

I glanced apprehensively at tot two. Her lip was sticking out more every second and was now like a soup plate, but it was no good, I had to go on.

'You must get a knife like a carving knife and

190

stick it straight into the stomach,' I declaimed desperately. 'Now I'll tell you just where to stick it in . . .'

But tot two had had enough. She threw back her head and bawled heartily till her big sister hurried down a few rows and led her away in floods of tears, her pigtails dangling forlornly. Tot one was undisturbed, utterly engrossed as she was with her thumb and the wisp of hair she was rub-rub-rubbing.

Anyway I was getting towards the last lap now.

'The future of the profession, I am convinced, will be less and less involved with the problems of the individual animal,' I went on, addressing myself now exclusively to the little sweetheart in the centre who kept her eyes fixed on me with open admiration. The thin boy went into another of his mighty yawns while his companion finished his last crisp and crumpled the bag noisily.

'We must also consider the emergence of small animal work in any of our plans for the future. Over the past few years the increase in this field has been . . .'

But I had to pause as there was a major disturbance at the back. The jolly feud between the gangsters had flared into ugly warfare. Fists flew, blood streamed, a few ripe oaths rocketed over the company. After a couple of minutes the combatants drew apart and sat glaring and snarling at each other as they dabbed their wounds.

'Whatever the uncertainties and despite the depressed state of agriculture I feel there will always be a place for the veterinary surgeon in our national economy.' That was it. I sat down and Helen, the curate and the little charmer in the middle applauded enthusiastically.

Mr Blenkinsopp rose, beaming delightedly around him. He congratulated me on my splendid talk and said how much they'd all enjoyed it and finished by saying he would now throw the meeting open for questions.

I settled back in my chair. So this was to be the lively discussion he had talked about. I hunted around anxiously from face to face but my audience stared back, dead-eyed; for the first time all evening there was dead silence.

The minutes ticked away and I felt the tension building in me, but at last there was a stirring in the middle of the hall. It was my darling girl; God bless and keep her, she was going to say something. I felt a sudden glow at the knowledge that my words had stimulated a response in at least one young mind.

She sat up in her seat, moistened her lips and smiled at me, bright eyed. She was indeed going to ask a question and as it turned out it was the only one of the evening. I leaned forward expectantly as she began to speak.

'Mr Herriot, I 'ave a little dog what's moultin'. What can I do for 'im?'

15

Probably the most dramatic occurrence in the history of veterinary practice was the disappearance of the draught horse. It is an almost incredible fact that this glory and mainstay of the profession just melted quietly away within a few years. And I was one of those who were there to see it happen.

When I first came to Darrowby the tractor had already begun to take over, but tradition dies hard in the agricultural world and there were still a lot of horses around. Which was just as well because my veterinary education had been geared to things equine with everything else a poor second. It had been a good scientific education in many respects but at times I wondered if the people who designed it still had a mental picture of the horse doctor with his top hat and frock coat busying himself in a world of horse-drawn trams and brewers' drays.

We learned the anatomy of the horse in great detail then that of the other animals much more superficially. It was the same with the other subjects; from animal husbandry with such insistence on a thorough knowledge of shoeing that we developed into amateur blacksmiths — right up to medicine and surgery where it was much more important to know about glanders and strangles than canine distemper. Even as we were learning, we youngsters knew it was ridiculous, with the draught horse already cast as a museum piece and the obvious potential of cattle and small animal work.

Still, after we had absorbed a vast store of equine lore it was a certain comfort that there were still a lot of patients on which we could try it out. I should think in my first two years I treated farm horses nearly every day and though I never was and never will be an equine expert there was a strange thrill in meeting with the age-old conditions whose names rang down almost from medieval times. Quittor, fistulous withers, poll evil, thrush, shoulder slip — vets had been wrestling with them for hundreds of years using very much the same drugs and procedures as myself. Armed with my firing iron and box of blister I plunged determinedly into what had always been the surging mainstream of veterinary life.

And now, in less than three years the stream had dwindled, not exactly to a trickle but certainly to the stage where the final dry-up was in sight. This meant, in a way, a lessening of the pressures on the veterinary surgeon because there is no doubt that horse work was the roughest and most arduous part of our life.

So that today, as I looked at the three-year-old gelding, it occurred to me that this sort of thing wasn't happening as often as it did. He had a long tear in his flank where he had caught himself on barbed wire and it gaped open whenever he moved. There was no getting away from the fact that it had to be stitched.

The horse was tied by the head in his stall, his right side against the tall wooden partition. One of the farm men, a hefty six footer, took a tight hold of the head collar and leaned back against the manger as I puffed some iodoform into the wound. The horse didn't seem to mind, which was a comfort because he was a massive animal emanating an almost tangible vitality and power. I threaded my needle with a length of silk, lifted one of the lips of the wound and passed it through. This was going to be no trouble, I thought as I lifted the flap at the other side and pierced it, but as I was drawing the needle through, the gelding made a convulsive leap and I felt as though a great wind had whistled across the front of my body. Then, strangely, he was standing there against the wooden boards as if nothing had happened.

On the occasions when I have been kicked I have never seen it coming. It is surprising how quickly those great muscular legs can whip out. But there was no doubt he had had a good go at me because my needle and silk was nowhere to be seen, the big man at the head was staring at me with wide eyes in a chalk white face and the front of my clothing was in an extraordinary state. I was wearing a gaberdine mac and it looked as if somebody had taken a razor blade and painstakingly cut the material into narrow strips which hung down in ragged strips to ground level. The great iron-shod hoof had missed my legs by an inch or two but my mac was a write-off.

I was standing there looking around me in a

kind of stupor when I heard a cheerful hail from the doorway.

'Now then, Mr Herriot, what's he done at you?' Cliff Tyreman, the old horseman, looked me up and down with a mixture of amusement and asperity.

'He's nearly put me in hospital, Cliff,' I replied shakily. 'About the closest near miss I've ever had. I just felt the wind of it.'

'What were you tryin' to do?'

'Stitch that wound, but I'm not going to try any more. I'm off to the surgery to get a chloroform muzzle.'

The little man looked shocked. 'You don't need no choloform. I'll haud him and you'll have no trouble.'

'I'm sorry, Cliff.' I began to put away my suture materials, scissors and powder. 'You're a good bloke, I know, but he's had one go at me and he's not getting another chance. I don't want to be lame for the rest of my life.'

The horseman's small, wiry frame seemed to bunch into a ball of aggression. He thrust forward his head in a characteristic posture and glared at me, 'I've never heard owt as daft in me life.' Then he swung round on the big man who was still hanging on to the horse's head, the ghastly pallor of his face now tinged with a delicate green. 'Come on out o' there, Bob! You're that bloody scared you're upsetting t'oss. Come on out of it and let me have 'im!'

Bob gratefully left the head and, grinning sheepishly moved with care along the side of the horse. He passed Cliff on the way and the little man's head didn't reach his shoulder.

Cliff seemed thoroughly insulted by the whole business. He took hold of the head collar and regarded the big animal with the disapproving stare of a schoolmaster at a naughty child. The horse, still in the mood for trouble, laid back his ears and began to plunge about the stall, his huge feet clattering ominously on the stone floor, but he came to rest quickly as the little man uppercutted him furiously in the ribs.

'Get stood up straight there, ye big bugger. What's the matter with ye?' Cliff barked and again he planted his tiny fist against the swelling barrel of the chest, a puny blow which the animal could scarcely have felt but which reduced him to quivering submission. 'Try to kick, would you, eh? I'll bloody fettle you!' He shook the head collar and fixed the horse with a hypnotic stare as he spoke. Then he turned to me. 'You can come and do your job, Mr Herriot, he won't hurt tha.'

I looked irresolutely at the huge, lethal animal. Stepping open-eyed into dangerous situations is something vets are called upon regularly to do and I suppose we all react differently. I know there were times when an over-vivid imagination made me acutely aware of the dire possibilities and now my mind seemed to be dwelling voluptuously on the frightful power in those enormous shining quarters, on the unyielding flintiness of the spatulate feet with their rims of metal. Cliff's voice cut into my musings.

'Come on, Mr Herriot, I tell ye he won't hurt tha.'

I reopened my box and tremblingly threaded another needle. I didn't seem to have much option; the little man wasn't asking me, he was telling me. I'd have to try again.

I couldn't have been a very impressive sight as I shuffled forwards, almost tripping over the tattered hula-hula skirt which dangled in front of me, my shaking hands reaching out once more for the wound, my heart thundering in my ears. But I needn't have worried. It was just as the little man had said; he didn't hurt me. In fact he never moved. He seemed to be listening attentively to the muttering which Cliff was directing into his face from a few inches' range. I powdered and stitched and clipped as though working on an anatomical specimen. Chloroform couldn't have done it any better.

As I retreated thankfully from the stall and began again to put away my instruments the monologue at the horse's head began to change its character. The menacing growl was replaced by a wheedling, teasing chuckle.

'Well, ye see, you're just a daft awd bugger, getting yourself all airigated over nowt. You're a good lad, really, aren't ye, a real good lad.' Cliff's hand ran caressingly over the neck and the towering animal began to nuzzle his cheek, as completely in his sway as any Labrador puppy.

When he had finished he came slowly from the stall, stroking the back, ribs, belly and quarters, even giving a playful tweak at the tail on parting while what had been a few minutes ago an explosive mountain of bone and muscle submitted happily.

I pulled a packet of Gold Flake from my pocket. 'Cliff, you're a marvel. Will you have a cigarette?'

'It 'ud be like givin' a pig a strawberry,' the little man replied, then he thrust forth his tongue on which reposed a half-chewed gobbet of tobacco. 'It's allus there. Ah push it in fust thing every mornin' soon as I get out of bed and there it stays. You'd never know, would you?'

I must have looked comically surprised because the dark eyes gleamed and the rugged little face split into a delighted grin. I looked at that grin — boyish, invincible — and reflected on the phenomenon that was Cliff Tyreman.

In a community in which toughness and durability was the norm he stood out as something exceptional. When I had first seen him nearly three years ago barging among cattle, grabbing their noses and hanging on effortlessly, I had put him down as an unusually fit middle-aged man; but he was in fact nearly seventy. There wasn't much of him but he was formidable; with his long arms swinging, his stumping, pigeon-toed gait and his lowered head he seemed always to be butting his way through life.

'I didn't expect to see you today,' I said. 'I heard you had pneumonia.'

He shrugged. 'Aye, summat of t'sort. First time I've ever been off work since I was a lad.'

'And you should be in your bed now, I should say.' I looked at the heaving chest and partly open mouth. 'I could hear you wheezing away when you were at the horse's head.'

'Nay, I can't stick that nohow. I'll be right in a day or two.' He seized a shovel and began busily clearing away the heap of manure behind the horse, his breathing loud and stertorous in the silence.

Harland Grange was a large, mainly arable farm in the low country at the foot of the Dale, and there had been a time when this stable had had a horse standing in every one of the long row of stalls. There had been over twenty with at least twelve regularly at work, but now there were only two, the young horse I had been treating and an ancient grey called Badger.

Cliff had been head horseman and when the revolution came he turned to tractoring and other jobs around the farm with no fuss at all. This was typical of the reaction of thousands of other farm workers throughout the country; they didn't set up a howl at having to abandon the skills of a lifetime and start anew — they just got on with it. In fact, the younger men seized avidly upon the new machines and proved themselves natural mechanics.

But to the old experts like Cliff, something had gone. He would say: 'It's a bloody sight easier sitting on a tractor — it used to play 'ell with me feet walking up and down them fields all day.' But he couldn't lose his love of horses; the fellow feeling between working man and working beast which had grown in him since childhood and was in his blood for ever.

My next visit to the farm was to see a fat bullock with a piece of turnip stuck in his throat but while I was there, the farmer, Mr Gilling, asked me to have a look at old Badger.

'He's had a bit of a cough lately. Maybe it's just his age, but see what you think.'

The old horse was the sole occupant of the stable now. 'I've sold the three year old,' Mr Gilling said. 'But I'll still keep the old 'un — he'll be useful for a bit of light carting.'

I glanced sideways at the farmer's granite features. He looked the least sentimental of men but I knew why he was keeping the old horse. It was for Cliff.

'Cliff will be pleased, anyway,' I said.

Mr Gilling nodded. 'Aye, I never knew such a feller for 'osses. He was never happier than when he was with them.' He gave a short laugh. 'Do you know, I can remember years ago when he used to fall out with his missus he'd come down to this stable of a night and sit among his 'osses. Just sit here for hours on end looking at 'em and smoking. That was before he started chewing tobacco.'

'And did you have Badger in those days?'

'Aye, we bred him. Cliff helped at his foaling — I remember the little beggar came arse first and we had a bit of a job pullin' him out.' He smiled again. 'Maybe that's why he was always Cliff's favourite. He always worked Badger himself — year in year out — and he was that proud of 'im that if he had to take him into the town for any reason he'd plait ribbons into his mane and hang all his brasses on him first.' He shook his head reminiscently.

The old horse looked round with mild interest as I went up to him. He was in his late twenties and everything about him suggested serene old age; the gaunt projection of the pelvic bones, the whiteness of face and muzzle, the sunken eye with its benign expression. As I was about to take his temperature he gave a sharp, barking cough and it gave me the first clue to his ailment. I watched the rise and fall of his breathing for a minute or two and the second clue was there to be seen; further examination was unnecessary.

'He's broken winded, Mr Gilling,' I said. 'Or he's got pulmonary emphysema to give it its proper name. Do you see that double lift of the abdomen as he breathes out? That's because his lungs have lost their elasticity and need an extra effort to force the air out.'

'What's caused it, then?'

'Well it's to do with his age, but he's got a bit of cold on him at the moment and that's brought it out.'

'Will he get rid of it in time?' the farmer asked.

'He'll be a bit better when he gets over his cold, but I'm afraid he'll never be quite right. I'll give you some medicine to put in his drinking water which will alleviate his symptoms.' I went out to the car for a bottle of the arsenical expectorant mixture which we used then.

It was about six weeks later that I heard from Mr Gilling again. He rang me about seven o'clock one evening.

'I'd like you to come out and have a look at old Badger,' he said.

'What's wrong? Is it his broken wind again?'

'No, it's not that. He's still got the cough but it doesn't seem to bother him much. No, I think he's got a touch of colic. I've got to go out but Cliff will attend to you.'

The little man was waiting for me in the yard. He was carrying an oil lamp. As I came up to him I exclaimed in horror.

'Good God, Cliff, what have you been doing to yourself?' His face was a patchwork of cuts and scratches and his nose, almost without skin, jutted from between two black eyes.

He grinned through the wounds, his eyes dancing with merriment. 'Came off me bike t'other day. Hit a stone and went right over handlebars, arse over tip.' He burst out laughing at the very thought.

'But damn it, man, haven't you been to a doctor? You're not fit to be out in that state.'

'Doctor? Nay, there's no need to bother them fellers. It's nowt much.' He fingered a gash on his jaw. 'Ah lapped me chin up for a day in a bit o' bandage, but it's right enough now.'

I shook my head as I followed him into the stable. He hung up the oil lamp then went over to the horse.

''Can't reckon t'awd feller up,' he said. 'You'd think there wasn't much ailing him but there's summat.'

There were no signs of violent pain but the animal kept transferring his weight from one hind foot to the other as if he did have a little abdominal discomfort. His temperature was normal and he didn't show symptoms of anything else.

I looked at him doubtfully. 'Maybe he has a bit of colic. There's nothing else to see, anyway. I'll

203

give him an injection to settle him down.'

'Right you are, maister, that's good.' Cliff watched me get my syringe out then he looked around him into the shadows at the far end of the stable.

'Funny seeing only one 'oss standing here. I remember when there was a great row of 'em and the barfins and bridles hangin' there on the stalls and the rest of the harness behind them all shinin' on t'wall.' He transferred his plug of tobacco to the other side of his mouth and smiled. 'By gaw, I were in here at six o'clock every morning feedin' them and gettin' them ready for work and ah'll tell you it was a sight to see, us all goin' off ploughing at the start o' the day. Maybe six pairs of 'osses setting off with their harness jinglin' and the ploughmen sittin' sideways on their backs. Like a regular procession it was.'

I smiled. 'It was an early start, Cliff.'

'Aye, by Gaw, and a late finish. We'd bring the 'osses home at night and give 'em a light feed and take their harness off, then we'd go and have our own teas and we'd be back 'ere again afterwards, curry-combing and dandy-brushin' all the sweat and dirt off 'em. Then we'd give them a right good stiff feed of chop and oats and hay to set 'em up for the next day.'

'There wouldn't be much left of the evening then, was there?'

'Nay, there wasn't. It was about like work and bed, I reckon, but it never bothered us.'

I stepped forward to give Badger the injection, then paused. The old horse had undergone a slight spasm, a barely perceptible stiffening of the muscles, and as I looked at him he cocked his tail for a second then lowered it.

'There's something else here,' I said. 'Will you bring him out of his stall, Cliff, and let me see him walk across the yard.'

And watching him clop over the cobbles I saw it again; the stiffness, the raising of the tail. Something clicked in my mind, I walked over and rapped him under the chin and as the membrana nictitans flicked across his eye then slid slowly back I knew.

I paused for a moment. My casual little visit had suddenly become charged with doom.

'Cliff,' I said. 'I'm afraid he's got tetanus.'

'Lockjaw, you mean?'

'That's right. I'm sorry, but there's no doubt about it. Has he had any wounds lately — especially in his feet?'

'Well he were dead lame about a fortnight ago and blacksmith let some matter out of his hoof. Made a right big 'ole.'

There it was. 'It's a pity he didn't get an anti-tetanus shot at the time,' I said. I put my hand into the animal's mouth and tried to prise it open but the jaws were clamped tightly together. 'I don't suppose he's been able to eat today.'

'He had a bit this morning but nowt tonight. What's the lookout for him, Mr Herriot?'

What indeed? If Cliff had asked me the same question today I would have been just as troubled to give him an answer. The facts are that seventy to eighty per cent of tetanus cases die and whatever you do to them in the way of treatment doesn't seem to make a whit of difference to those figures. But I didn't want to sound entirely defeatist.

'It's a very serious condition as you know, Cliff, but I'll do all I can. I've got some antitoxin in the car and I'll inject that into his vein and if the spasms get very bad I'll give him a sedative. As long as he can drink there's a chance for him because he'll have to live on fluids — gruel would be fine.'

For a few days Badger didn't get any worse and I began to hope. I've seen tetanus horses recover and it is a wonderful experience to come in one day and find that the jaws have relaxed and the hungry animal can once more draw food into its mouth.

But it didn't happen with Badger. They had got the old horse into a big loose box where he could move around in comfort and each day as I looked over the half door I felt myself willing him to show some little sign of improvement; but instead, after the first few days he began to deteriorate. A sudden movement or the approach of any person would throw him into a violent spasm so that he would stagger stiff-legged round the box like a big wooden toy, his eyes terrified, saliva drooling from between his fiercely clenched teeth. One morning I was sure he would fall and I suggested putting him in slings. I had to go back to the surgery for the slings and it was just as I was entering Skeldale House that the phone rang.

It was Mr Gilling. 'He's beat us to it, I'm

afraid. He's flat out on the floor and I doubt it's a bad job, Mr Herriot. We'll have to put him down, won't we?'

'I'm afraid so.'

'There's just one thing. Mallock will be taking him away but old Cliff says he doesn't want Mallock to shoot 'im. Wants you to do it. Will you come?'

I got out the humane killer and drove back to the farm, wondering at the fact that the old man should find the idea of my bullet less repugnant than the knacker man's. Mr Gilling was waiting in the box and by his side Cliff, shoulders hunched, hands deep in his pockets. He turned to me with a strange smile.

'I was just saying to t'boss how grand t'awd lad used to look when I got 'im up for a show. By Gaw you should have seen him with 'is coat polished and the feathers on his legs scrubbed as white as snow and a big blue ribbon round his tail.'

'I can imagine it, Cliff,' I said. 'Nobody could have looked after him better.'

He took his hands from his pockets, crouched by the prostrate animal and for a few minutes stroked the white-flecked neck and pulled at the ears while the old sunken eye looked at him impassively.

He began to speak softly to the old horse but his voice was steady, almost conversational, as though he was chatting to a friend.

'Many's the thousand miles I've walked after you, awd lad, and many's the talk we've had together. But I didn't have to say much to tha, did I? I reckon you knew every move I made, everything I said. Just one little word and you always did what ah wanted you to do.'

He rose to his feet. 'I'll get on with me work now, boss,' he said firmly, and strode out of the box.

I waited awhile so that he would not hear the bang which signalled the end of Badger, the end of the horses of Harland Grange and the end of the sweet core of Cliff Tyreman's life.

As I was leaving I saw the little man again. He was mounting the iron seat of a roaring tractor and I shouted to him above the noise.

'The boss says he's going to get some sheep in and you'll be doing a bit of shepherding. I think you'll enjoy that.'

Cliff's undefeated grin flashed out as he called back to me.

'Aye, I don't mind learnin' summat new. I'm nobbut a lad yet!'

16

This was a different kind of ringing. I had gone to sleep as the great bells in the church tower down the street pealed for the Christmas midnight mass, but this was a sharper, shriller sound.

It was difficult at first to shake off the mantle of unreality in which I had wrapped myself last night. Last night — Christmas Eve. It had been like a culmination of all the ideas I had ever held about Christmas — a flowering of emotions I had never experienced before. It had been growing in me since the afternoon call to a tiny village where the snow lay deep on the single street and on the walls and on the ledges of the windows where the lights on the tinselled trees glowed red and blue and gold; and as I left it in the dusk I drove beneath the laden branches of a group of dark spruce as motionless as though they had been sketched against the white background of the fields. And when I reached Darrowby it was dark and around the market place the little shops were bright with decorations and the light from the windows fell in a soft yellow wash over the trodden snow of the cobbles. People, anonymously muffled, were hurrying about, doing their last minute shopping, their feet slithering over the rounded stones.

I had known many Christmases in Scotland

but they had taken second place to the New Year celebrations; there had been none of this air of subdued excitement which started days before with folks shouting good wishes and coloured lights winking on the lonely fell-sides and the farmers' wives plucking the fat geese, the feathers piled deep around their feet. And for fully two weeks you heard the children piping carols in the street then knocking on the door for sixpences. And best of all, last night the Methodist choir had sung out there, filling the night air with rich, thrilling harmony.

Before going to bed and just as the church bells began, I closed the door of Skeldale House behind me and walked again into the market place. Nothing stirred now in the white square stretching smooth and cold and empty under the moon, and there was a Dickensian look about the ring of houses and shops put together long before anybody thought of town planning; tall and short, fat and thin, squashed in crazily around the cobbles, their snow-burdened roofs jagged and uneven against the frosty sky.

As I walked back, the snow crunching under my feet, the bells clanging, the sharp air tingling in my nostrils, the wonder and mystery of Christmas enveloped me in a great wave. Peace on earth, goodwill towards men; the words became meaningful as never before and I saw myself suddenly as a tiny particle in the scheme of things; Darrowby, the farmers, the animals and I seemed for the first time like a warm, comfortable entity. I hadn't been drinking but I almost floated up the stairs of

Skeldale House to my bedroom.

The temperature up there was about the same as in the street. It was always like that and I had developed the habit of hurling off my clothes and leaping into bed before the freezing air could get at me, but tonight my movements were leisurely and when I finally crawled between the sheets I was still wallowing in my Yuletide euphoria. There wouldn't be much work tomorrow; I'd have a long lie — maybe till nine — and then a lazy day, a glorious hiatus in my busy life. As I drifted into sleep it was as though I was surrounded by the smiling faces of my clients looking down at me with an all-embracing benevolence; and strangely I fancied I could hear singing, sweet and haunting, just like the Methodist choir — God Rest Ye Merry Gentlemen . . .

But now there was this other bell which wouldn't stop. Must be the alarm. But as I pawed at the clock the noise continued and I saw that it was six o'clock. It was the phone of course. I lifted the receiver.

A metallic voice, crisp and very wideawake, jarred in my ear. 'Is that the vet?'

'Yes, Herriot speaking,' I mumbled.

'This is Brown, Willet Hill. I've got a cow down with milk fever. I want you here quick.'

'Right, I'll see to it.'

'Don't take ower long.' Then a click at the far end.

I rolled on to my back and stared at the ceiling. So this was Christmas Day. The day when I was going to step out of the world for a spell and luxuriate in the seasonal spirit. I hadn't bargained for this fellow jerking me brutally back to reality. And not a word of regret or apology. No 'sorry to get you out of bed', or anything else, never mind 'Merry Christmas'. It was just a bit hard.

Mr Brown was waiting for me in the darkness of the farmyard. I had been to his place a few times before and as my headlights blazed on him I was struck, as always, by his appearance of perfect physical fitness. He was a gingery man of about forty with high cheekbones set in a sharp-featured clear-skinned face. Red hair peeped from under a check cap and a faint auburn down covered his cheeks, his neck, the backs of his hands. It made me feel a bit more sleepy just to look at him.

He didn't say good morning but nodded briefly then jerked his head in the direction of the byre. 'She's in there' was all he said.

He watched in silence as I gave the injections and it wasn't until I was putting the empty bottles into my pocket that he spoke.

'Don't suppose I'll have to milk her today?'

'No,' I replied. 'Better leave the bag full.'

'Anything special about feedin'?'

'No, she can have anything she likes when she wants it.' Mr Brown was very efficient. Always wanted to know every detail.

As we crossed the yard he halted suddenly and turned to face me. Could it be that he was going to ask me in for a nice hot cup of tea?

'You know,' he said, as I stood ankle deep in the snow, the frosty air nipping at my ears. 'I've had a few of these cases lately. Maybe there's summat wrong with my routine. Do you think I'm steaming up my cows too much?'

'It's quite possible.' I hurried towards the car. One thing I wasn't going to do was deliver a lecture on animal husbandry at this moment.

My hand was on the door handle when he said 'I'll give you another ring if she's not up by dinner time. And there's one other thing — that was a hell of a bill I had from you fellers last month, so tell your boss not to be so savage with 'is pen.' Then he turned and walked quickly towards the house.

Well that was nice, I thought as I drove away. Not even thanks or goodbye, just a complaint and a promise to haul me away from my roast goose if necessary. A sudden wave of anger surged in me. Bloody farmers! There were some miserable devils among them. Mr Brown had doused my festive feelings as effectively as if he had thrown a bucket of water over me.

As I mounted the steps of Skeldale House the darkness had paled to a shivery grey. Mrs Hall met me in the passage. She was carrying a tray.

'I'm sorry,' she said. 'There's another urgent job. Mr Farnon's had to go out, too. But I've got a cup of coffee and some fried bread for you. Come in and sit down — you've got time to eat it before you go.'

I sighed. It was going to be just another day after all. 'What's this about, Mrs Hall?' I asked, sipping the coffee.

'It's old Mr Kirby,' she replied. 'He's in a right state about his nanny goat.'

'Nanny goat!'

'Aye, he says she's choking.'

'Choking! How the heck can she be choking?' I shouted.

'I'm sure I don't know. And I wish you wouldn't shout at me, Mr Herriot. It's not my fault.'

'I'm sorry, Mrs Hall, I'm really sorry.' I finished the coffee sheepishly. My feeling of goodwill was at a very low ebb.

Mr Kirby was a retired farmer, but he had sensibly taken a cottage with a bit of land where he kept enough stock to occupy his time — a cow, a few pigs and his beloved goats. He had always had goats, even when he was running his dairy herd; he had a thing about them.

The cottage was in a village high up the Dale. Mr Kirby met me at the gate.

'Ee, lad,' he said. 'I'm right sorry to be bothering you this early in the morning and Christmas an' all, but I didn't have no choice. Dorothy's real bad.'

He led the way to a stone shed which had been converted into a row of pens. Behind the wire of one of them a large white Saanen goat peered out at us anxiously and as I watched her she gulped, gave a series of retching coughs, then stood trembling, saliva drooling from her mouth.

The farmer turned to me, wide-eyed. 'You see, I had to get you out, didn't I? If I left her till tomorrow she'd be a goner.'

'You're right, Mr Kirby,' I replied. 'You couldn't leave her. There's something in her throat.'

214

We went into the pen and as the old man held the goat against the wall I tried to open her mouth. She didn't like it very much and as I prised her jaws apart she startled me with a loud, long-drawn human-sounding cry. It wasn't a big mouth but I have a small hand and, as the sharp back teeth tried to nibble me, I poked a finger deep into the pharynx.

There was something there all right. I could just touch it but I couldn't get hold of it. Then the animal began to throw her head about and I had to come out; I stood there, saliva dripping from my hand, looking thoughtfully at Dorothy.

After a few moments I turned to the farmer. 'You know, this is a bit baffling. I can feel something in the back of her throat, but it's soft — like cloth. I'd been expecting to find a bit of twig, or something sharp sticking in there — it's funny what a goat will pick up when she's pottering around outside. But if it's cloth, what the heck is holding it there? Why hasn't she swallowed it down?'

'Aye, it's a rum 'un, isn't it?' The old man ran a gentle and along the animal's back. 'Do you think she'll get rid of it herself? Maybe it'll just slip down?'

'No, I don't. It's stuck fast, God knows how, but it is. And I've got to get it out soon because she's beginning to blow up. Look there.' I pointed to the goat's left side, bulged by the tympanitic rumen, and as I did so, Dorothy began another paroxysm of coughs which seemed almost to tear her apart.

Mr Kirby looked at me with a mute appeal,

215

but just at that moment I didn't see what I could do. Then I opened the door of the pen. 'I'm going to get my torch from the car. Maybe I can see something to explain this.'

The old man held the torch as I once more pulled the goat's mouth open and again heard the curious child-like wailing. It was when the animal was in full cry that I noticed something under the tongue — a thin, dark band.

'I can see what's holding the thing now,' I cried. 'It's hooked round the tongue with string or something.' Carefully I pushed my forefinger under the band and began to pull.

It wasn't string. It began to stretch as I pulled carefully at it . . . like elastic. Then it stopped stretching and I felt a real resistance . . . whatever was in the throat was beginning to move. I kept up a gentle traction and very slowly the mysterious obstruction came sliding up over the back of the tongue and into the mouth, and when it came within reach I let go the elastic, grabbed the sodden mass and hauled it forth. It seemed as if there was no end to it — a long snake of dripping material nearly two feet long — but at last I had it out on to the straw of the pen.

Mr Kirby seized it and held it up and as he unravelled the mass wonderingly he gave a sudden cry.

'God 'elp us, it's me summer drawers!'

'Your what?'

'Me summer drawers. Ah don't like them long johns when weather gets warmer and I allus change into these little short 'uns. Missus was

216

havin' a clearout afore the end of t'year and she didn't know whether to wash 'em or mek 'em into dusters. She washed 'em at t'finish and Dorothy must have got 'em off the line.' He held up the tattered shorts and regarded them ruefully. 'By Gaw, they've seen better days, but I reckon Dorothy's fettled them this time.'

Then his body began to shake silently, a few low giggles escaped from him and finally he gave a great shout of laughter. It was an infectious laugh and I joined in as I watched him. He went on for quite a long time and when he had finished he was leaning weakly against the wire netting.

'Me poor awd drawers,' he gasped, then leaned over and patted the goat's head. 'But as long as you're all right, lass, I'm not worried.'

'Oh, she'll be OK.' I pointed to her left flank. 'You can see her stomach's going down already.' As I spoke, Dorothy belched pleasurably and began to nose interestedly at her hay rack.

The farmer gazed at her fondly. 'Isn't that grand to see! She's ready for her grub again. And if she hadn't got her tongue round the elastic that lot would have gone right down and killed her.'

'I really don't think it would, you know,' I said. 'It's amazing what ruminants can carry around in their stomachs. I once found a bicycle tyre inside a cow when I was operating for something else. The tyre didn't seem to be bothering her in the least.'

'I see.' Mr Kirby rubbed his chin. 'So Dorothy might have wandered around with me drawers

217

inside her for years.'

'It's possible. You'd never have known what became of them.'

'By gaw, that's right.' Mr Kirby said, and for a moment I thought he was going to start giggling again, but he mastered himself and seized my arm. 'But I don't know what I'm keeping you out here for, lad. You must come in and have a bit o' Christmas cake.'

Inside the tiny living-room of the cottage I was ushered to the best chair by the fireside where two rough logs blazed and crackled.

'Bring cake out for Mr Herriot, mother,' the farmer cried as he rummaged in the pantry. He reappeared with a bottle of whisky at the same time as his wife bustled in carrying a cake thickly laid with icing and ornamented with coloured spangles, toboggans, reindeers.

Mr Kirby unscrewed the stopper. 'You know, mother, we're lucky to have such men as this to come out on a Christmas mornin' to help us.'

'Aye, we are that.' The old lady cut a thick slice of the cake and placed it on a plate by the side of an enormous wedge of Wensleydale cheese.

Her husband meanwhile was pouring my drink. Yorkshiremen are amateurs with whisky and there was something delightfully untutored in the way he was sloshing it into the glass as if it was lemonade; he would have filled it to the brim if I hadn't stopped him.

Drink in hand, cake on knee, I looked across at the farmer and his wife who were sitting in upright kitchen chairs watching me with quiet benevolence. The two faces had something in

218

common — a kind of beauty. You would find faces like that only in the country; deeply wrinkled and weathered, clear-eyed, alight with a cheerful serenity.

I raised my glass. 'A happy Christmas to you both.'

The old couple nodded and replied smilingly. 'And the same to you, Mr Herriot.'

'Aye, and thanks again, lad,' said Mr Kirby. 'We're right grateful to you for runnin' out here to save awd Dorothy. We've maybe mucked up your day for you but it would've mucked up ours if we'd lost the old lass, wouldn't it, mother?'

'Don't worry, you haven't spoiled anything for me.' I said. 'In fact you've made me realize again that it really is Christmas.' And as I looked around the little room with the decorations hanging from the low-beamed ceiling I could feel the emotions of last night surging slowly back, a warmth creeping through me that had nothing to do with the whisky.

I took a bite of the cake and followed it with a moist slice of cheese. When I had first come to Yorkshire I had been aghast when offered this unheard-of combination, but time had brought wisdom and I had discovered that the mixture when chewed boldly together was exquisite; and, strangely, I had also found that there was nothing more suitable for washing it finally over the tonsils than a draught of raw whisky.

'You don't mind t'wireless, Mr Herriot?' Mrs Kirby asked. 'We always like to have it on Christmas morning to hear t'old hymns but I'll turn it off if you like.'

'No please leave it, it sounds grand.' I turned to look at the old radio with its chipped wooden veneer, the ornate scroll-work over the worn fabric; it must have been one of the earliest models and it gave off a tinny sound, but the singing of the church choir was none the less sweet . . . 'Hark the Herald Angels Sing' — flooding the little room, mingling with the splutter of the logs and the soft voices of the old people.

They showed me a picture of their son, who was a policeman over in Houlton and their daughter who was married to a neighbouring farmer. They were bringing their grand-children up for Christmas dinner as they always did and Mrs Kirby opened a box and ran a hand over the long row of crackers. The choir started on 'Once in Royal David's City', I finished my whisky and put up only feeble resistance as the farmer plied the bottle again. Through the small window I could see the bright berries of a holly tree pushing through their covering of snow.

It was really a shame to have to leave here and it was sadly that I drained my glass for the second time and scooped up the last crumbs of cake and icing from my plate.

Mr Kirby came out with me and at the gate of the cottage he stopped and held out his hand.

'Thank ye lad, I'm right grateful,' he said. 'And all the very best to you.'

For a moment the rough dry palm rasped against mine, then I was in the car, starting the engine. I looked at my watch; it was still only half past nine but the first early sunshine was sparkling from a sky of palest blue.

Beyond the village the road climbed steeply then curved around the rim of the valley in a wide arc, and it was here that you came suddenly upon the whole great expanse of the Plain of York spread out almost at your feet. I always slowed down here and there was always something different to see, but today the vast chequerboard of fields and farms and woods stood out with a clarity I had never seen before. Maybe it was because this was a holiday and down there no factory chimney smoked, no lorries belched fumes, but the distance was magically foreshortened in the clear, frosty air and I felt I could reach out and touch the familiar landmarks far below.

I looked back at the enormous white billows and folds of the fells, crowding close, one upon another into the blue distance, every crevice uncannily defined, the highest summits glittering where the sun touched them. I could see the village with the Kirbys' cottage at the end. I had found Christmas and peace and goodwill and everything back there.

Farmers? They were the salt of the earth.

17

Marmaduke Skelton was an object of interest to me long before our paths crossed. For one thing I hadn't thought people were ever called Marmaduke outside of books and for another he was a particularly well-known member of the honourable profession of unqualified animal doctors.

Before the Veterinary Surgeons' Act of 1948 anybody who fancied his chance at it could dabble in the treatment of animal disease. Veterinary students could quite legally be sent out to cases while they were seeing practice, certain members of the lay public did a bit of veterinary work as a sideline while others did it as a full time job. These last were usually called 'quacks'.

The disparaging nature of the term was often unjust because, though some of them were a menace to the animal population, others were dedicated men who did their job with responsibility and humanity and after the Act were brought into the profession's fold as Veterinary Practitioners.

But long before all this there were all sorts and types among them. The one I knew best was Arthur Lumley, a charming little ex-plumber who ran a thriving small animal practice in Brawton, much to the chagrin of Mr Angus Grier MRCVS. Arthur used to drive around in a small van. He always wore a white coat and looked very clinical and efficient, and on the side of the van in foot-high letters which would have got a qualified man a severe dressing down from the Royal College was the legend, 'Arthur Lumley MKC, Canine and Feline Specialist'. The lack of 'letters' after their name was the one thing which differentiated these men from qualified vets in the eyes of the general public and I was interested to see that Arthur did have an academic attainment. However the degree of MKC was unfamiliar to me and he was somewhat cagey when I asked him about it; I did find out eventually what it stood for: Member of the Kennel Club.

Marmaduke Skelton was of a vastly different breed. I had been working long enough round the Scarburn district to become familiar with some of the local history and it seemed that when Mr and Mrs Skelton were producing a family in the early 1900s they must have thought their offspring were destined for great things; they named their four sons Marmaduke, Sebastian, Cornelius and, incredibly, Alonzo. The two middle brothers drove lorries for the Express Dairy and Alonzo was a small farmer; one of my vivid memories is the shock of surprise when I was filling up the forms after his tuberculin test and asked him for his first name. The exotic appellation pronounced in gruff Yorkshire was so incongruous that I thought he was pulling my leg; in fact I was going to make a light comment but something in his eye prompted me to leave it alone.

Marmaduke, or Duke as he was invariably called, was the colourful member of the family. I had heard a lot about him on my visits to Scarburn farms; he was a 'right good hand' at calving, foaling and lambing, and 'as good as any vitnery' in the diagnosis and treatment of animals' ailments. He was also an expert castrator, docker and pig-killer. He made a nice living at his trade and, of course, in Ewan Ross he had the ideal professional opposition; a veterinary surgeon who worked only when he felt like it and who didn't bother to go to a case unless he was in the mood. Much as the farmers liked and in many cases revered Ewan, they were often forced to fall back on Duke's services.

If Duke had confined his activities to treating his patients I don't think Ewan would ever have spared him a thought; but Skelton liked to enliven his farm visits with sneers about the old Scotch vet who had never been much good and was definitely getting past it now. Maybe even that didn't get very far under Ewan's skin but at the mention of his rival's name his mouth would harden a little and a ruminative expression creep into the blue eyes.

And it wasn't easy to like Duke. There were the tales you heard about his savage brawls and about how he knocked his wife and children around when the mood was on him. I didn't find his appearance engaging either when I first saw him swaggering across Scarburn market place; a black bull of a man, a shaggy Heathcliffe with fierce, darting eyes and a hint of braggadocio in the bright red handkerchief tied round his neck.

But on this particular afternoon I wasn't thinking about Duke Skelton, in fact I wasn't thinking about anything much as I sprawled in a chair by the Rosses' fireside. I had just finished one of Ginny's lunches; something with the unassuming name of fish pie but in truth a magical concoction in which the humble haddock was elevated to unimagined heights by the admixture of potatoes, tomatoes, eggs, macaroni and things only Ginny knew. Then the apple crumble and the chair close to the fire with the heat from the flames beating on my face.

The thoughts I had were slumbrous ones; that this house and the people in it had come to have a magnetic attraction for me; that if this had been a big successful practice the phone would have been dinging and Ewan would be struggling into his coat as he chewed his last bite. And an unworthy thought as I glanced through the window at the white garden and the snow-burdened trees; that if I didn't hurry back to Darrowby, Siegfried might do double the work and finish the lot before I got home.

Playing with the soothing picture of the muffled figure of my boss battling round the farms I watched Ginny placing a coffee cup by her husband's elbow. Ewan smiled up into her face and just then the phone rang.

Like most vets I am bell-happy and I jumped, but Ewan didn't. He began quietly to sip his coffee as Ginny picked up the receiver and he didn't change expression when his wife came over and said, 'It's Tommy Thwaite. One of his cows has put its calf bed out.'

These dread tidings would have sent me leaping round the room but Ewan took a long swallow at his coffee before replying.

'Thank you, dear. Will you tell him I'll have a look at her shortly.'

He turned to me and began to tell me something funny which had happened to him that morning and when he had finished he went into his characteristic laugh — showing nothing apart from a vibration of the shoulders and a slight popping of the eyes. Then he relaxed in his chair and recommenced his leisurely sipping.

Though it wasn't my case my feet were itching. A bovine prolapsed uterus was not only an urgent condition but it held such grim promise of hard labour that I could never get it over quickly enough. Some were worse than others and I was always in a hurry to find out what was in store.

Ewan, however, appeared to be totally incurious. In fact he closed his eyes and I thought for a moment he was settling down for a post prandial nap. But it was only a gesture of resignation at the wrecking of his afternoon's repose and he gave a final stretch and got up.

'Want to come with me, Jim?' he asked in his soft voice.

I hesitated for a moment then, callously abandoning Siegfried to his fate, I nodded eagerly and followed Ewan into the kitchen.

He sat down and pulled on a pair of thick woollen over-socks which Ginny had been warming by the stove, then he put on his

Wellingtons, a short overcoat, yellow gloves and a check cap. As he strolled along the narrow track which had been dug through the garden snow he looked extraordinarily youthful and debonair.

He didn't go into his dispensary this time and I wondered what equipment he would use, thinking at the same time of Siegfried's words: 'Ewan has his own way of doing everything.'

At the farm Mr Thwaite trotted over to meet us. He was understandably agitated but there was something else; a nervous rubbing of the hands, an uneasy giggle as he watched my colleague opening the car boot.

'Mr Ross,' he blurted out at last, 'I don't want you to be upset, but I've summat to tell you.' He paused for a moment. 'Duke Skelton's in there with my cow.'

Ewan's expression did not nicker. 'Oh, right. Then you won't need me.' He closed the boot, opened the door and got back into the car.

'Hey, hey, I didn't mean you to go away!' Mr Thwaite ran round and cried through the glass. 'Duke just happened to be in t'village and he said he'd help me out.'

'Fine,' Ewan said, winding down the window, 'I don't mind in the least. I'm sure he'll do a good job for you.'

The farmer screwed up his face in misery. 'But you don't understand. He's been in there for about an hour and a half and he's no further forward. He's not doin' a bit o' good and he's about buggered an' all. I want you to take over, Mr Ross.'

'No, I'm sorry,' Ewan gave him a level stare. 'I couldn't possibly interfere. You know how it is, Tommy. He's begun the job — I've got to let him finish.' He started the engine.

'No, no, don't go!' shouted Mr Thwaite, beating the car roof with his hands. 'Duke's whacked, I tell ye. If you drive away now ah'm going to lose one of ma best cows. You've got to help me, Mr Ross!' He seemed on the verge of tears.

My colleague looked at him thoughtfully as the engine purred. Then he bent forward and turned off the ignition. 'All right, I'll tell you what — I'll go in there and see what he says. If he wants me to help, then I will.'

I followed him into the byre and as we paused just inside the door Duke Skelton looked up from his work. He had been standing head down, one hand resting on the rump of a massive cow, his mouth hanging open, his great barrel chest heaving. The thick hair over his shoulders and ribs was matted with blood from the huge everted uterus which dangled behind the animal. Blood and filth streaked his face and covered his arms and as he stared at us from under his shaggy brows he looked like something from the jungle.

'Well now, Mr Skelton,' Ewan mumured conversationally. 'How are you getting on?'

Duke gave him a quick malevolent glance. 'Ah'm doin' all right.' The words rumbled from deep down through his gaping lips.

Mr Thwaite stepped forward, smiling ingratiatingly, 'Come on, Duke, you've done your best.

228

I think you should let Mr Ross give you a 'and now.'

'Well ah don't.' The big man's jaw jutted suddenly. 'If I was lookin' for help I wouldn't want 'IM.' He turned away and seized the uterus. Hoisting it in his arms he began to push at it with fierce concentration.

Mr Thwaite turned to us with an expression of despair and opened his mouth to lament again, but Ewan silenced him with a raised hand, pulling a milking stool from a corner and squatted down comfortably against a wall. Unhurriedly he produced his little pouch and, one-handed, began to make a cigarette; as he licked the paper, screwed up the end and applied a match he gazed with blank eyes at the sweating, struggling figure a few feet from him.

Duke had got the uterus about halfway back. Grunting and gasping, legs straddled, he had worked the engorged mass inch by inch inside the vulva till he had just about enough cradled in his arms for one last push; and as he stood there taking a breather with the great muscles of his shoulders and arms rigid his immense strength was formidably displayed. But he wasn't as strong as that cow. No man is as strong as a cow and this cow was one of the biggest I had ever seen with a back like a table top and rolls of fat round her tail-head.

I had been in this position myself and I knew what was coming next. I didn't have to wait long. Duke took a long wheezing breath and made his assault, heaving desperately, pushing with arms and chest, and for a second or two he seemed to be winning as the mass disappeared steadily inside. Then the cow gave an almost casual strain and the whole thing welled out again till it hung down bumping against the animal's hocks.

As Duke almost collapsed against her pelvis in the same attitude as when we first came in I felt pity for the man. I found him uncharming but I felt for him. That could easily be me standing there; my jacket and shirt hanging on that nail, my strength ebbing, my sweat mingling with the blood. No man could do what he was trying to do. You could push back a calf bed with the aid of an epidural anaesthetic to stop the straining or you could sling the animal up to a beam with a block and tackle; you couldn't just stand there and do it from scratch as this chap was trying to do.

I was surprised Duke hadn't learned that with all his experience; but apparently it still hadn't dawned on him even now because he was going through all the motions of having another go. This time he got even further — a few more inches inside before the cow popped it out again. The animal appeared to have a sporting streak because there was something premeditated about the way she played her victim along before timing her thrust at the very last moment. Apart from that she seemed somewhat bored by the whole business; in fact with the possible exception of Ewan she was the calmest among us.

Duke was trying again. As he bent over wearily and picked up the gory organ I wondered how often he had done this since he arrived nearly two hours ago. He had guts, there was no doubt. But the end was near. There was a frantic urgency about his movements as though he knew himself it was his last throw and as he yet again neared his goal his grunts changed to an agonized whimpering, an almost tearful sound as though he were appealing to the recalcitrant mass, beseeching it to go away inside and stay away, just this once.

And when the inevitable happened and the poor fellow, panting and shaking, surveyed once more the ruin of his hopes I had the feeling that somebody had to do something.

Mr Thwaite did it. 'You've had enough, Duke,' he said. 'For God's sake come in the house and get cleaned up. Missus'll give you a bit o' dinner and while you're having it Mr Ross'll see what he can do.'

The big man, arms hanging limp by his sides, chest heaving, stared at the farmer for a few seconds then he turned abruptly and snatched his clothes from the wall.

'Aw right,' he said and began to walk slowly towards the door. He stopped opposite Ewan but didn't look at him. 'But ah'll tell you summat, Maister Thwaite. If ah can't put that calf bed back this awd bugger never will.'

Ewan drew on his cigarette and peered up at him impassively. He didn't follow him with his eyes as he left the byre but leaned back against the wall, puffed out a thin plume of smoke and watched it rise and disappear among the shadows in the roof.

Mr Thwaite was soon back. 'Now, Mr Ross,'

he said a little breathlessly, 'I'm sorry about you havin' to wait but we can get on now. I expect you'll be needin' some fresh hot water and is there anything else you want?'

Ewan dropped his cigarette on the cobbles and ground it with his foot. 'Yes, you can bring me a pound of sugar.'

'What's that?'

'A pound of sugar.'

'A pound of . . . right, right . . . I'll get it.'

In no time at all the farmer returned with an unopened paper bag. Ewan split the top with his finger, walked over to the cow and began to dust the sugar all over the uterus. Then he turned to Mr Thwaite again.

'And I'll want a pig stool, too. I expect you have one.'

'Oh aye, we have one, but what the hangment . . . ?'

Ewan cocked a gentle eye at him. 'Bring it in, then. It's time we got this job done.'

As the farmer disappeared at a stiff gallop I went over to my colleague. 'What's going on, Ewan? What the devil are you chucking that sugar about for?'

'Oh it draws the serum out of the uterus. You can't beat it when the thing's engorged like that.'

'It does?' I glanced unbelievingly at the bloated organ. 'And aren't you going to give her an epidural . . . and some pituitrin . . . and a calcium injection?'

'Och no,' Ewan replied with his slow smile. 'I never bother about those things.'

I didn't get the chance to ask him what he

wanted with the pig stool because just then Mr Thwaite trotted in with one under his arm.

Most farms used to have them. They were often called 'creels' and the sides of bacon were laid on them at pig-killing time. This was a typical specimen — like a long low table with four short legs and a slatted concave top. Ewan took hold of it and pushed it carefully under the cow just in front of the udder while I stared at it through narrowed eyes. I was getting out of my depth.

Ewan then walked unhurriedly out to his car and returned with a length of rope and two objects wrapped in the inevitable brown paper. As he draped the rope over the partition, pulled on a rubber parturition gown and began to open the parcels I realized I was once again watching Ewan setting out his stall.

From the first parcel he produced what looked like a beer tray but which I decided couldn't possibly be; but when he said, 'Here, hold this a minute, Jim,' and I read the emblazoned gold scroll, 'John Smith's Magnet Pale Ale' I had to change my mind. It was a beer tray.

He began to unfold the brown paper from the other object and my brain reeled a little as he fished out an empty whisky bottle and placed it on the tray. Standing there with my strange burden I felt like the stooge in a conjuring act and I wouldn't have been a bit surprised if my colleague had produced a live rabbit next.

But all he did was to fill the whisky bottle with some of the clean hot water from the bucket.

Next he looped the rope round the cow's

horns, passed it round the body a couple of times then leaned back and pulled. Without protest the big animal collapsed gently on top of the pig stool and lay there with her rear end stuck high in the air.

'Right now, we can start,' Ewan murmured, and as I threw down my jacket and began to tear off my tie he turned to me in surprise.

'Here, here, what do you think you're doing?'

'Well I'm going to give you a hand, of course.'

One corner of his mouth twitched upwards. 'It's kind of you, Jim, but there's no need to get stripped off. This will only take a minute. I just want you and Mr Thwaite to keep the thing level for me.'

He gently hoisted the organ which to my fevered imagination had shrunk visibly since the sugar, on to the beer tray and gave the farmer and me an end each to hold.

Then he pushed the uterus back.

He did literally only take a minute or not much more. Without effort, without breaking sweat or exerting visible pressure he returned that vast mass to where it belonged while the cow, unable to strain or do a thing about it, just lay there with an aggrieved expression on her face. Then he took his whisky bottle, passed it carefully into the vagina and disappeared up to arm's length where he began to move his shoulder vigorously.

'What the hell are you doing now?' I whispered agitatedly into his ear from my position at the end of the beer tray.

'I'm rotating each horn to get it back into

place and pouring a little hot water from the bottle into the ends of the horns to make sure they're completely involuted.'

'Oh, I see.' I watched as he removed the bottle, soaped his arms in the bucket and began to take off his overall.

'But aren't you going to stitch it in?' I blurted out.

Ewan shook his head. 'No, Jim. If you put it back properly it never comes out again.'

He was drying his hands when the byre door opened and Duke Skelton slouched in. He was washed and dressed, with his red handkerchief knotted again round his neck and he glared fierce-eyed at the cow which, tidied up and unperturbed, looked now just like all the other cows in the row. His lips moved once or twice before he finally found his voice.

'Aye, it's all right for some people,' he snarled. 'Some people with their bloody fancy injections and instruments! It's bloody easy that way, isn't it.' Then he swung round and was gone.

As I heard his heavy boots clattering across the yard it struck me that his words were singularly inapt. What was there even remotely fancy about a pig stool, a pound of sugar, a whisky bottle and a beer tray?

18

'I work for cats.'

That was how Mrs Bond introduced herself on my first visit, gripping my hand firmly and thrusting out her jaw defiantly as though challenging me to make something of it. She was a big woman with a strong, high-cheekboned face and a commanding presence and I wouldn't have argued with her anyway, so I nodded gravely as though I fully understood and agreed, and allowed her to lead me into the house.

I saw at once what she meant. The big kitchen-living-room had been completely given over to cats. There were cats on the sofas and chairs and spilling in cascades on to the floor, cats sitting in rows along the window sills and right in the middle of it all, little Mr Bond, pallid, wispy-moustached, in his shirt sleeves reading a newspaper.

It was a scene which was going to become very familiar. A lot of the cats were obviously uncastrated Toms because the atmosphere was vibrant with their distinctive smell — a fierce pungency which overwhelmed even the sickly wisps from the big saucepans of nameless cat food bubbling on the stove. And Mr Bond was always there, always in his shirt sleeves and reading his paper, a lonely little island in a sea of cats.

I had heard of the Bonds, of course. They were

Londoners who for some obscure reason had picked on North Yorkshire for their retirement. People said they had a 'bit o' brass' and they had bought an old house on the outskirts of Darrowby where they kept themselves to themselves — and the cats. I had heard that Mrs Bond was in the habit of taking in strays and feeding them and giving them a home if they wanted it and this had predisposed me in her favour, because in my experience the unfortunate feline species seemed to be fair game for every kind of cruelty and neglect. They shot cats, threw things at them, starved them and set their dogs on them for fun. It was good to see somebody taking their side.

My patient on this first visit was no more than a big kitten, a terrified little blob of black and white crouching in a corner.

'He's one of the outside cats,' Mrs Bond boomed.

'Outside cats?'

''Yes. All these you see here are the inside cats. The others are the really wild ones who simply refuse to enter the house. I feed them of course but the only time they come indoors is when they are ill.'

'I see.'

'I've had frightful trouble catching this one. I'm worried about his eyes — there seemed to be a skin growing over them, and I do hope you can do something for him. His name, by the way, is Alfred.'

'Alfred? Ah yes, quite.' I advanced cautiously on the little half-grown animal and was greeted by a waving set of claws and a series of open-mouthed spittings. He was trapped in his corner or he would have been off with the speed of light.

Examining him was going to be a problem. I turned to Mrs Bond. 'Could you let me have a sheet of some kind? An old ironing sheet would do. I'm going to have to wrap him up.'

'Wrap him up?' Mrs Bond looked very doubtful but she disappeared into another room and returned with a tattered sheet of cotton which looked just right.

I cleared the table of an amazing variety of cat feeding dishes, cat books, cat medicines and spread out the sheet, then I approached my patient again. You can't be in a hurry in a situation like this and it took me perhaps five minutes of wheedling and 'Puss-pussing' while I brought my hand nearer and nearer. When I got as far as being able to stroke his cheek I made a quick grab at the scruff of his neck and finally bore Alfred, protesting bitterly and lashing out in all directions, over to the table. There, still holding tightly to his scruff, I laid him on the sheet and started the wrapping operation.

This is something which has to be done quite often with obstreperous felines and, although I say it, I am rather good at it. The idea is to make a neat, tight roll, leaving the relevant piece of cat exposed; it may be an injured paw, perhaps the tail, and in this case of course the head. I think it was the beginning of Mrs Bond's unquestioning faith in me when she saw me quickly enveloping that cat till all you could see of him was a small black and white head protruding from an immovable cocoon of cloth. He and I were now facing each other, more or less eyeball to eyeball, and Alfred couldn't do a thing about it.

As I say, I rather pride myself on this little expertise and even today my veterinary colleagues have been known to remark: 'Old Herriot may be limited in many respects but by God he can wrap a cat.'

As it turned out, there wasn't a skin growing over Alfred's eyes. There never is.

'He's got a paralysis of the third eyelid, Mrs Bond. Animals have this membrane which flicks across the eye to protect it. In this case it hasn't gone back, probably because the cat is in low condition — maybe had a touch of cat flu or something else which has weakened him. I'll give him an injection of vitamins and leave you some powder to put in his food if you could keep him in for a few days. I think he'll be all right in a week or two.'

The injection presented no problems with Alfred furious but helpless inside his sheet and I had come to the end of my first visit to Mrs Bond's.

It was the first of many. The lady and I established an immediate rapport which was strengthened by the fact that I was always prepared to spend time over her assorted charges; crawling on my stomach under piles of logs in the outhouses to reach the outside cats, coaxing them down from trees, stalking them endlessly through the shrubbery. But from my point of view it was rewarding in many ways.

For instance there was the diversity of names she had for her cats. True to her London upbringing she had named many of the Toms after the great Arsenal team of those days. There was Eddie Hapgood, Cliff Bastin, Ted Drake, Wilf Copping, but she did slip up in one case because Alex James had kittens three times a year with unfailing regularity.

Then there was her way of calling them home. The first time I saw her at this was on a still summer evening. The two cats she wanted me to see were out in the garden somewhere and I walked with her to the back door where she halted, clasped her hands across her bosom, closed her eyes and gave tongue in a mellifluous contralto.

'Bates, Bates, Bates, Ba-hates.' She actually sang out the words in a reverent monotone except for a delightful little lilt on the 'Ba-hates'. Then once more she inflated her ample rib cage like an operatic prima donna and out it came again, delivered with the utmost feeling.

'Bates, Bates, Bates, Ba-hates.'

Anyway it worked, because Bates the cat came trotting from behind a clump of laurel. There remained the other patient and I watched Mrs Bond with interest.

She took up the same stance, breathed in, closed her eyes, composed her features into a sweet half-smile and started again.

'Seven-times-three, Seven-times-three, Seven-times-three-hee.' It was set to the same melody as Bates with the same dulcet rise and fall at the end. She didn't get the quick response this time, though, and had to go through the performance again and again, and as the notes lingered on the still evening air the effect was startlingly like a muezzin calling the faithful to prayer.

At length she was successful and a fat tortoiseshell slunk apologetically along the wall-side into the house.

'By the way, Mrs Bond,' I asked, making my voice casual. 'I didn't quite catch the name of that last cat.'

'Oh, Seven-times-three?' She smiled reminiscently. 'Yes, she is a dear. She's had three kittens seven times running, you see, so I thought it rather a good name for her, don't you?'

'Yes, yes, I do indeed. Splendid name, splendid.'

Another thing which warmed me towards Mrs Bond was her concern for my safety. I appreciated this because it is a rare trait among animal owners. I can think of the trainer after one of his racehorses had kicked me clean out of a loose box examining the animal anxiously to see if it had damaged its foot; the little old lady dwarfed by the bristling, teeth-bared Alsatian saying: 'You'll be gentle with him won't you and I hope you won't hurt him — he's very nervous'; the farmer, after an exhausting calving which I feel certain has knocked about two years off my life expectancy, grunting morosely: 'I doubt you've tired that cow out, young man.'

Mrs Bond was different. She used to meet me at the door with an enormous pair of gauntlets to protect my hands against scratches and it was an inexpressible relief to find that somebody cared.

It became part of the pattern of my life; walking up the garden path among the innumerable slinking, wild-eyed little creatures which were the outside cats, the ceremonial acceptance of the gloves at the door, then the entry into the charged atmosphere of the kitchen with little Mr Bond and his newspaper just visible among the milling furry bodies of the inside cats. I was never able to ascertain Mr Bond's attitude to cats — come to think of it he hardly ever said anything — but I had the impression he could take them or leave them.

The gauntlets were a big help and at times they were a veritable godsend. As in the case of Boris. Boris was an enormous blue-black member of the outside cats and my bête noire in more senses than one. I always cherished a private conviction that he had escaped from a zoo; I had never seen a domestic cat with such sleek, writhing muscles, such dedicated ferocity. I'm sure there was a bit of puma in Boris somewhere.

It had been a sad day for the cat colony when he turned up. I have always found it difficult to dislike any animal; most of the ones which try to do us a mischief are activated by fear, but Boris was different; he was a malevolent bully and after his arrival the frequency of my visits increased because of his habit of regularly beating up his colleagues. I was forever stitching up tattered ears, dressing gnawed limbs.

We had one trial of strength fairly early. Mrs Bond wanted me to give him a worm dose and I had the little tablet all ready held in forceps.

How I ever got hold of him I don't quite know, but I hustled him on to the table and did my wrapping act at lightning speed, swathing him in roll upon roll of stout material. Just for a few seconds I thought I had him as he stared up at me, his great brilliant eyes full of hate. But as I pushed my loaded forceps into his mouth he clamped his teeth viciously down on them and I could feel claws of amazing power tearing inside the sheet. It was all over in moments. A long leg shot out and ripped its way down my wrist. I let go my tight hold of the neck and in a flash Boris sank his teeth through the gauntlet into the ball of my thumb and was away. I was left standing there stupidly, holding the fragmented worm tablet in a bleeding hand and looking at the bunch of ribbons which had once been my wrapping sheet. From then on Boris loathed the very sight of me and the feeling was mutual.

But this was one of the few clouds in a serene sky. I continued to enjoy my visits there and life proceeded on a tranquil course except, perhaps, for some legpulling from my colleagues. They could never understand my willingness to spend so much time over a lot of cats. And of course this fitted in with the general attitude because Siegfried didn't believe in people keeping pets of any kind. He just couldn't understand their mentality and propounded his views to anybody who cared to listen. He himself, of course, kept five dogs and two cats. The dogs, all of them, travelled everywhere with him in the car and he fed dogs and cats every day with his own hands

— wouldn't allow anybody else to do the job. In the evening all seven animals would pile themselves round his feet as he sat in his chair by the fire. To this day he is still as vehemently anti-pet as ever, though another generation of waving dogs' tails almost obscures him as he drives around and he also has several cats, a few tanks of tropical fish and a couple of snakes. '

Tristan saw me in action at Mrs Bond's on only one occasion. I was collecting some long forceps from the instrument cupboard when he came into the room.

'Anything interesting, Jim?' he asked.

'No, not really. I'm just off to see one of the Bond cats. It's got a bone stuck between its teeth.'

The young man eyed me ruminatively for a moment. 'Think I'll come with you. I haven't seen much small animal stuff lately.'

As we went down the garden at the cat establishment I felt a twinge of embarrassment. One of the things which had built up my happy relationship with Mrs Bond was my tender concern for her charges. Even with the wildest and the fiercest I exhibited only gentleness, patience and solicitude; it wasn't really an act, it came quite naturally to me. However I couldn't help wondering what Tristan would think of my cat bedside manner.

Mrs Bond in the doorway had summed up the situation in a flash and had two pairs of gauntlets waiting. Tristan looked a little surprised as he received his pair but thanked the lady with typical charm. He looked still more surprised when he entered the kitchen, sniffed the rich atmosphere and surveyed the masses of furry creatures occupying almost every available inch of space.

'Mr Herriot, I'm afraid it's Boris who has the bone in his teeth,' Mrs Bond said.

'Boris!' My stomach lurched. 'How on earth are we going to catch him?'

'Oh I've been rather clever,' she replied. 'I've managed to entice him with some of his favourite food into a cat basket.'

Tristan put his hand on a big wicker cage on the table. 'In here, is he?' he asked casually. He slipped back the catch and opened the lid. For something like a third of a second the coiled creature within and Tristan regarded each other tensely, then a sleek black body exploded silently from the basket past the young man's left ear on to the top of a tall cupboard.

'Christ!' said Tristan. 'What the hell was that?'

'That,' I said, 'was Boris, and now we've got to get hold of him again.' I climbed on to a chair, reached slowly on to the cupboard top and started 'Puss-puss-puss'ing in my most beguiling tone.

After about a minute Tristan appeared to think he had a better idea; he made a sudden leap and grabbed Boris's tail. But only briefly, because the big cat freed himself in an instant and set off on a whirlwind circuit of the room; along the tops of cupboards and dressers, across the curtains, careering round and round like a wall of death rider.

Tristan stationed himself at a strategic point

and as Boris shot past he swiped at him with one of the gauntlets.

'Missed the bloody thing!' he shouted in chagrin. 'But here he comes again . . . take that, you black sod! Damn it, I can't nail him!'

The docile little inside cats, startled by the scattering of plates and tins and pans and by Tristan's cries and arm wavings, began to run around in their turn, knocking over whatever Boris had missed. The noise and confusion even got through to Mr Bond because just for a moment he raised his head and looked around him in mild surprise at the hurtling bodies before returning to his newspaper.

Tristan, flushed with the excitement of the chase had really begun to enjoy himself. I cringed inwardly as he shouted over to me happily.

'Send him on, Jim, I'll get the bugger next time round!'

We never did catch Boris. We just had to leave the piece of bone to work its own way out, so it wasn't a successful veterinary visit. But Tristan as we got back into the car smiled contentedly.

'That was great, Jim. I didn't realize you had such fun with your pussies.'

Mrs Bond on the other hand, when I next saw her, was rather tight-lipped over the whole thing.

'Mr Herriot,' she said, 'I hope you aren't going to bring that young man with you again.'

19

I always liked having a student with us. These young men had to see at least six months' practice on their way through college and most of their vacations were spent going round with a vet.

We, of course, had our own resident student in Tristan but he was in a different category. I often envied him his remarkable brain because he didn't have to be taught anything — he seemed to know things, to absorb knowledge without apparent effort or indeed without showing interest. If you took Tristan to a case he usually spent his time on the farm sitting in the car reading his *Daily Mirror* and smoking Woodbines.

There were all types among the others — some from the country some from the towns, some dull-witted, some bright — but as I say, I liked having them.

For one thing they were good company in the car. A big part of a country vet's life consists of solitary driving and it was a relief to be able to talk to somebody. It was wonderful, too, to have a gate-opener. Some of the outlying farms were approached through long, gated roads — one which always struck terror into me had eight gates — and it is hard to convey the feeling of sheer luxury when somebody else leaped out and opened them.

And there was another little pleasure; asking the students questions. My own days of studying and examinations were still fresh in my memory and on top of that I had all the vast experience of nearly three years of practice. It gave me a feeling of power to drop casual little queries about the cases we saw and watch the lads squirm as I had so recently squirmed myself. I suppose that even in those early days I was forming a pattern for later life; unknown to myself I was falling into the way of asking a series of my own pet questions as all examiners are liable to do and many years later I overheard one youngster asking another: 'Has he grilled you on the causes of fits in calves yet? Don't worry, he will.' That made me feel suddenly old but there was compensation on another occasion when a newly qualified ex-student rushed up to me and offered to buy me all the beer I could drink. 'You know what the examiner asked me in the final oral? The causes of fits in calves! By God I paralysed him — he had to beg me to stop talking.'

And students were useful in other ways. They ran and got things out of the car boot, they pulled a rope at calvings, they were skilled assistants at operations, they were a repository for my worries and doubts; it isn't too much to say that during their brief visits they revolutionized my life.

So this Easter I waited on the platform of Darrowby station with pleasant anticipation. This lad had been recommended by one of the Ministry officials. 'A really first class chap. Final year London — several times gold medallist. He's seen mixed and town practice and thought he ought to have a look at some of the real rural stuff. I said I'd give you a ring. His name is Richard Carmody.'

Veterinary students came in a variety of shapes and sizes but there were a few features most of them had in common and I already had a mental picture of an eager-faced lad in tweed jacket and rumpled slacks carrying a rucksack. He would probably jump on to the platform as soon as the train drew up. But this time there was no immediate sign of life and a porter had begun to load a stack of egg boxes into the guard's van before one of the compartment doors opened and a tall figure descended in leisurely manner.

I was doubtful about his identity but he seemed to place me on sight. He walked over, held out a hand and surveyed me with a level gaze.

'Mr Herriot?'

'Yes . . . er . . . yes. That's right.'

'My name is Carmody.'

'Ah yes, good. How are you?' We shook hands and I took in the fine check suit and tweedy hat, the shining brogues and pigskin case. This was a very superior student, in fact a highly impressive young man. About a couple of years younger than myself but with a mature air in the set of his broad shoulders and the assurance on his strong, high-coloured face.

I led him across the bridge out on to the station yard; He didn't actually raise his eyebrows when he saw my car but he shot a cold

249

glance at the mud-spattered vehicle, at the cracked windscreen and smooth tyres; and when I opened the door for him I thought for a moment he was going to wipe the seat before sitting down.

At the surgery I showed him round. I was only the assistant but I was proud of our modest set-up and most people were impressed by their first sight of it. But Carmody said, 'Hm', in the little operating room, 'Yes, I see', in the dispensary, and 'Quite' at the instrument cupboard. In the stockroom he was more forthcoming. He reached out and touched a packet of our beloved Adrevan worm medicine for horses.

'Still using this stuff, eh?' he said with a faint smile.

He didn't go into any ecstasies but he did show signs of approval when I took him out through the French windows into the long, high-walled garden where the daffodils glowed among the unkempt tangle and the wisteria climbed high over the old bricks of the tall Georgian house. In the cobbled yard at the foot of the garden he looked up at the rooks making their din high in the overhanging elms and he gazed for a few moments through the trees to where you could see the bare ribs of the fells still showing the last white runnels of winter.

'Charming,' he murmured. 'Charming.'

I was glad enough to see him to his lodgings that evening. I felt I needed time to readjust my thinking.

When we started out next morning I saw he

had discarded his check suit but was still very smart in a hacking jacket and flannels.

'Haven't you any protective clothing?' I asked.

'I've got these.' He indicated a spotless pair of Wellingtons in the back of the car.

'Yes, but I mean an oilskin or a coat of some kind. Some of our jobs are pretty dirty.'

He smiled indulgently. 'Oh, I'm sure I'll be all right. I've been round the farms before, you know.'

I shrugged my shoulders and left it at that.

Our first visit was to a lame calf. The little animal was limping round its pen, holding up a fore leg and looking very woebegone. The knee was visibly swollen and as I palpated it there seemed to be a lumpiness in the fluid within as if there might be a flocculus of pus among it. The temperature was a hundred and four.

I looked up at the farmer. 'This is joint ill. He probably got an infection through his navel soon after birth and it's settled in his knee. We'll have to take care of him because his internal organs such as the liver and lungs can be affected. I'll give him an injection and leave you some tablets for him.'

I went out to the car and when I came back Carmody was bending over the calf, feeling at the distended knee and inspecting the navel closely. I gave my injection and we left.

'You know,' Carmody said as we drove out of the yard, 'that wasn't joint ill.'

'Really?' I was a bit taken aback. I didn't mind students discussing the pros and cons of my diagnoses as long as they didn't do it in

251

front of the farmer, but I had never had one tell me bluntly that I was wrong. I made a mental note to try to keep this fellow away from Siegfried; one remark like that and Siegfried would hurl him unhesitatingly out of the car, big as he was.

'How do you make that out, then?' I asked him.

'Well there was only the one joint involved and the navel was perfectly dry. No pain or swelling there. I should say he just sprained that knee.'

'You may be right, but wouldn't you say the temperature was a bit high for a sprain?'

Carmody grunted and shook his head slightly. Apparently he had no doubts.

A few gates cropped up in the course of our next batch of calls and Carmody got out and opened them just like any ordinary being except that he did it with a certain leisurely elegance. Watching his tall figure as he paced across, his head held high, the smart hat set at just the right angle, I had to admit again that he had enormous presence. It was remarkable at his age.

Shortly before lunch I saw a cow that the farmer had said on the phone might have TB. 'She's gone down t'nick ever since she calved, guv'nor. I doubt she's a screw, but you'd better have a look at her, anyroad.'

As soon as I walked into the byre I knew what the trouble was. I have been blessed with an unusually sensitive nose and the sickly sweet smell of ketone hit me right away. It has always afforded me a childish pleasure to be able to say suddenly in the middle of a tuberculin test,

'There's a cow in here about three weeks calved that isn't doing very well,' and watch the farmer scratch his head and ask me how I knew.

I had another little triumph today. 'Started going off her cake first didn't she?' and the farmer nodded assent. 'And the flesh has just melted off her since then?'

'That's right,' the farmer said, 'I've never seen a cow go down as quick.'

'Well you can stop worrying, Mr Smith. She hasn't got TB, she's got slow fever and we'll be able to put her right for you.'

Slow fever is the local term for acetonaemia and the farmer smiled in relief. 'Damn. I'm glad! I thowt she was dog meat. I nearly rang Mallock this morning.'

I couldn't reach for the steroids which we use today, but I injected six ounces of glucose and 100 units of insulin intravenously — it was one of my pet remedies and might make modern vets laugh. But it used to work. The cow, dead-eyed and gaunt, was too weak to struggle as the farmer held her nose.

When I had finished I ran my hand over the jutting bones, covered, it seemed, only by skin.

'She'll soon fatten up now,' I said. 'But cut her down to once a day milking — that's half the battle. And if that doesn't work, stop milking her entirely for two or three days.'

'Yes, I reckon she's putting it in t'bucket instead of on her back.'

'That's it exactly, Mr Smith.'

Carmody didn't seem to appreciate this interchange of home-spun wisdom and fidgeted

253

impatiently. I took my cue and headed for the car.

'I'll see her in a couple of days,' I cried as we drove away, and waved to Mrs Smith who was looking out from the farmhouse doorway. Carmody however raised his hat gravely and held it a few inches above his head till we had left the yard, which was definitely better. I had noticed him doing this at every place we had visited and it looked so good that I was playing with the idea of starting to wear a hat so that I could try it too.

I glanced sideways at my companion. Most of a morning's work done and I hadn't asked him any questions. I cleared my throat.

'By the way, talking about that cow we've just seen, can you tell me something about the causes of acetonaemia?'

Carmody regarded me impassively. 'As a matter of fact I can't make up my mind which theory I endorse at the moment. Stevens maintains it is the incomplete oxidation of fatty acids, Sjollema leans towards liver intoxication and Janssen implicates one of the centre of the autonomic nervous system. My own view is that if we could only pin-point the exact cause of the production of diacetic acid and beta-oxybutyric acid in the metabolism we'd be well on the way to understanding the problem. Don't you agree?'

I closed my mouth which had begun to hang open.

'Oh yes, I do indeed . . . it's that oxy . . . that old beta-oxy . . . yes, that's what it is, without a doubt.' I slumped lower in my seat and decided not to ask Carmody any more questions; and as the stone walls flipped past the windows I began to face up to the gradually filtering perception that this was a superior being next to me. It was depressing to ponder on the fact that not only was he big, good-looking, completely sure of himself but brilliant as well. Also, I thought bitterly, he had every appearance of being rich.

We rounded the corner of a lane and came up to a low huddle of stone buildings. It was the last call before lunch and the gate into the yard was closed.

'We might as well go through,' I murmured. 'Do you mind?'

The student heaved himself from the car, unlatched the gate and began to bring it round. And he did it as he seemed to do everything: coolly, unhurriedly, with natural grace. As he passed the front of the car I was studying him afresh, wondering again at his style, his massive composure, when, apparently from nowhere, an evil looking little black cur dog glided silently out, sank its teeth with dedicated venom into Carmody's left buttock and slunk away.

Not even the most monolithic dignity can survive being bitten deeply and without warning in the backside. Carmody screamed, leaped in the air clutching his rear, then swarmed to the top of the gate with the agility of a monkey. Squatting on the top spar, his natty hat tipped over one eye, he glared about him wildly.

'What the hell?' he yelled. 'What the bloody hell?'

'It's all right,' I said, hurrying towards him and resisting the impulse to throw myself on the ground and roll about. 'It was just a dog.'

'Dog? What dog? Where?' Carmody's cries took on a frantic note.

'It's gone — disappeared. I only saw it for a couple of seconds.' And indeed, as I looked around it was difficult to believe that that flitting little black shadow had ever existed.

Carmody took a bit of coaxing down from the top of the gate and when he finally did reach ground level he limped over and sat down in the car instead of seeing the case. And when I saw the tattered cloth on his bottom I couldn't blame him for not risking a further attack. If it had been anybody else I'd have told him to drop his pants so that I could slap on some iodine but in this instance I somehow couldn't bring myself to do it. I left him sitting there.

20

When Carmody turned up for the afternoon round he had completely recovered his poise. He had changed his flannels and adopted a somewhat lopsided sitting position in the car but apart from that the dog episode might never have happened. In fact we had hardly got under way when he addressed me with a touch of arrogance.

'Look, I'm not going to learn much just watching you do things. Do you think I could carry out injections and the like? I want actual experience with the animals themselves.'

I didn't answer for a moment but stared ahead through the maze of fine cracks on the windscreen. I couldn't very well tell him that I was still trying to establish myself with the farmers and that some of them had definite reservations about my capabilities. Then I turned to him.

'OK. I'll have to do the diagnosing but whenever possible you can carry on from there.'

He soon had his first taste of action. I decided that a litter of ten weeks old pigs might benefit from an injection of E coli antiserum and handed him the bottle and syringe. And as he moved purposefully among the little animals I thought with gloomy satisfaction that though I may not be au fait with all the small print in the text books I did know better than to chase pigs into the dirty end of the pen to catch them. Because with Carmody in close pursuit the squealing creatures leaped from their straw bed and charged in a body towards a stagnant lake of urine against the far wall. And as the student grabbed at their hind legs the pigs scrabbled among the filth, kicking it back over him in a steady shower. He did finally get them all injected but at the end his smart outfit was liberally spattered and I had to open the windows wide to tolerate his presence in the car.

The next visit was to a big arable farm in the low country, and it was one of the few places where they had hung on to their horses; the long stable had several stalls in use and the names of the horses on the wall above; Boxer, Captain, Bobby, Tommy, and the mares Bonny and Daisy. It was Tommy the old cart horse we had to see and his trouble was a 'stoppage'.

Tommy was an old friend of mine; he kept having mild bouts of colic with constipation and I often wondered if he had a faecolith lurking about in his bowels somewhere. Anyway, six drachms of Istin in a pint of water invariably restored him to normal health and I began automatically to shake up the yellow powder in a drenching bottle. Meanwhile the farmer and his man turned the horse round in his stall, ran a rope under his nose band, threw it over a beam in the stable roof and pulled the head upwards.

I handed the bottle to Carmody and stepped back. The student looked up and hesitated. Tommy was a big horse and the head, pulled high, was far beyond reach; but the farm man pushed a ramshackle kitchen chair wordlessly forward and Carmody mounted it and stood swaying precariously.

I watched with interest. Horses are awkward things to drench at any time and Tommy didn't like Istin, even though it was good for him. On my last visit I had noticed that he was becoming very clever at holding the bitter mixture at the back of his throat instead of swallowing it. I had managed to foil him by tapping him under the chin just as he was toying with the idea of coughing it out and he had gulped it down with an offended look. But it was more and more becoming a battle of wits.

Carmody never really had a chance. He started off well enough by grasping the horse's tongue and thrusting the bottle past the teeth, but Tommy outwitted him effortlessly by inclining his head and allowing the liquid to flow from the far side of his mouth.

'It's coming out t'other side, young man!' the farmer cried with some asperity.

The student gasped and tried to direct the flow down the throat but Tommy had summed him up immediately as an amateur and was now in complete command of the situation. By judicious rolling of the tongue and a series of little coughs and snorts he kept ridding himself of most of the medicine and I felt a pang of pity at the sight of Carmody weaving about on the creaking chair as the yellow fluid cascaded over his clothes.

At the end, the farmer squinted into the empty bottle.

'Well I reckon t'oss got SOME of it,' he muttered sourly.

Carmody eyed him impassively for a moment, shook a few ounces of Istin solution from somewhere up his sleeve and strode out of the stable.

At the next farm I was surprised to detect a vein of sadism in my makeup. The owner, a breeder of pedigree Large White pigs, was exporting a sow abroad and it had to be subjected to various tests including a blood sample for Brucellosis. Extracting a few cc's of blood from the ear vein of a struggling pig is a job which makes most vets shudder and it was clearly a dirty trick to ask a student to do it, but the memory of his coldly confident request at the beginning of the afternoon seemed to have stilled my conscience. I handed him the syringe with scarcely a qualm.

The pigman slipped a noose into the sow's mouth and drew it tight over the snout and behind the canine teeth. This common method of restraint isn't at all painful but the sow was one of those who didn't like any form of mucking about. She was a huge animal and as soon as she felt the rope she opened her mouth wide in a long-drawn, resentful scream. The volume of sound was incredible and she kept it up effortlessly without any apparent need to draw breath. Conversation from then on was out of the question and I watched in the appalling din as Carmody put an elastic tourniquet at the base of the sow's ear, swabbed the surface with spirit and then poked with his needle at the small blood vessel. Nothing happened. He tried again but the syringe remained obstinately empty. He had a few more attempts then, as I felt the top of my head was going to come loose I wandered from the pen into the peace of the yard.

I took a leisurely stroll round the outside of the piggery, pausing for a minute or two to look at the view at the far end where the noise was comparatively faint. When I returned to the pen the screaming hit me again like a pneumatic drill and Carmody, sweating and slightly pop-eyed, looked up from the ear where he was still jabbing fruitlessly. It seemed to me that everybody had had enough. Using sign language I indicated to the student that I'd like to have a go and by a happy chance my first effort brought a dark welling of blood into the syringe. I waved to the pigman to remove the rope and the moment he did so the big sow switched off the noise magically and began to nose, quite unperturbed, among the straw.

'Nothing very exciting at the next place,' I kept the triumph out of my voice as we drove away. 'Just a bullock with a tumour on its jaw. But it's an interesting herd — all Galloways, and this group we're going to see have been wintered outside. They're the toughest animals in the district.'

Carmody nodded. Nothing I said seemed to rouse much enthusiasm in him. For myself this herd of untamed black cattle always held a certain fascination; contacts with them were always coloured by a degree of uncertainty — sometimes you could catch them to examine them, sometimes you couldn't.

As we approached the farm I could see a bunch of about thirty bullocks streaming down the scrubby hillside on our right. The farm men were driving them down through the scattered gorse bushes and the sparse groups of trees to where the stone walls met in a rough V at the front.

One of them waved to me. 'We're going to try to get a rope on 'im down in the corner while he's among his mates. He's a wick bugger — you'd never get near him in t'field.'

After a lot of shouting and waving and running about the bullocks were finally cornered and they stood in a tight, uneasy pack, their shaggy black polls bobbing among the steam rising from their bodies.

'There he is! You can see the thing on his face.' A man pointed to a big beast about the middle of the bunch and began to push his way towards him. My admiration for the Yorkshire farm worker rose another notch as I watched him squeezing between the plunging, kicking animals. 'When I get the rope on his head you'll all have to get on t'other end — one man'll never hold 'im.' He gasped as he fought his way forward.

He was obviously an expert because as soon as he got within reach he dropped the halter on to the bullock's head with practised skill. 'Right!' he shouted. 'Give me a hand with him. We have 'im now.'

But as he spoke the beast gave a great bellow and began to charge from the pack. The man cried out despairingly and disappeared among the hairy bodies. The rope whipped free out of reach of everybody. Except Carmody. As the bullock shot past him he grabbed the trailing rope with a reflex action and hung on.

I watched, fascinated, as man and beast careered across the field. They were travelling away from me towards the far slope, the animal head down, legs pistoning, going like a racehorse, the student also at full speed but very upright, both hands on the rope in front of him, a picture of resolution.

The men and I were helpless spectators and we stood in a silent group as the beast turned left suddenly and disappeared behind a clump of low trees. It was gone for only a few moments but it seemed a long time and when it reappeared it was going faster than ever, hurtling over the turf like a black thunderbolt. Carmody, incredibly, was still there on the end of the rope and still very upright but his strides had increased to an impossible length till he seemed to be touching the ground only every twenty feet or so.

I marvelled at his tenacity but obviously the end was near. He took a last few soaring, swooping steps then he was down on his face. But he didn't let go. The bullock, going better than ever, had turned towards us now, dragging the inert form apparently without effort, and I winced as I saw it was headed straight for a long row of cow pats.

It was when Carmody was skidding face down through the third heap of muck that I suddenly began to like him. And when he finally did have to release his hold and lay for a moment motionless on the grass I hurried over to help him up. He thanked me briefly then looked calmly across the field at a sight which is familiar to every veterinary surgeon — his patient thundering out of sight across the far horizon.

The student was almost unrecognizable. His clothes and face were plastered with filth except where the saffron streaks of the Istin showed up like war paint, he smelt abominably, he had been bitten in the backside, nothing had really gone right for him all day yet he was curiously undefeated. I smiled to myself. It was no good judging this bloke by ordinary standards; I could recognize the seeds of greatness when I saw them.

★   ★   ★

Carmody stayed with us for two weeks and after that first day I got on with him not so badly. Of course it wasn't the same relationship as with other students; there was always a barrier of reserve. He spent a lot of time squinting down the practice microscope at blood films, skin scrapings, milk smears, and by the end of each day he had collected a fresh supply of samples from the cases he had seen. He would come and drink a polite beer with me after an evening call but there was none of the giggling over the day's events as with the other young lads. I had the feeling always that he would rather have been writing up his case book and working out his findings.

But I didn't mind. I found an interest in being in contact with a truly scientific mind. He was as far removed as he could be from the traditional studious swot — his was a cold, superior intellect and there was something rewarding in watching him at work.

I didn't see Carmody again for over twenty years. I picked out his name in the Record when he qualified with top marks then he disappeared into the great world of research for a while to emerge with a PhD and over the years he added a string of further degrees and qualifications. Every now and then an unintelligible article would appear in the professional journals under his name and it became commonplace when reading scientific papers to see references to what Dr Carmody had said on the subject.

When I finally did see him he was the guest of honour at a professional banquet, an international celebrity heavy with honours. From where I was sitting at the far end of one of the side tables I listened to his masterly speech with a feeling of inevitability; the wide grasp of his subject, the brilliant exposition — I had seen it all coming those many years ago.

Afterwards when we had left the tables he moved among us and I gazed with something like awe at the majestic figure approaching. Carmody had always been big, but with the tail coat tight across the massive shoulders and the vast expanse of gleaming shirt front stretched over the curving abdomen he was almost overpowering. As he passed he stopped and looked at me.

'It's Herriot, isn't it?' the handsome, high-coloured face still had that look of calm power.

'Yes, it is. It's good to see you again.'

We shook hands. 'And how is the practice at Darrowby?'

'Oh, as usual,' I replied. 'Bit too busy at times. We could do with some help if ever you felt like it.'

Carmody nodded gravely. 'I'd like that very much. It would be good for me.'

He was about to move on when he paused. 'Perhaps you'd let me know any time you want a pig bled.' For a moment we looked into each other's eyes and I saw a small flame flicker briefly in the frosty blue. Then he was gone.

As I looked at the retreating back a hand gripped my arm. It was Brian Miller, a happily obscure practitioner like myself.

'Come on, Jim, I'll buy you a drink,' he said.

We went into the bar and ordered two beers.

'That Carmody!' Brian said. 'The man's got a tremendous brain, but by God he's a cold fish.'

I sipped at the beer and looked thoughtfully into my glass for a few seconds.

'Oh I don't know,' I said. 'He certainly gives that impression, but Carmody's all right.'

21

The big room at Skeldale House was full. It seemed to me that this room with its graceful alcoves, high, carved ceiling and french windows lay at the centre of our life in Darrowby. It was where Siegfried, Tristan and I gathered when the day's work was done, toasting our feet by the white wood fireplace with the glass-fronted cupboard on top, talking over the day's events. It was the heart of our bachelor existence, sitting there in a happy stupor, reading, listening to the radio, Tristan usually flipping effortlessly through the *Daily Telegraph* crossword.

It was where Siegfried entertained his friends and there was a constant stream of them — old and young, male and female. But tonight it was Tristan's turn and the pack of young people with drinks in their hands were there at his invitation. And they wouldn't need much persuasion. Though just about the opposite of his brother in many ways he had the same attractiveness which brought the friends running at the crook of a finger.

The occasion was the Daffodil Ball at the Drovers' Arms and we were dressed in our best. This was a different kind of function from the usual village institute hop with the farm lads in their big boots and music from a scraping fiddle and piano. It was a proper dance with a popular local band — Lenny Butterfield and his Hot

Shots — and was an annual affair to herald the arrival of spring.

I watched Tristan dispensing the drinks. The bottles of whisky, gin and sherry which Siegfried kept in the fireplace cupboard had taken some severe punishment but Tristan himself had been abstemious. An occasional sip from a glass of light ale perhaps, but nothing more. Drinking, to him, meant the bulk intake of draught bitter; all else was mere vanity and folly. Dainty little glasses were anathema and even now when I see him at a party where everybody is holding small drinks Tristan somehow contrives to have a pint in his hand.

' 'Nice little gathering, Jim,' he said, appearing at my elbow. 'A few more blokes than girls but that won't matter much.'

I eyed him coldly. I knew why there were extra men. It was so that Tristan wouldn't have to take the floor too often. It fitted in with his general dislike of squandering energy that he was an unenthusiastic dancer; he didn't mind walking a girl round the floor now and again during the evening but he preferred to spend most of the time in the bar.

So, in fact, did a lot of the Darrowby folk. When we arrived at the Drovers the bar was congested while only a dedicated few circled round the ballroom. But as time went on more and more couples ventured out and by ten o'clock the dance floor was truly packed.

And I soon found I was enjoying myself. Tristan's friends were an effervescent bunch; likeable young men and attractive girls; I just couldn't help having a good time.

Butterfield's famed band in their short red jackets added greatly to the general merriment. Lenny himself looked about fifty-five and indeed all four of the Hot Shots ensemble were rather elderly, but they made up for their grey hairs by sheer vivacity. Not that Lenny's hair was grey; it was dyed a determined black and he thumped the piano with dynamic energy, beaming out at the company through his horn-rimmed glasses, occasionally bawling a chorus into the microphone by his side, announcing the dances, making throaty wisecracks. He gave value for money.

There was no pairing off in our party and I danced with all the girls in turn. At the peak of the evening I was jockeying my way around the floor with Daphne and the way she was constructed made it a rewarding experience. I never have been one for skinny women but I suppose you could say that Daphne's development had strayed a little too far in the other direction. She wasn't fat, just lavishly endowed.

Battling through the crush, colliding with exuberant neighbours, bouncing deliriously off Daphne, with everybody singing as they danced and the Hot Shots pouring out an insistent boom-boom beat, I felt I hadn't a care in the world. And then I saw Helen.

She was dancing with the inevitable Richard Edmundson, his shining gold head floating above the company like an emblem of doom. And it was uncanny how in an instant my cosy little world disintegrated leaving a chill gnawing emptiness.

When the music stopped I returned Daphne to her friends and went to find Tristan. The comfortable little bar in the Drovers was overflowing and the temperature like an oven. Through an almost impenetrable fog of cigarette smoke I discerned my colleague on a high stool holding court with a group of perspiring revellers. Tristan himself looked cool and, as always, profoundly content. He drained his glass, smacked his lips gently as though it had been the best pint of beer he'd ever tasted, then, as he reached across the counter and courteously requested a refill he spotted me struggling towards him.

When I reached his stool he laid an affable hand on my shoulder, 'Ah, Jim, nice to see you. Splendid dance, this, don't you think?'

I didn't bring up the fact that I hadn't seen him on the floor yet, but making my voice casual I mentioned that Helen was there.

Tristan nodded benignly. 'Yes, saw her come in. Why don't you go and dance with her?'

'I can't do that. She's with a partner — young Edmundson.'

'Not at all.' Tristan surveyed his fresh pint with a critical eye and took an exploratory sip. 'She's with a party, like us. No partner.'

'How do you know that?'

'I watched all the fellows hang their coats out there while the girls went upstairs. No reason at all why you shouldn't have a dance with her.'

'I see.' I hesitated for a few moments then

made my way back to the ballroom.

But it wasn't as easy as that. I had to keep doing my duty with the girls in our group and whenever I headed for Helen she was whisked away by one of her men friends before I got near her. At times I fancied she was looking over at me but I couldn't be sure; the only thing I knew for certain was that I wasn't enjoying myself any more; the magic and gaiety had gone and I felt a rising misery at the thought that this was going to be another of my frustrating contacts with Helen when all I could do was look at her hopelessly. Only, this time was worse — I hadn't even spoken to her.

I was almost relieved when the manager came up and told me there was a call for me. I went to the phone and spoke to Mrs Hall. There was a bitch in trouble whelping and I had to go. I looked at my watch — after midnight, so that was the end of the dance for me.

I stood for a moment listening to the muffled thudding from the dance floor then slowly pulled on my coat before going in to say good-bye to Tristan's friends. I exchanged a few words with them, waved, then turned back and pushed the swing door open.

Helen was standing there, about a foot away from me. Her hand was on the door, too. I didn't wonder whether she was going in or out but stared dumbly into her smiling blue eyes,

'Leaving already, Jim?' she said.

'Yes, I've got a call, I'm afraid.'

'Oh what a shame. I hope it's nothing very serious.'

I opened my mouth to speak, but her dark beauty and the very nearness of her suddenly filled my world and a wave of hopeless longing swept over and submerged me. I slid my hand a few inches down the door and gripped hers as a drowning man might, and wonderingly I felt her fingers come round and entwine themselves tightly in mine.

And in an instant there was no band, no noise, no people, just the two of us standing very close in the doorway.

'Come with me,' I said.

Helen's eyes were very large as she smiled that smile I knew so well.

'I'll get my coat,' she murmured.

This wasn't really me, I thought, standing on the hall carpet watching Helen trotting quickly up the stairs, but I had to believe it as she reappeared on the landing pulling on her coat. Outside, on the cobbles of the market place my car, too, appeared to be taken by surprise because it roared into life at the first touch of the starter.

I had to go back to the surgery for my whelping instruments and in the silent moonlit street we got out and opened the big white door to Skeldale House.

And once in the passage it was the most natural thing in the world to take her in my arms and kiss her gratefully and unhurriedly. I had waited a long time for this and the minutes flowed past unnoticed as we stood there, our feet on the black and red eighteenth-century tiles, our heads almost touching the vast picture of the

Death of Nelson which dominated the entrance.

We kissed again at the first bend of the passage under the companion picture of the Meeting of Wellington and Blucher at Waterloo. We kissed at the second bend by the tall cupboard where Siegfried kept his riding coats and boots. We kissed in the dispensary in between searching for my instruments. Then we tried it out in the garden and this was the best of all with the flowers still expectant in the moonlight and the fragrance of the moist earth and grass rising about us.

I have never driven so slowly to a case. About ten miles an hour with Helen's head on my shoulder and all the scents of spring drifting in through the open window. And it was like sailing from stormy seas into a sweet, safe harbour, like coming home.

The light in the cottage window was the only one showing in the sleeping village, and when I knocked at the door Bert Chapman answered. Bert was a council roadman — one of the breed for whom I felt an abiding affinity.

The council men were my brethren of the roads. Like me they spent most of their lives on the lonely by-ways around Darrowby and I saw them most days of the week, repairing the tarmac, cutting back the grass verges in the summer, gritting and snow ploughing in the winter. And when they spotted me driving past they would grin cheerfully and wave as if the very sight of me had made their day. I don't know whether they were specially picked for good nature but I don't think I have ever met a more equable body of men.

One old farmer remarked sourly to me once. 'There's no wonder the buggers are 'appy, they've got nowt to do.' An exaggeration, of course, but I knew how he felt; compared with farming every other job was easy.

I had seen Bert Chapman just a day or two ago, sitting on a grassy bank, his shovel by his side, a vast sandwich in his hand. He had raised a corded forearm in salute, a broad smile bisecting his round, sun-reddened face. He had looked eternally carefree but tonight his smile was strained.

'I'm sorry to bother you this late, Mr Herriot,' he said as he ushered us into the house, 'but I'm gettin' a bit worried about Susie. Her pups are due and she's been making a bed for them and messing about all day but nowt's happened. I was goin' to leave her till morning but about midnight she started panting like 'ell — I don't like the look of her.'

Susie was one of my regular patients. Her big, burly master was always bringing her to the surgery, a little shame-faced at his solicitude, and when I saw him sitting in the waiting room looking strangely out of place among the ladies with their pets, he usually said 'T'missus asked me to bring Susie.' But it was a transparent excuse.

'She's nobbut a little mongrel, but very faithful,' Bert said, still apologetic, but I could understand how he felt about Susie, a shaggy little ragamuffin whose only wile was to put her paws on my knees and laugh up into my face with her tail lashing. I found her irresistible.

But she was a very different character tonight. As we went into the living room of the cottage the little animal crept from her basket, gave a single indeterminate wag of her tail then stood miserably in the middle of the floor, her ribs heaving. As I bent to examine her she turned a wide panting mouth and anxious eyes up to me.

I ran my hand over her abdomen. I don't think I have ever felt a more bloated little dog; she was as round as a football, absolutely bulging with pups, ready to pop, but nothing was happening.

'What do you think?' Bert's face was haggard under his sunburn and he touched the dog's head briefly with a big calloused hand.

'I don't know yet, Bert,' I said. 'I'll have to have a feel inside. Bring me some hot water, will you?'

I added some antiseptic to the water, soaped my hand and with one finger carefully explored the vagina. There was a pup there, all right; my finger tip brushed across the nostrils, the tiny mouth and tongue; but he was jammed in that passage like a cork in a bottle.

Squatting back on my heels I turned to the Chapmans.

'I'm afraid there's a big pup stuck fast. I have a feeling that if she could get rid of this chap the others would come away. They'd probably be smaller.'

'Is there ony way of shiftin' him, Mr Herriot?' Bert asked.

I paused for a moment. 'I'm going to put forceps on his head and see if he'll move. I don't

275

like using forceps but I'm going to have one careful try and if it doesn't work I'll have to take her back to the surgery for a caesarean.'

'An operation?' Bert said hollowly. He gulped and glanced fearfully at his wife. Like many big men he had married a tiny woman and at this moment Mrs Chapman looked even smaller than her four foot eleven inches as she huddled in her chair and stared at me with wide eyes.

'Oh I wish we'd never had her mated,' she wailed, wringing her hands. 'I told Bert five year old was too late for a first litter but he wouldn't listen. And now we're maybe going to lose 'er.'

I hastened to reassure her. 'No, she isn't too old, and everything may be all right. Let's just see how we get on.'

I boiled the instrument for a few minutes on the stove then kneeled behind my patient again. I poised the forceps for a moment and at the flash of steel a grey tinge crept under Bert's sunburn and his wife coiled herself into a ball in her chair. Obviously they were non-starters as assistants so Helen held Susie's head while I once more reached in towards the pup. There was desperately little room but I managed to direct the forceps along my finger till they touched the nose. Then very gingerly I opened the jaws and pushed them forward with the very gentlest pressure until I was able to clamp them on either side of the head.

I'd soon know now. In a situation like this you can't do any pulling, you can only try to ease the thing along. This I did and I fancied I felt just a bit of movement; I tried again and there was no doubt about it, the pup was coming towards me. Susie, too, appeared to sense that things were taking a turn for the better. She cast off her apathy and began to strain lustily.

It was no trouble after that and I was able to draw the pup forth almost without resistance.

'I'm afraid this one'll be dead,' I said, and as the tiny creature lay across my palm there was no sign of breathing. But, pinching the chest between thumb and forefinger I could feel the heart pulsing steadily and I quickly opened his mouth and blew softly down into his lungs.

I repeated this a few times then laid the pup on his side in the basket. I was just thinking it was going to be no good when the little rib cage gave a sudden lift, then another and another.

'He's off!' Bert exclaimed happily. 'That's champion! We want these puppies alive tha knows. They're by Jack Dennison's terrier and he's a grand 'un.'

'That's right,' Mrs Chapman put in, 'No matter how many she has, they're all spoken for. Everybody wants a pup out of Susie.'

'I can believe that,' I said. But I smiled to myself. Jack Dennison's terrier was another hound of uncertain ancestry, so this lot would be a right mixture. But none the worse for that.

I gave Susie half a cc of pituitrin. 'I think she needs it after pushing against that fellow for hours. We'll wait and see what happens now.'

And it was nice waiting. Mrs Chapman brewed a pot of tea and began to slap butter on to home-made scones. Susie, partly aided by my pituitrin, pushed out a pup in a self-satisfied manner about every fifteen minutes. The pups themselves soon set up a bawling of surprising volume for such minute creatures. Bert, relaxing visibly with every minute, filled his pipe and regarded the fast-growing family with a grin of increasing width.

'Ee, it is kind of you young folks to stay with us like this.' Mrs Chapman put her head on one side and looked at us worriedly, 'I should think you've been dying to get back to your dance all this time.'

I thought of the crush at the Drovers. The smoke, the heat, the nonstop boom-boom of the Hot Shots and I looked around the peaceful little room with the old-fashioned black grate, the low, varnished beams, Mrs Chapman's sewing box, the row of Bert's pipes on the wall. I took a firmer grasp of Helen's hand which I had been holding under the table for the last hour.

'Not at all, Mrs Chapman,' I said. 'We haven't missed it in the least.' And I have never been more sincere.

It must have been about half past two when I finally decided that Susie had finished. She had six fine pups which was a good score for a little thing like her and the noise had abated as the family settled down to feast on her abundant udder.

I lifted the pups out one by one and examined them. Susie didn't mind in the least but appeared to be smiling with modest pride as I handled her brood. When I put them back with her she inspected them and sniffed them over busily before rolling on to her side again.

'Three dogs and three bitches,' I said. ''Nice even litter.'

Before leaving I took Susie from her basket and palpated her abdomen. The degree of deflation was almost unbelievable; a pricked balloon could not have altered its shape more spectacularly and she had made a remarkable metamorphosis to the lean, scruffy little extrovert I knew so well.

When I released her she scurried back and curled herself round her new family who were soon sucking away with total absorption.

Bert laughed. 'She's fair capped wi' them pups.' He bent over and prodded the first arrival with a horny forefinger. 'I like the look o' this big dog pup. I reckon we'll keep this 'un for ourselves, mother. He'll be company for t'awd lass.'

It was time to go. Helen and I moved over to the door and little Mrs Chapman with her fingers on the handle looked up at me.

'Well, Mr Herriot,' she said, 'I can't thank you enough for comin' out and putting our minds at rest. I don't know what I've done wi' this man of mine if anything had happened to his little dog.'

Bert grinned sheepishly. 'Nay,' he muttered. 'Ah was never really worried.'

His wife laughed and opened the door and as we stepped out into the silent scented night she gripped my arm and looked up at me roguishly.

'I suppose this is your young lady,' she said.

I put my arm round Helen's shoulders.

'Yes,' I said firmly, 'this is my young lady.'

22

It was almost as though I were looking at my own cows because as I stood in the little new byre and looked along the row of red and roan backs I felt a kind of pride.

'Frank,' I said. 'They look marvellous. You wouldn't think they were the same animals.'

Frank Metcalfe grinned. 'Just what I was thinking meself. It's wonderful what a change of setting'll do for livestock.'

It was the cows' first day in the new byre. Previously I had seen them only in the old place — a typical Dales cowhouse, centuries old with a broken cobbled floor and gaping holes where the muck and urine lay in pools, rotting wooden partitions between the stalls and slit windows as though the place had been built as a fortress. I could remember Frank sitting in it milking, almost invisible in the gloom, the cobwebs hanging in thick fronds from the low roof above him.

In there, the ten cows had looked what they were — a motley assortment of ordinary milkers — but today they had acquired a new dignity and style.

'You must feel it's been worth all your hard work,' I said, and the young farmer nodded and smiled. There was a grim touch about the smile as though he was reliving for a moment the hours and weeks and months of back-breaking labour he had put in there. Because Frank Metcalfe had done it all himself. The rows of neat, concreted standings, the clean, level sweep of floor, the whitewashed, cement-rendered walls all bathed in light from the spacious windows had been put there by his own two hands.

'I'll show you the dairy,' Frank said.

We went into a small room which he had built at one end and I looked admiringly at the gleaming milk cooler, the spotless sinks and buckets, the strainer with its neat pile of filter pads.

'You know,' I said. 'This is how milk should be produced. All those mucky old places I see every day on my rounds — they nearly make my hair stand on end.'

Frank leaned over and drew a jet of water from one of the taps. 'Aye, you're right. It'll all be like this and better one day and it'll pay the farmers better too. I've got me TT licence now and the extra fourpence a gallon will make a hell of a difference. I feel I'm ready to start.'

And when he did start, I thought, he'd go places. He seemed to have all the things it took to succeed at the hard trade of farming — intelligence, physical toughness, a love of the land and animals and the ability to go slogging on endlessly when other people were enjoying their leisure. I felt these qualities would overcome his biggest handicap which was simply that he didn't have any money.

Frank wasn't a farmer at all to start with. He was a steel worker from Middlesbrough. When he had first arrived less than a year ago with his young wife to take over the isolated small holding at Bransett I had been surprised to learn that he hailed from the city because he had the dark, sinewy look of the typical Dalesman — and he was called Metcalfe.

He had laughed when I mentioned this. 'Oh, my great grandfather came from these parts and I've always had a hankering to come back.'

As I came to know him better I was able to fill in the gaps in that simple statement. He had spent all his holidays up here as a small boy and though his father was a foreman in the steelworks and he himself had served his time at the trade the pull of the Dales had been like a siren song welling stronger till he had been unable to resist it any longer. He had worked on farms in his spare time, read all he could about agriculture and finally had thrown up his old life and rented the little place high in the fells at the end of a long, stony track.

With its primitive house and tumbledown buildings it seemed an unpromising place to make a living and in any case I hadn't much faith in the ability of townspeople to suddenly turn to farming and make a go of it; in my short experience I had seen quite a few try and fail. But Frank Metcalfe had gone about the job as though he had been at it all his life, repairing the broken walls, improving the grassland, judiciously buying stock on his shoe-string budget; there was no sign of the bewilderment and despair I had seen in so many others.

I had mentioned this to a retired farmer in Darrowby and the old man chuckled. 'Aye, you've got to have farmin' inside you. There's very few people as can succeed at it unless it's in their blood. It matters nowt that young Metcalfe's been brought up in a town, he's still got it in 'im — he's got it through the titty, don't you see, through the titty.'

Maybe he was right, but whether Frank had it through the titty or through study and brains he had transformed the holding in a short time. When he wasn't milking, feeding, mucking out, he was slaving at that little byre, chipping stones, mixing cement, sand and dust clinging to the sweat on his face. And now, as he said, he was ready to start.

As we came out of the dairy he pointed to another old building across the yard. 'When I'm straightened out I aim to convert that into another byre. I've had to borrow a good bit but now I'm TT I should be able to clear it off in a couple, of years. Sometime in the future if all goes well I might be able to get a bigger place altogether.'

He was about my own age and a natural friendship had sprung up between us. We used to sit under the low beams of his cramped living room with its single small window and sparse furniture and as his young wife poured cups of tea he liked to talk of his plans. And, listening to him, I always felt that a man like him would do well not only for himself but for farming in general.

I looked at him now as he turned his head and gazed for a few moments round his domain. He didn't have to say: 'I love this place, I feel I

283

belong here.' It was all there in his face, in the softening of his eyes as they moved over the huddle of grass fields cupped in a hollow of the fells. These fields, clawed by past generations from the rough hillside and fighting their age-old battle with heather and bracken, ran up to a ragged hem of cliff and scree and above you could just see the lip of the moor — a wild land of bog and peat hag. Below, the farm track disappeared round the bend of a wooded hill. The pastures were poor and knuckles of rock pushed out in places through the thin soil, but the clean, turf-scented air and the silence must have been like a deliverance after the roar and smoke of the steel-works.

'Well we'd better see that cow, Frank,' I said. 'The new byre nearly made me forget what I came for.'

'Aye, it's this red and white 'un. My latest purchase and she's never been right since I got her. Hasn't come on to her milk properly and she seems dozy, somehow.'

The temperature was a hundred and three and as I put the thermometer away I sniffed. 'She smells a bit, doesn't she?'

'Aye,' Frank said. 'I've noticed that myself.'

'Better bring me some hot water, then I'll have a feel inside.'

The uterus was filled with a stinking exudate and as I withdrew my arm there was a gush of yellowish, necrotic material. 'Surely she must have had a bit of a discharge,' I said.

Frank nodded. 'Yes, she has had, but I didn't pay much attention — a lot of them do it when

284

they're clearing up after calving.'

I drained the uterus by means of a rubber tube and irrigated it with antiseptic, then I pushed in a few acriflavine pessaries. 'That'll help to clean her up, and I think she'll soon be a lot better in herself, but I'm going to take a blood sample from her.'

'Why's that?'

'Well it may be nothing, but I don't like the look of that yellow stuff. It consists of decayed cotyledones — you know, the berries on the calf bed — and when they're that colour it's a bit suspicious of Brucellosis.'

'Abortion, you mean?'

'It's possible, Frank. She may have calved before her time or she may have calved normally but still been infected. Anyway the blood will tell us. Keep her isolated in the meantime.'

A few days later at breakfast time in Skeldale House I felt a quick stab of anxiety as I opened the lab report and read that the agglutination test on the blood had given a positive result. I hurried out to the farm.

'How long have you had this cow?' I asked.

'Just over three weeks,' the young farmer replied.

'And she's been running in the same field as your other cows and the in-calf heifers?'

'Yes, all the time.'

I paused for a moment. 'Frank, I'd better tell you the implications. I know you'll want to know what might happen. The source of infection in Brucellosis is the discharges of an infected cow and I'm afraid this animal of yours will have

285

thoroughly contaminated that pasture. Any or all of your animals may have picked up the bug.'

'Does that mean they'll abort?'

'Not necessarily. It varies tremendously. Many cows carry their calves through despite infection.' I was doing my best to sound optimistic.

Frank dug his hands deep into his pockets. His thin, dark-complexioned face was serious. 'Damn, I wish I'd never seen the thing. I bought her at Houlton market — God knows where she came from, but it's too late to talk like that now. What can we do about the job?'

'The main thing is to keep her isolated and away from the other stock. I wish there was some way to protect the others but there isn't much we can do. There are only two types of vaccine — live ones which can only be given to empty cows and yours are all in-calf, and dead ones which aren't reckoned to be of much use.'

'Well I'm the sort that doesn't like to just sit back and wait. The dead vaccine won't do any harm if it doesn't do any good, will it?'

'No.'

'Right, let's do 'em all with it and we'll hope for the best.'

Hoping for the best was something vets did a lot of in the thirties. I vaccinated the entire herd and we waited.

Nothing happened for a full eight weeks. Summer lengthened into autumn and the cattle were brought inside. The infected cow improved, her discharge cleared up and she began to milk a bit better. Then Frank rang early one morning.

'I've found a dead calf laid in the channel

when I went in to milk. Will you come?'

It was a thinly-haired seven months foetus that I found. The cow looked sick and behind her dangled the inevitable retained placenta. Her udder which, if she had calved normally would have been distended with milk, the precious milk which Frank depended on for his livelihood, was almost empty.

Obsessed by a feeling of helplessness I could only offer the same old advice; isolate, disinfect — and hope.

A fortnight later one of the in-calf heifers did it — she was a pretty little Jersey cross which Frank had hoped would push up his butter fat percentage — and a week after that one of the cows slipped a calf in her sixth month of pregnancy.

It was when I was visiting this third case that I met Mr Bagley. Frank introduced him somewhat apologetically. 'He says he has a cure for this trouble, Jim. He wants to talk to you about it.'

In every sticky situation there is always somebody who knows better than the vet. Subconsciously I suppose I had been waiting for a Mr Bagley to turn up and I listened patiently.

He was very short with bandy legs in cloth leggings, and he looked up at me intently. 'Young man, I've been through this on ma own farm and ah wouldn't be here today if I hadn't found the remedy.'

'I see, and what was that, Mr Bagley?'

'I have it 'ere.' The little man pulled a bottle from his jacket pocket. 'It's a bit mucky — it's been stood in t'cow house window for a year or two.'

I read the label. 'Professor Driscoll's Abortion Cure. Give two tablespoonsful to each cow in the herd in a pint of water and repeat on the following day.' The professor's face took up most of the label. He was an aggressive-looking, profusely whiskered man in a high Victorian collar and he glared out at me belligerently through a thick layer of dust. He wasn't so daft, either, because lower down the bottle I read. 'If an animal has aborted a dose of this mixture will prevent further trouble.' He knew as well as I did that they didn't often do it more than once.

'Yes,' Mr Bagley said. 'That's the stuff. Most of my cows did it on me but I kept goin' with the medicine and they were right as a bobbin next time round.'

'But they would be in any case. They develop an immunity you see.'

Mr Bagley put his head on one side and gave a gentle unbelieving smile. And who was I to argue, anyway? I hadn't a thing to offer.

'OK, Frank,' I said wearily. 'Go ahead — like my vaccine, I don't suppose it can do any harm.'

A fresh bottle of Driscoll's cure was purchased and little Mr Bagley supervised the dosing of the herd. He was cock-a-hoop when, three weeks later, one of the cows calved bang on time.

'Now then, what do you say, young man? Ma stuffs working already, isn't it?'

'Well I expected some of them to calve normally,' I replied and the little man pursed his lips as though he considered me a bad loser.

288

But I wasn't really worried about what he thought; all I felt was an unhappy resignation. Because this sort of thing was always happening in those days before the modern drugs appeared. Quack medicines abounded on the farms and the vets couldn't say a lot about them because their own range of pharmaceuticals was pitifully inadequate.

And in those diseases like abortion which had so far defeated all the efforts of the profession at control the harvest for the quack men was particularly rich. The farming press and country newspapers were filled with confident advertisements of red drenches, black draughts, pink powders which were positively guaranteed to produce results. Professor Driscoll had plenty of competition.

When shortly afterwards another cow calved to time Mr Bagley was very nice about it. 'We all 'ave to learn, young man, and you haven't had much practical experience. You just hadn't heard of my medicine and I'm not blaming you, but I think we're on top of t'job now.'

I didn't say anything. Frank was beginning to look like a man who could see a gleam of hope and I wasn't going to extinguish it by voicing my doubts. Maybe the outbreak had run its course — these things were unpredictable.

But the next time I heard Frank on the phone all my gloomy forebodings were realized. 'I want you to come out and cleanse three cows.'

'Three!'

'Aye, they did it one after the other — bang, bang, bang. And all before time. It's an absolute bugger, Jim — I don't know what I'm going to do.'

He met me as I got out of the car at the top of the track. He looked ten years older, his face pale and haggard as though he hadn't slept. Mr Bagley was there, too, digging a hole in front of the byre door.

'What's he doing?' I asked.

Frank looked down at his boots expressionlessly. 'He's burying one of the calves. He says it does a lot of good if you put it in front of the door.' He looked at me with an attempt at a smile. 'Science can do nowt for me so we might as well try a bit of black magic.'

I felt a few years older myself as I picked my way round the deep grave Mr Bagley was digging. The little man looked up at me as I passed. 'This is a very old remedy,' he explained. 'Ma medicine seems to be losing its power so we'll have to try summat stronger. The trouble is,' he added with some asperity. 'I was called in on this case far too late.'

I removed the putrefying afterbirths from the three cows and got off the place as soon as possible. I felt such a deep sense of shame that I could hardly meet Frank's eye. And it was even worse on my next visit a fortnight later because as I walked across the yard I was conscious of a strange smell polluting the sweet hill air. It was a penetrating, acrid stink and though it rang a bell somewhere I couldn't quite identify it. As Frank came out of the house he saw me sniffing and looking round.

'Not very nice is it?' he said with a tired smile.

'I don't believe you've met our goat.'

'You've got a goat?'

'Well, we've got the loan of one — an old Billy. I don't see him around right now but by God you can always smell him. Mr Bagley dug 'im up somewhere — says he did one of his neighbours a world of good when he was having my trouble. Burying the calves wasn't doing any good so he thought he'd better bring on the goat. It's the smell that does the trick, he says.'

'Frank, I'm sorry,' I said. 'It's still going on, then?'

He shrugged his shoulders. 'Aye, two more since I saw you. But I'm past worrying now, Jim, and for God's sake stop looking so bloody miserable yourself. You can't do anything, I know that. Nobody can do anything.'

Driving home, I brooded on his words. Contagious Bovine Abortion has been recognized for centuries and I had read in old books of the filthy scourge which ravaged and ruined the ancient farmers just as it was doing to Frank Metcalfe today. The experts of those days said it was due to impure water, improper feeding, lack of exercise, sudden frights. They did note, however, that other cows which were allowed to sniff at the foetuses and afterbirth were likely to suffer the same fate themselves. But beyond that it was a black tunnel of ignorance.

We modern vets, on the other hand, knew all about it. We knew it was caused by a Gram negative bacillus called Brucella abortus whose habits and attributes we had studied till we knew its every secret; but when it came to helping a farmer in Frank's situation we were about as much use as our colleagues of old who wrote those quaint books. True, dedicated researchers were working to find a strain of the bacillus which would form a safe and efficient vaccine to immunize cattle in calfhood and as far back as 1930 a certain strain 19 had been developed from which much was hoped. But even now it was still in the experimental stage. If Frank had had the luck to be born twenty years later the chances are that those cows he bought would have all been vaccinated and protected by that same strain 19. Nowadays we even have an efficient dead vaccine for the pregnant cows.

Best of all there is now a scheme under way for the complete eradication of Brucellosis and this has brought the disease to the notice of the general public. People are naturally interested mainly in the public health aspect and they have learned about the vast spectrum of illnesses which the infected milk, can cause in humans. But few townsmen know what Brucellosis can do to farmers.

The end of Frank's story was not far away. Autumn was reaching into winter and the frost was sparkling on the steps of Skeldale House when he called one night to see me. We went into the big room and I opened a couple of bottles of beer.

'I thought I'd come and tell you, Jim,' he said in a matter of fact tone. 'I'm having to pack up.'

'Pack up?' Something in me refused to accept what he was saying.

'Aye, I'm going back to me old job in

Middlesbrough. There's nowt else to do.'

I looked at him helplessly. 'It's as bad as that, is it?'

'Well just think.' He smiled grimly. 'I have three cows which calved normally out of the whole herd. The rest are a mucky, discharging, sickly lot with no milk worth talking about. I've got no calves to sell or keep as replacements. I've got nowt.'

I hesitated. 'There's no hope of raising the wind to get you over this?'

'No, Jim. If I sell up now I'll just about be able to pay the bank what I owe them. The rest I borrowed from my old man and I'm not goin' back to him for more. I promised him I'd return to the steelworks if this didn't work out and that's what I'm goin' to do.'

'Oh hell, Frank,' I said. 'I can't tell you how sorry I am. You haven't had a scrap of luck all the way through.'

He looked at me and smiled with no trace of self pity. 'Aye well,' he said. 'These things happen.'

I almost jumped at the words. 'These things happen!' That's what farmers always said after a disaster. That old man in Darrowby had been right. Frank really did have it through the titty.

And in truth he wasn't the only man to be bankrupted in this way. What had hit Frank was called an 'abortion storm' and the same sort of thing had driven a legion of good men to the wall. Some of them hung on, tightened their belts, spent their life savings and half starved till the storm abated and they could start again. But

293

Frank had no savings to see him through; his venture had been a gamble from the beginning and he had lost.

I never heard of him again. At first I thought he might write, but then I realized that once the agonizing break had been made it had to be complete.

★ ★ ★

From some parts of the northern Pennines you can see away over the great sprawl of Teesside and when the fierce glow from the blast furnaces set the night sky alight I used to think of Frank down there and wonder how he was getting on. He'd make a go of it all right, but how often did his mind turn to the high-blown green hollow where he had hoped to build something worth while and to live and bring up his children?

Some people called Peters bought the little farm at Bransett after he left. Strangely enough they were from Teesside, too, but Mr Peters was a wealthy director of the ICI and used the place only as a weekend retreat. It was ideal for the purpose because he had a young family all keen on riding and the fields were soon being grazed by an assortment of horses and ponies. In the summer Mrs Peters used to spend months on end up there with the children. They were nice people who cared for their animals and I was a frequent visitor.

The dwelling house was renovated almost out of recognition and I drank coffee instead of tea in the living-room which had become a place of grace and charm with an antique table, chintz covers and pictures on the walls. The old outbuildings were converted into loose boxes with shining, freshly painted doors.

The only thing which got no attention was Frank's little new byre; it was used as a storage place for corn and bedding for the horses.

I always felt a tug at my heart when I looked in there at the thick dust on the floor, the windows almost opaque with dirt, the cobwebs everywhere, the rusting water bowls, the litter of straw bales, peat moss and sacks of oats where once Frank's cows had stood so proudly.

It was all that was left of a man's dream.

23

After the night of the Daffodil Ball I just seemed to drift naturally into the habit of dropping in to see Helen on an occasional evening. And before I knew what was happening I had developed a pattern; around eight o'clock my feet began to make of their own accord for Heston Grange. Of course I fought the impulse — I didn't go every night; there was my work which often occupied me round the clock, there was a feeling of propriety, and there was Mr Alderson.

Helen's father was a vague little man who had withdrawn into himself to a great extent since his wife's death a few years ago. He was an expert stockman and his farm could compare with the best, but a good part of his mind often seemed to be elsewhere. And he had acquired some little peculiarities; when things weren't going well he carried on long muttered conversations with himself but when he was particularly pleased about something he was inclined to break into a loud, tuneless humming. It was a penetrating sound and on my professional visits I could often locate him by tracking down this characteristic droning among the farm buildings.

At first when I came to see Helen I'm sure he never even noticed me — I was just one of the crowd of young men who hung around his daughter; but as time went on and my visits became more frequent he suddenly seemed to become conscious of me and began to regard me with an interest which deepened rapidly into alarm. I couldn't blame him, really. He was devoted to Helen and it was natural that he should desire a grand match for her. Richard Edmundson represented just that. His family were rich, powerful people and Richard was very keen indeed. Compared to him, an unknown, impecunious young vet was a poor bargain.

When Mr Alderson was around, my visits were uncomfortable affairs, and it was a pity because I instinctively liked him. He had an amiable, completely inoffensive nature which was very appealing and under other conditions we would have got along very well. But there was no getting round the fact that he resented me. And it wasn't because he wanted to hang on to Helen — he was an unselfish man and anyway, he had an excellent housekeeper in his sister who had been recently widowed and had come to live with the Aldersons. Auntie Lucy was a redoubtable character and was perfectly capable of running the household and looking after the two younger children. It was just that he had got used to the comfortable assumption that one day his daughter would marry the son of his old friend and have a life of untroubled affluence; and he had a stubborn streak which rebelled fiercely against any prospect of change.

So it was always a relief when I got out of the house with Helen. Everything was right then; we went to the little dances in the village institutes, we walked for miles along the old grassy mine tracks among the hills, or sometimes she came

297

on my evening calls with me. There wasn't anything spectacular to do in Darrowby but there was a complete lack of strain, a feeling of being self-sufficient in a warm existence of our own that made everything meaningful and worthwhile.

Things might have gone on like this indefinitely but for a conversation I had with Siegfried. We were sitting in the big room at Skeldale House as we often did before bedtime, talking over the day's events when he laughed and slapped his knee.

'I had old Harry Forster in tonight paying his bill. He was really funny — sat looking round the room and saying 'It's a nice little nest you have here, Mr Farnon, a nice little nest,' and then, very sly 'It's time there was a bird in this nest, you know, there should be a little bird in here.''

I laughed too. 'Well, you should be used to it by now. You're the most eligible bachelor in Darrowby. People are always having a dig at you — they won't be happy till they've got you married off.'

'Wait a minute, not so fast.' Siegfried eyed me thoughtfully. 'I don't think for a moment that Harry was talking about me, it was you he had in mind.'

'What do you mean?'

'Well just think. Didn't you say you had run into the old boy one night when you were walking over his land with Helen. He'd be on to a thing like that in a flash. He thinks it's time you were hitched up, that's all.'

I lay back in my chair and gave myself over to

laughter. 'Me! Married! That'll be the day. Can you imagine it? Poor old Harry.'

Siegfried leaned forward. 'What are you laughing at, James? He's quite right — it's time you were married.'

'What's that?' I looked at him incredulously. 'What are you on about now?'

'It's quite simple,' he said. 'I'm saying you ought to get married, and soon.'

'Oh come on Siegfried, you're joking!'

'Why should I be?'

'Well damn it, I'm only starting my career, I've no money, no nothing, I've never even thought about it.'

'You've never even . . . well tell me this, are you courting Helen Alderson or aren't you?'

'Well I'm . . . I've been . . . oh I suppose you could call it that.'

Siegfried settled back comfortably on his chair, put his finger tips together and assumed a judicial expression. 'Good, good. You admit you're courting the girl. Now let us take it a step further. She is, from my own observation, extremely attractive — in fact she nearly causes a traffic pile-up when she walks across the cobbles on market day. It's common knowledge that she is intelligent, equable and an excellent cook. Perhaps you would agree with this?'

'Of course I would,' I said, nettled at his superior air. 'But what's this all about? Why are you going on like a High Court judge?'

'I'm only trying to establish my point, James, which is that you seem to have an ideal wife lined up and you are doing nothing about it. In fact, not to put a too fine point on it, I wish you'd stop playing around and let us see a little action.'

'But it's not as simple as that,' I said, my voice rising, 'I've told you already I'd have to be a lot better off, and anyway, give me a chance, I've only been going to the house for a few weeks — surely you don't start thinking of getting married as soon as that. And there's another thing — her old man doesn't like me.'

Siegfried put his head on one side and I gritted my teeth as a saintly expression began to settle on his face. 'Now my dear chap, don't get angry, but there's something I have to tell you for your own good. Caution is often a virtue, but in your case you carry it too far. It's a little flaw in your character and it shows in a multitude of ways. In your wary approach to problems in your work, for instance — you are always too apprehensive, proceeding fearfully step by step when you should be plunging boldly ahead. You keep seeing dangers when there aren't any — you've got to learn to take a chance, to lash out a bit. As it is, you are confined to a narrow range of activity by your own doubts.'

'The original stick-in-the-mud in fact, eh?'

'Oh come now, James, I didn't say that, but while we're talking, there's another small point I want to bring up. I know you won't mind my saying this. Until you get married I'm afraid I shall fail to get the full benefit of your assistance in the practice because frankly you are becoming increasingly besotted and bemused to the extent

300

that I'm sure you don't know what you're doing half the time.'

'What the devil are you talking about? I've never heard such . . . '

'Kindly hear me out, James. What I'm saying is perfectly true — you're walking about like a man in a dream and you've developed a disturbing habit of staring into space when I'm talking to you. There's only one cure, my boy.'

'And it's a simple little cure, isn't it!' I shouted. 'No money, no home, but leap into matrimony with a happy cry. There's not a thing to worry about!'

'Ah-ah, you see, there you go again, looking for difficulties.' He gave a little laugh and gazed at me with pitying affection. 'No money you say. Well one of these days you'll be a partner here. Your plate will be out on those railings in front of the house, so you'll never be short of your daily bread. And as regards a home — look at all the empty rooms in this house. You could set up a private suite upstairs without any trouble. So that's just a piffling little detail.'

I ran my hand distractedly through my hair. My head was beginning to swim. 'You make it all sound easy.'

'But it IS easy!' Siegfried shot upright in his chair. 'Go out and ask that girl without further delay and get her into church before the month is out!' He wagged a finger at me. 'Learn to grasp the nettle of life, James. Throw off your hesitant ways and remember:' He clenched his fist and struck an attitude. 'There is a tide in the affairs of men which, taken at the flood . . . '

'OK, OK,' I said, rising wearily from my chair, 'That's enough, I get the message. I'm going to bed now.'

★ ★ ★

And I don't suppose I am the first person to have had his life fundamentally influenced by one of Siegfried's chance out-bursts. I thought his opinions ridiculous at the time but he planted a seed which germinated and flowered almost overnight. There is no doubt he is responsible for the fact that I was the father of a grown-up family while I was still a young man, because when I brought the subject up with Helen she said yes she'd like to marry me and we set our eyes on an early date. She seemed surprised at first — maybe she had the same opinion of me as Siegfried and expected it would take me a few years to get off the ground.

Anyway, before I had time to think much more about it everything was neatly settled and I found I had made a magical transition from jeering at the whole idea to making plans for furnishing our prospective bedsitter at Skeldale House.

It was a blissful time with only one cloud on the horizon; but that cloud bulked large and forbidding. As I walked hand in hand with Helen, my thoughts in the air, she kept bringing me back to earth with an appealing look.

'You know, Jim, you'll really have to speak to Dad. It's time he knew.'

24

I had been warned long before I qualified that country practice was a dirty, stinking job. I had accepted the fact and adjusted myself to it but there were times when this side of my life obtruded itself and became almost insupportable. Like now, when even after a long hot bath I still smelt.

As I hoisted myself from the steaming water I sniffed at my arm and there it was; the malodorous memory of that horrible cleansing at Tommy Dearlove's striking triumphantly through all the soap and antiseptic almost as fresh and pungent as it had been at four o'clock this afternoon. Nothing but time would move it.

But something in me rebelled at the idea of crawling into bed in this state and I looked with something like desperation along the row of bottles on the bathroom shelf. I stopped at Mrs Hall's bath salts, shining violent pink in their big glass jar. This was something I'd never tried before and I tipped a small handful into the water round my feet. For a moment my head swam as the rising steam was suddenly charged with an aggressive sweetness then on an impulse I shook most of the jar's contents into the bath and lowered myself once more under the surface.

For a long time I lay there smiling to myself in triumph as the oily liquid lapped around me.

Not even Tommy Dearlove's cleansing could survive this treatment.

The whole process had a stupefying effect on me and I was half asleep even as I sank back on the pillow. There followed a few moments of blissful floating before a delicious slumber claimed me. And when the bedside phone boomed in my ear the sense of injustice and personal affront was even stronger than usual. Blinking sleepily at the clock which said 1.15 AM I lifted the receiver and mumbled into it, but I was jerked suddenly wide awake when I recognized Mr Alderson's voice. Candy was calving and something was wrong. Would I come right away.

There has always been a 'this is where I came in' feeling about a night call. And as my lights swept the cobbles of the deserted market place it was there again; a sense of returning to fundamentals, of really being me. The silent houses, the tight drawn curtains, the long, empty street giving way to the stone walls of the country road flipping endlessly past on either side. At these times I was usually in a state of suspended animation, just sufficiently awake to steer the car in the right direction, but tonight I was fully alert, my mind ticking over anxiously.

Because Candy was something special. She was the house cow, a pretty little Jersey and Mr Alderson's particular pet. She was the sole member of her breed in the herd but whereas the milk from the Shorthorns went into the churns to be collected by the big dairy, Candy's rich yellow offering found its way on to the family porridge every morning or appeared heaped up on trifles and fruit pies or was made into butter, a golden creamy butter to make you dream.

But apart from all that, Mr Alderson just liked the animal. He usually stopped opposite her on his way down the byre and began to hum to himself and gave her tail head a brief scratch as he passed. And I couldn't blame him because I sometimes wish all cows were Jerseys; small, gentle, doe-eyed creatures you could push around without any trouble; with padded corners and fragile limbs. Even if they kicked you it was like a love tap compared with the clump from a craggy Friesian.

I just hoped it would be something simple with Candy, because my stock wasn't high with Mr Alderson and I had a nervous conviction that he wouldn't react favourably if I started to make a ham-fisted job of calving his little favourite. I shrugged away my fears; obstetrics in the Jersey were usually easy.

Helen's father was an efficient farmer. As I pulled up in the yard I could see into the lighted loose box where two buckets of water were steaming in readiness for me. A towel was draped over the half door and Stan and Bert, the two long-serving cowmen, were standing alongside their boss. Candy was lying comfortably in deep straw. She wasn't straining and there was nothing visible at the vulva but the cow had a preoccupied, inward look as though all was not well with her.

I closed the door behind me. 'Have you had a feel inside her, Mr Alderson?'

'Aye, I've had me hand in and there's nowt there.'

'Nothing at all?'

'Not a thing. She'd been on for a few hours and not showing so I popped me hand in and there's no head, no legs, nowt. And not much room, either. That's when I rang you.'

This sounded very strange. I hung my jacket on a nail and began thoughtfully to unbutton my shirt. It was when I was pulling it over my head that I noticed Mr Alderson's nose wrinkling. The farm men, too, began to sniff and look at each other wonderingly. Mrs Hall's bath salts, imprisoned under my clothing had burst from their bondage in a sickly wave, filling the enclosed space with their strident message. Hurriedly I began to wash my arms in the hope that the alien odour might pass away but it seemed to get worse, welling from my warm skin, competing incongruously with the honest smells of cow, hay and straw. Nobody said anything. These men weren't the type to make the ribald remark which would have enabled me to laugh the thing off. There was no ambiguity about this scent; it was voluptuously feminine and Bert and Stan stared at me open-mouthed. Mr Alderson, his mouth turned down at the corners, his nostrils still twitching, kept his eyes fixed on the far wall.

Cringing inwardly I knelt behind the cow and in a moment my embarrassment was forgotten. The vagina was empty; a smooth passage narrowing rapidly to a small, ridged opening just wide enough to admit my hand. Beyond I could feel the feet and head of a calf. My spirits plummeted. Torsion of the uterus. There was going to be no easy victory for me here.

I sat back on my heels and turned to the farmers. 'She's got a twisted calf bed. There's a live calf in there all right but there's no way out for it — I can barely get my hand through.'

'Aye, I thought it was something peculiar.' Mr Alderson rubbed his chin and looked at me doubtfully. 'What can we do about it, then?'

'We'll have to try to correct the twist by rolling the cow over while I keep hold of the calf. It's a good job there's plenty of us here.'

'And that'll put everything right, will it?'

I swallowed. I didn't like these jobs. Sometimes rolling worked and sometimes it didn't and in those days we hadn't quite got round to performing caesareans on cows. If I was unsuccessful I had the prospect of telling Mr Alderson to send Candy to the butcher. I banished the thought quickly.

'It'll put everything right,' I said. It had to. I stationed Bert at the front legs, Stan at the hind and the farmer holding the cow's head on the floor. Then I stretched myself on the hard concrete, pushed in a hand and grasped the calf's foot.

'Now roll her,' I gasped, and the men pulled the legs round in a clockwise direction. I held fiercely to the little feet as the cow flopped on to her other side. Nothing seemed to be happening inside.

'Push her on to her chest,' I panted.

Stan and Bert expertly tucked the legs under

the cow and rolled her on to her brisket and as she settled there I gave a yell of pain.

'Get her back, quick! We're going the wrong way!' The smooth band of tissue had tightened on my wrist in a numbing grip of frightening power. For a moment I had the panicky impression that I'd never get out of there again.

But the men worked like lightning. Within seconds Candy was stretched out on her original side, the pressure was off my arm and we were back where we started.

I gritted my teeth and took a fresh grip on the calf's foot. 'OK, try her the other way.'

This time the roll was anti-clockwise and we went through 180 degrees without anything happening. I only just kept my grasp on the foot — the resistance this time was tremendous. Taking a breather for a few seconds I lay face down while the sweat sprang out on my back, sending out fresh exotic vapours from the bath salts.

'Right. One more go!' I cried and the men hauled the cow further over.

And oh it was beautiful to feel everything magically unravelling and my arm lying free in a wide uterus with all the room in the world and the calf already beginning to slide towards me.

Candy summed up the situation immediately and for the first time gave a determined heaving strain. Sensing victory just round the corner she followed up with another prolonged effort which popped the calf wet and wriggling into my arms.

'By gum, it was quick at t'finish,' Mr Alderson murmured wonderingly. He seized a wisp of hay and began to dry off the little creature.

Thankfully I soaped my arms in one of the buckets. After every delivery there is a feeling of relief but in this case it was overwhelming. It no longer mattered that the loose box smelt like a ladies' hairdressing salon, I just felt good. I said goodnight to Bert and Stan as they returned to their beds, giving a final incredulous sniff as they passed me. Mr Alderson was pottering about, having a word with Candy then starting again on the calf which he had already rubbed down several times. He seemed fascinated by it. And I couldn't blame him because it was like something out of Disney; a pale gold fawn, unbelievably tiny with large dark limpid eyes and an expression of trusting innocence. It was a heifer, too.

The farmer lifted it as if it were a whippet dog and laid it by the mother's head. Candy nosed the little animal over, rumbling happily in her throat, then she began to lick it. I watched Mr Alderson. He was standing, hands clasped behind him, rocking backwards and forwards on his heels, obviously enchanted by the scene. Any time now, I thought. And I was right; the tuneless humming broke out, even louder than usual, like a joyful paean.

I stiffened in my wellingtons. There would never be a better time. After a nervous cough I spoke up firmly.

'Mr Alderson,' I said and he half turned his head. 'I would like to marry your daughter.'

The humming was switched off abruptly and he turned slowly till he was facing me. He didn't speak but his eyes searched my face unhappily. Then he bent stiffly, picked up the buckets one by one, tipped out the water and made for the door.

'You'd better come in the house,' he said.

The farmhouse kitchen looked lost and forsaken with the family abed. I sat in a high backed wooden chair by the side of the empty hearth while Mr Alderson put away his buckets, hung up the towel and washed his hands methodically at the sink, then he pottered through to the parlour and I heard him bumping and clinking about in the sideboard. When he reappeared he bore a tray in front of him on which a bottle of whisky and two glasses rattled gently. The tray lent the simple procedure an air of formality which was accentuated by the heavy cut crystal of the glasses and the virgin, unopened state of the bottle.

Mr Alderson set the tray down on the kitchen table which he dragged nearer to us before settling in the chair at the other side of the fireplace. Nobody said anything. I waited in the lengthening silence while he peered at the cap of the bottle like a man who had never seen one before then unscrewed it with slow apprehension as though he feared it might blow up in his face.

Finally he poured out two measures with the utmost gravity and precision, ducking his head frequently to compare the levels in the two glasses, and with a last touch of ceremony proffered the laden tray.

I took my drink and waited expectantly.

Mr Alderson looked into the lifeless fireplace

310

for a minute or two then he directed his gaze upwards at the oil painting of the paddling cows which hung above the mantelpiece. He pursed his lips as though about to whistle but appeared to change his mind and without salutation took a gulp of his whisky which sent him into a paroxysm of coughing from which it took him some time to recover. When his breathing had returned to normal he sat up straight and fixed me with streaming eyes. He cleared his throat and I felt a certain tension.

'Aye well,' he said, 'it's grand hay weather.'

I agreed with him and he looked round the kitchen with the interested stare of a total stranger. Having completed his inspection he took another copious swallow from his glass, grimaced, closed his eyes, shook his head violently a few times, then leaned forward.

'Mind you,' he said, 'a night's rain would do a lot o' good.'

I gave my opinion that it undoubtedly would and the silence fell again. It lasted even longer this time and my host kept drinking his whisky as though he was getting used to it. And I could see that it was having a relaxing effect; the strained lines on his face were beginning to smooth out and his eyes were losing their hunted look.

Nothing more was said until he had replenished our glasses, balancing the amounts meticulously again. He took a sip at his second measure then he looked down at the rug and spoke in a small voice.

'James,' he said, 'I had a wife in a thousand.'

I was so surprised I hardly knew what to say. 'Yes, I know,' I murmured. 'I've heard a lot about her.'

Mr Alderson went on, still looking down, his voice full of gentle yearning.

'Yes, she was the grandest lass for miles around and the bonniest.' He looked up at me suddenly with the ghost of a smile. 'Nobody thought she'd ever have a feller like me, you know. But she did.' He paused and looked away. 'Aye, she did.'

He began to tell me about his dead wife. He told me calmly, without self pity, but with a wistful gratitude for the happiness he had known. And I discovered that Mr Alderson was different from a lot of the farmers of his generation because he said nothing about her being a 'good worker'. So many of the women of those times seemed to be judged mainly on their working ability and when I had first come to Darrowby I had been shocked when I commiserated with a newly widowed old man. He had brushed a tear from his eye and said, 'Aye, she was a grand worker.'

But Mr Alderson said only that his wife had been beautiful, that she had been kind, and that he had loved her very much. He talked about Helen, too, about the things she had said and done when she was a little girl, about how very like her mother she was in every way. He never said anything about me but I had the feeling all the time that he meant it to concern me; and the very fact that he was talking so freely seemed a sign that the barriers were coming down.

Actually he was talking a little too freely. He was halfway down his third huge whisky and in my experience Yorkshiremen just couldn't take the stuff. I had seen burly ten pint men from the local pub keel over after a mere sniff at the amber fluid and little Mr Alderson hardly drank at all. I was getting worried.

But there was nothing I could do, so I let him ramble on happily. He was lying right back in his chair now, completely at ease, his eyes, alight with his memories, gazing somewhere above my head. In fact I am convinced he had forgotten I was there because after one long passage he dropped his eyes, caught sight of me and stared for a moment without recognition. When he did manage to place me it seemed to remind him of his duties as a host. But as he reached again for the bottles he caught sight of the clock on the wall.

'Well dang it, it's four o'clock. We've been here long enough. It's hardly worth goin' to bed, but I suppose we'd better have an hour or two's sleep.' He tipped the last of the whisky down his throat, jumped briskly to his feet, looked around him for a few moments in a business-like sort of way then pitched head first with a sickening clatter among the fire irons.

Frozen with horror, I started forward to help the small figure scrabbling on the hearth but I needn't have worried because he bounced back to his feet in a second or two and looked me in the eye as if nothing had happened.

'Well, I'd better be off,' I said. 'Thanks for the drink.' There was no point in staying longer as I realized that the chances of Mr Alderson saying 'Bless you, my son' or anything like that were remote. But I had a comforting impression that all was going to be well.

As I made my way to the door the farmer made a creditable attempt to usher me out but his direction was faulty and he tacked helplessly away from me across the kitchen floor before collapsing against a tall dresser. From under a row of willow pattern dinner plates his face looked at me with simple bewilderment.

I hesitated then turned back. 'I'll just walk up the stairs with you, Mr Alderson,' I said in a matter of fact voice and the little man made no resistance as I took his arm and guided him towards the door in the far corner.

As we creaked our way upstairs he stumbled and would have gone down again had I not grabbed him round the waist. As I caught him he looked up at me and grunted 'Thanks, lad,' and we grinned at each other for a moment before restarting the climb.

I supported him across the landing to his bedroom door and he stood hesitating as though about to say something. But finally he just nodded to me a couple of times before ducking inside.

I waited outside the door, listening in some anxiety to the bumps and thumps from within; but I relaxed as a loud, tuneless humming came through the panels. Everything most certainly was going to be all right.

25

'Well, do you want t'job or don't you?'

Walt Barnett towered over me in the surgery doorway and his eyes flickered from my head to my feet and up again without expression. The cigarette dangling from his lower lip seemed to be a part of him as did the brown trilby hat and the shining navy blue serge suit stretched tightly over his bulky form. He must have weighed nearly twenty stone and with his red beefy brutal mouth and overbearing manner he was undeniably formidable.

'Well, er . . . yes. Of course we want the job,' I replied. 'I was just wondering when we could fit it in.' I went over to the desk and began to look through the appointment book. 'We're pretty full this week and I don't know what Mr Farnon has fixed for the week after. Maybe we'd better give you a ring.'

The big man had burst in on me without warning or greeting and barked, 'I 'ave a fine big blood 'oss to geld. When can you do 'im?'

I had looked at him hesitantly for a few moments, taken aback partly by the arrogance of his approach, partly by his request. This wasn't good news to me; I didn't like castrating fine big blood 'osses — I much preferred the ordinary cart colts and if you came right down to it I had a particular preference for Shetland ponies. But it was all part of living and if it had

315

to be done it had to be done.

'You can give me a ring if you like, but don't be ower long about it.' The hard unsmiling stare still held me. 'And I want a good job doin', think on!'

'We always try to do a good job, Mr Barnett,' I said, fighting a rising prickle of resentment at his attitude.

'Aye well I've heard that afore and I've had some bloody balls-ups,' he said. He gave me a final truculent nod, turned and walked out, leaving the door open.

I was still standing in the middle of the room seething and muttering to myself when Siegfried walked in. I hardly saw him at first and when he finally came into focus I found I was glowering into his face.

'What's the trouble, James?' he asked. 'A little touch of indigestion, perhaps?'

'Indigestion? No . . . no . . . Why do you say that?'

'Well you seemed to be in some sort of pain, standing there on one leg with your face screwed up.'

'Did I look like that? Oh it was just our old friend Walt Barnett. He wants us to cut a horse for him and he made the request in his usual charming way — he really gets under my skin, that man.'

Tristan came in from the passage, 'Yes, I was out there and I heard him. He's a bloody big lout.'

Siegfried rounded on him. 'That's enough! I don't want to hear that kind of talk in here.'

Then he turned back to me. 'And really, James, even if you were upset I don't think it's an excuse for profanity.'

'What do you mean?'

'Well, some of the expletives I heard you muttering there were unworthy of you.' He spread his hands in a gesture of disarming frankness. 'Heaven knows I'm no prude but I don't like to hear such language within these walls.' He paused and his features assumed an expression of deep gravity. 'After all, the people who come in here provide us with our bread and butter and they should be referred to with respect.'

'Yes, but . . .'

'Oh I know some are not as nice as others but you must never let them irritate you. You've heard the old saying, 'The customer is always right.' Well I think it's a good working axiom and I always abide by it myself.' He gazed solemnly at Tristan and me in turn. 'So I hope I make myself clear. No swearing in the surgery — particularly when it concerns the clients.'

'It's all right for you!' I burst out heatedly. 'But you didn't hear Barnett. I'll stand so much, but . . .'

Siegfried put his head on one side and a smile of ethereal beauty crept over his face. 'My dear old chap, there you go again, letting little things disturb you. I've had to speak to you about this before, haven't I? I wish I could help you, I wish I could pass on my own gift of remaining calm at all times.'

'What's that you said?'

'I said I wanted to help you, James, and I will.' He held up a forefinger. 'You've probably often wondered why I never get angry or excited.'

'Eh?'

'Oh I know you have — you must have. Well I'll let you into a little secret.' His smile took on a roguish quality. 'If a client is rude to me I simply charge him a little more. Instead of getting all steamed up like you do I tell myself that I'm putting ten bob extra on the bill and it works like magic.'

'Is that so?'

'Yes indeed, my boy.' He thumped my shoulder then became very serious. 'Of course I realize that I have an advantage right at the start — I have been blessed with a naturally even temperament while you are blown about in all directions by every little wind of circumstance. But I do think that this is something you could cultivate, so work at it, James, work at it. All this fretting and fuming is bad for you — your whole life would change if you could just acquire my own tranquil outlook.'

I swallowed hard. 'Well thank you, Siegfried,' I said. 'I'll try.'

★ ★ ★

Walt Barnett was a bit of a mystery man in Darrowby. He wasn't a farmer, he was a scrap merchant, a haulier, a dealer in everything from linoleum to second hand cars, and there was only one thing the local people could say for certain about hum — he had brass, lots of brass.

They said everything he touched turned to money.

He had bought a decaying mansion a few miles outside the town where he lived with a downtrodden little wife and where he kept a floating population of livestock; a few bullocks, some pigs and always a horse or two. He employed all the vets in the district in turn, probably because he didn't think much of any of us; a feeling which, I may say, was mutual. He never seemed to do any physical work and could be seen most days of the week shambling around the streets of Darrowby, hands in pockets, cigarette dangling, his brown trilby on the back of his head, his huge body threatening to burst through that shiny navy suit.

After my meeting with him we had a busy few days and it was on the following Thursday that the phone rang in the surgery. Siegfried lifted it and immediately his expression changed. From across the floor I could clearly hear the loud hectoring tones coming through the receiver and as my colleague listened a slow flush spread over his cheeks and his mouth hardened. Several times he tried to put in a word but the torrent of sound from the far end was unceasing. Finally he raised his voice and broke in but instantly there was a click and he found himself speaking to a dead line.

Siegfried crashed the receiver into its rest and swung round. 'That was Barnett — playing hell because we haven't rung him.' He stood staring at me for a few moments, his face dark with anger.

'The bloody bastard!' he shouted. 'Who the hell does he think he is? Abusing me like that, then hanging up on me when I try to speak!'

For a moment he was silent then he turned to me. 'I'll tell you this, James, he wouldn't have spoken to me like that if he'd been in this room with me.' He came over to me and held out his hands, fingers crooked menacingly. 'I'd have wrung his bloody neck, big as he is! I would have, I tell you, I'd have strangled the bugger!'

'But Siegfried,' I said. 'What about your system?'

'System? What system?'

'Well, you know the trick you have when people are unpleasant — you put something on the bill, don't you?'

Siegfried let his hands fall to his sides and stared at me for some time, his chest rising and falling with his emotion. Then he patted me on the shoulder and turned away towards the window where he stood looking out at the quiet street.

When he turned back to me he looked grim but calmer. 'By God, James, you're right. That's the answer. I'll cut Barnett's horse for him but I'll charge him a tenner.'

I laughed heartily. In those days the average charge for castrating a horse was a pound, or if you wanted to be more professional, a guinea.

'What are you laughing at?' my employer inquired sourly.

'Well . . . at your joke. I mean, ten pounds . . . ha-ha-ha!'

'I'm not joking, I'm going to charge him a tenner.'

'Oh come on, Siegfried, you can't do that.'

'You just watch me,' he said. 'I'm going to sort that bugger.'

* * *

Two mornings later I was going through the familiar motions of preparing for a castration; boiling up the emasculator and laying it on the enamel tray along with the scalpel, the roll of cotton wool, the artery forceps, the tincture of iodine, the suture materials, the tetanus antitoxin and syringes. For the last five minutes Siegfried had been shouting at me to hurry.

'What the hell are you doing through there, James? Don't forget to put in an extra bottle of chloroform. And bring the sidelines in case he doesn't go down. Where have you hidden those spare scalpel blades, James?'

The sunshine streamed across the laden tray, filtering through the green tangle of the wisteria which fell untidily across the surgery window. Reminding me that it was May and that there was nowhere a May morning came with such golden magic as to the long garden at Skeldale House; the high brick walls with their crumbling mortar and ancient stone copings enfolding the sunlight in a warm clasp and spilling it over the untrimmed lawns, the banks of lupins and bluebells, the masses of fruit blossom. And right at the top the rooks cawing in the highest branches of the elms.

Siegfried, chloroform muzzle looped over one shoulder, made a final check of the items on the tray then we set off. In less than half an hour we were driving through the lodge gates of the old mansion then along a mossy avenue which wandered among pine and birch trees up to the house which looked out from its wooded background over the rolling miles of fell and moor.

Nobody could have asked for a more perfect place for the operation; a high-walled paddock deep in lush grass. The two-year-old, a magnificent chestnut, was led in by two characters who struck me as typical henchmen for Mr Barnett. I don't know where he had dug them up but you didn't see faces like that among the citizens of Darrowby. One was a brown goblin who, as he conversed with his companion, repeatedly jerked his head and winked one eye as though they were sharing some disreputable secret. The other had a head covered with ginger stubble surmounting a countenance of a bright scrofulous red which looked as though a piece would fall off if you touched it; and deep in the livid flesh two tiny eyes darted.

The two of them regarded us unsmilingly and the dark one spat luxuriously as we approached.

'It's a nice morning,' I said.

Ginger just stared at me while Winker nodded knowingly and closed one eye as if I had uttered some craftiness which appealed to him.

The vast hunched figure of Mr Barnett hovered in the background, cigarette drooping, the bright sunshine striking brilliant shafts of light from the tight sheen of the navy suit.

I couldn't help comparing the aspect of the trio of humans with the natural beauty and dignity of the horse. The big chestnut tossed his head then stood looking calmly across the paddock, the large fine eyes alight with intelligence, the noble lines of the face and neck blending gently into the grace and power of the body. Observations I had heard about the higher and lower animals floated about in my mind.

Siegfried walked around the horse, patting him and talking to him, his eyes shining with the delight of the fanatic.

'He's a grand sort, Mr Barnett,' he said.

The big man glowered at him. 'Aye well, don't spoil 'im, that's all. I've paid a lot o' money for that 'oss.'

Siegfried gave him a thoughtful look then turned to me.

'Well, let's get on. We'll drop him over there on that long grass. Are you ready, James?'

I was ready, but I'd be a lot more at ease if Siegfried would just leave me alone. In horse work I was the anaesthetist and my colleague was the surgeon. And he was good; quick, deft, successful. I had no quarrel with the arrangement; he could get on with his job and let me do mine. But there was the rub; he would keep butting into my territory and I found it wearing.

Anaesthesia in the large animals has a dual purpose; it abolishes pain and acts as a means of restraint. It is obvious that you can't do much with these potentially dangerous creatures unless they are controlled.

That was my job. I had to produce a sleeping patient ready for the knife and very often I thought it was the most difficult part. Until the animal was properly under I always felt a certain tension and Siegfried didn't help in this respect. He would hover at my elbow, offering advice as to the quantity of chloroform and he could never bear to wait until the anaesthetic had taken effect. He invariably said, 'He isn't going to go down, James.' Then, 'Don't you think you should strap a foreleg up?'

Even now, thirty years later, when I am using such intravenous drugs as thiopentone he is still at it. Stamping around impatiently as I fill my syringe, poking over my shoulder with a long forefinger into the jugular furrow. 'I'd shove it in just there, James.'

I stood there irresolute, my employer by my side, the chloroform bottle in my pocket, the muzzle dangling from my hand. It would be wonderful, I thought, if just once I could be on my own to get on with it. And, after all, I had worked for him for nearly three years — surely I knew him well enough to be able to put it to him.

I cleared my throat. 'Siegfried, I was just wondering. Would you care to go and sit down over there for a few minutes till I get him down?'

'What's that?'

'Well I thought it would be a good idea if you left me to it. There's a bit of a crowd round the horse's head — I don't want him excited. So why don't you relax for a while. I'll give you a shout when he's down.'

Siegfried raised a hand. 'My dear chap, anything you say. I don't know what I'm hanging around here for anyway. I never interfere with your end as you well know.' He turned about and, tray under arm, marched off to where he had parked his car on the grass about fifty yards away. He strode round behind the Rover and sat down on the turf, his back against the metal. He was out of sight.

Peace descended. I became suddenly aware of the soft warmth of the sun on my forehead, of the bird song echoing among the nearby trees. Unhurriedly I fastened on the muzzle under the head collar and produced my little glass measure.

This once I had plenty of time. I'd start him off with just a couple of drachms to get him used to the smell of it without frightening him. I poured the clear fluid on to the sponge.

'Walk him slowly round in a circle,' I said to Ginger and Winker. 'I'm going to give him a little bit at a time, there's no hurry. But keep a good hold of that halter shank in case he plays up.'

There was no need for my warning. The two-year-old paced round calmly and fearlessly and every minute or so I trickled a little extra on to the sponge. After a while his steps became laboured and he began to sway drunkenly as he walked. I watched him happily; this was the way I liked to do it. Another little dollop would just about do the trick. I measured out another half ounce and walked over to the big animal.

His head nodded sleepily as I gave it to him.

'You're just about ready aren't you, old lad,' I was murmuring when the peace was suddenly shattered.

'He isn't going to go down, you know, James!' It was a booming roar from the direction of the car and as I whipped round in consternation I saw a head just showing over the bonnet. There was another cry.

'Why don't you strap up a . . . ?'

At that moment the horse lurched and collapsed quietly on the grass and Siegfried came bounding knife in hand from his hiding place like a greyhound.

'Sit on his head!' he yelled. 'What are you waiting for, he'll be up in a minute! And get that rope round that hind leg! And bring my tray! And fetch the hot water!' He panted up to the horse then turned and bawled into Ginger's face, 'Come on, I'm talking to you. MOVE!'

Ginger went off at a bow-legged gallop and cannoned into Winker who was rushing forward with the bucket. Then they had a brief but frenzied tug of war with the rope before they got it round the pastern.

'Pull the leg forward,' cried my employer, bending over the operation site, then a full blooded bellow, 'Get the bloody foot out of my eye, will you! What's the matter with you, you wouldn't pull a hen off its nest the way you're going.'

I knelt quietly at the head, my knee on the neck. There was no need to hold him down; he was beautifully out, his eyes blissfully closed as Siegfried worked with his usual lightning expertise. There was a mere few seconds of silence broken only by the tinkling of instruments as they fell back on the tray, then my colleague glanced along the horse's back. 'Open the muzzle, James.'

The operation was over.

I don't think I've ever seen an easier job. By the time we had washed our instruments in the bucket the two-year-old was on his feet, cropping gently at the grass.

'Splendid anaesthetic, James,' said Siegfried, drying off the emasculator. 'Just right. And what a grand sort of horse.'

We had put our gear back in the boot and were ready to leave when Walt Barnett heaved his massive bulk over towards us. He faced Siegfried across the bonnet of the car.

'Well that were nowt of a job,' he grunted, slapping a cheque book down on the shining metal, 'How much do you want?'

There was an arrogant challenge in the words and, faced with the dynamic force, the sheer brutal presence of the man, most people who were about to charge a guinea would have changed their minds and said a pound.

'Well, I'm askin' yer,' he repeated. 'How much do you want?'

'Ah yes,' said Siegfried lightly. 'That'll be a tenner.'

The big man put a meaty hand on the cheque book and stared at my colleague. 'What?'

'That'll be a tenner,' Siegfried said again.

'Ten pounds?' Mr Barnett's eyes opened wider.

'Yes,' said Siegfried, smiling pleasantly. 'That's right. Ten pounds.'

There was a silence as the two men faced each other across the bonnet. The bird song and the noises from the wood seemed abnormally loud as the seconds ticked away and nobody moved. Mr Barnett was glaring furiously and I looked from the huge fleshy face which seemed to have swollen even larger across to the lean, strong-jawed, high-cheek-boned profile of my employer. Siegfried still wore the remains of a lazy smile but down in the grey depths of his eye a dangerous light glinted.

Just when I was at screaming point the big man dropped his head suddenly and began to write. When he handed the cheque over he was shaking so much that the slip of paper fluttered as though in a high wind.

'Here y'are, then,' he said hoarsely.

'Thank you so much.' Siegfried read the cheque briefly then stuffed it carelessly into a side pocket. 'Isn't it grand to have some real May weather, Mr Barnett. Does us all good. I'm sure.'

Walt Barnett mumbled something and turned away. As I got into the car I could see the great expanse of navy blue back moving ponderously towards the house.

'He won't have us back, anyway,' I said.

Siegfried started the engine and we moved away. 'No, James, I should think he'd get his twelve bore out if we ventured down this drive again. But that suits me — I think I can manage to get through the rest of my life without Mr Barnett.'

Our road took us through the little village of Baldon and Siegfried slowed down outside the. pub, a yellow-washed building standing a few yards back from the road with a wooden sign reading The Gross Keys and a large black dog sleeping on the sunny front step.

My boss looked at his watch. 'Twelve fifteen — they'll just have opened. A cool beer would be rather nice wouldn't it. I don't think I've been in this place before.'

After the brightness outside, the shaded interior was restful, with only stray splinters of sunshine filtering through the curtains on to the flagged floor, the fissured oak tables, the big fireplace with its high settle.

'Good morning to you, landlord,' boomed my employer, striding over to the bar. He was in his most ducal mood and I felt it was a pity he didn't have a silver-knobbed stick to rap on the counter.

The man behind the counter smiled and knuckled a forelock in the approved manner. 'Good morning to you, sir, and what can I get for you gentlemen?'

I half expected Siegfried to say, 'Two stoups of your choicest brew, honest fellow,' but instead he just turned to me and murmured 'I think two halves of bitter, eh James?'

The man began to draw the beer.

'Won't you join us?' Siegfried inquired.

'Thank ye sir, I'll 'ave a brown ale with you.'

'And possibly your good lady, too?' Siegfried smiled over at the landlord's wife who was stacking glasses at the end of the counter.

'That's very kind of you, I will.' She looked up, gulped, and an expression of wonder crept over her face. Siegfried hadn't stared at her — it had only been a five second burst from the grey eyes — but the bottle rattled against the glass as she poured her small port and she spent the rest of the time gazing at him dreamily.

'That'll be five and sixpence,' the landlord said.

'Right.' My employer plunged a hand into his bulging side pocket and crashed down on the counter an extraordinary mixture of crumpled bank notes, coins, veterinary instruments, thermometers, bits of string. He stirred the mass with a forefinger, flicking out a half crown and two florins across the woodwork.

'Wait a minute!' I exclaimed. 'Aren't those my curved scissors? I lost them a few days . . .'

Siegfried swept the pile out of sight into his pocket.

'Nonsense! What makes you think that?'

'Well, they look exactly like mine. Unusual shape — lovely long, flat blades. I've been looking everywhere . . .'

'James!' He drew himself up and faced me with frozen hauteur. 'I think you've said enough. I may be capable of stooping to some pretty low actions but I'd like to believe that certain things are beneath me. And stealing a colleague's curved scissors is one of them.'

I relapsed into silence. I'd have to bide my time and take my chance later. I was fairly sure I'd recognized a pair of my dressing forceps in there too.

In any case, something else was occupying Siegfried's mind. He narrowed his eyes in intense thought then delved into his other pocket and produced a similar collection which he proceeded to push around the counter anxiously.

'What's the matter?' I asked.

'That cheque I've just taken. Did I give it to you?'

'No, you put it in that pocket. I saw you.'

'That's what I thought. Well it's gone.'

'Gone?'

'I've lost the bloody thing!'

I laughed. 'Oh you can't have. Go through your other pockets — it must be on you somewhere.'

Siegfried made a systematic search but it was in vain.

'Well James,' he said at length. 'I really have lost it, but I've just thought of a simple solution. I will stay here and have one more beer while you slip back to Walt Barnett and ask him for another cheque.'

26

Considering we spent our honeymoon tuberculin testing it was a big success. It compared favourably, at any rate, with the experiences of a lot of people I know who celebrated this milestone in their lives by cruising for a month on sunny seas and still wrote it off as a dead loss. For Helen and me it had all the ingredients; laughter, fulfilment and camaraderie, and yet it only lasted a week. And, as I say, we spent it tuberculin testing.

The situation had its origins one morning at the breakfast table when Siegfried, red-eyed after a bad night with a colicky mare, was opening the morning mail. He drew his breath in sharply as a thick roll of forms fell from an official envelope.

'God almighty! Look at all that testing!' He smoothed out the forms on the table cloth and read feverishly down the long list of farm premises. 'And they want us to start this lot around Ellerthorpe next week without fail — it's very urgent.' He glanced at me for a moment. 'That's when you're getting married, isn't it?'

I shifted uncomfortably in my chair. 'Yes, I'm afraid it is.'

Siegfried snatched a piece of toast from the rack and began to slap butter on it. 'Well this is just great isn't it? The practice going mad, a week's testing right at the top of the Dale, away in the back of beyond, and your wedding smack in the middle of it. You'll be drifting gaily off on your honeymoon without a care in the world while I'm rushing around here nearly disappearing up my own backside!' He bit a piece from the toast and began to chew it worriedly.

'I'm sorry, Siegfried,' I said. 'I didn't mean to land you in the cart like this. I couldn't know the practice was going to get so busy right now and I never expected them to throw all this testing at us.'

Siegfried paused in his chewing and pointed a finger at me. 'That's just it, James, that's your trouble — you don't look ahead. You just go belting straight on without a thought. Even when it comes to a bloody wedding you're not worried — oh no, let's get on with it, to hell with the consequences.' He paused to cough up a few crumbs which he had inhaled in his agitation. 'In fact I can't see what all the hurry is — you've got all the time in the world to get married, you're just a boy. And another thing — you hardly know this girl, you've only been seeing her regularly for a few weeks.'

'But wait a minute, you said . . . '

'No, let me finish, James. Marriage is a very serious step, not to be embarked upon without long and serious thought. Why in God's name does it have to be next week? Next year would have been soon enough and you could have enjoyed a nice long engagement. But no, you've got to rush in and tie the knot and it isn't so easily untied you know.'

'Oh hell, Siegfried, this is too bad! You know perfectly well it was you who . . . '

'One moment more. Your precipitate marital arrangements are going to cause me a considerable headache but believe me I wish you well. I hope all turns out for the best despite your complete lack of foresight, but at the same time I must remind you of the old saying: 'Marry in haste, repent at leisure.''

I could stand no more. I leaped to my feet, thumped a fist on the table and yelled at him.

'But damn it, it was your idea! I was all for leaving it for a bit but you . . . '

Siegfried wasn't listening. He had been cooling off all the time and now his face broke into a seraphic smile. 'Now, now, now, James, you're getting excited again. Sit down and calm yourself. You mustn't mind my speaking to you like this — you are very young and it's my duty. You haven't done anything wrong at all; I suppose it's the most natural thing in the world for people of your age to act without thinking ahead, to jump into things with never a thought of the morrow. It's just the improvidence of youth.' Siegfried was about six years older than me but he had donned the mantle of the omniscient greybeard without effort.

I dug my fingers into my knees and decided not to pursue the matter. I had no chance anyway, and besides, I was beginning to feel a bit worried about clearing off and leaving him snowed under with work. I got up and walked to the window where I watched old Will Varley pushing a bicycle up the street with a sack of potatoes balanced on the handle-bars as I had watched him a hundred times before. Then I turned back to my employer. I had had one of my infrequent ideas

'Look, Siegfried, I wouldn't mind spending my honeymoon round Ellerthorpe. It's wonderful up there at this time of the year and we could stay at the Wheat Sheaf. I could do the testing from there.'

He looked at me in astonishment. 'Spend it at Ellerthorpe? And testing? It's impossible — what would Helen say?'

'She wouldn't mind. In fact she could do the writing for me. We were only going off touring in the car so we haven't made any plans, and anyway it's funny, but Helen and I have often said we'd like to stay at the Wheat Sheaf some time — there's something about that little pub.'

Siegfried shook his head decisively. 'No, James I won't hear of it. In fact you're beginning to make me feel guilty. I'll get through the work all right so forget about it and go away and have a good time.'

'No, I've made up my mind. I'm really beginning to like the idea.' I scanned the list quickly. 'I can start testing at Allen's and do all those smaller ones around there on Tuesday, get married on Wednesday and go back for the second injection and readings on Thursday and Friday. I can knock hell out of that list by the end of the week.'

Siegfried looked at me as though he was seeing me for the first time. He argued and protested but for once I got my way. I fished the Ministry notification cards from the desk drawer and began to make the arrangements for my honeymoon.

★ ★ ★

On Tuesday at 12 noon I had finished testing the Allens' huge herd scattered for miles over the stark fells at the top of the Dale and was settling down with the hospitable folk for the inevitable 'bit o' dinner'. Mr Allen was at the head of the scrubbed table, and facing me were his two sons, Jack, aged about twenty, and Robbie, about seventeen. The young men were superbly fit and tough and I had been watching all morning in something like awe as they man-handled the wild, scattered beasts, chasing and catching tirelessly hour after hour. I had stared incredulously as Jack had run down a galloping heifer on the open moor, seized its horns and borne it slowly to the ground for me to inject; it struck me more than once that it was a pity that an Olympic selector was unlikely to stray into this remote corner of high Yorkshire — he would have found some world-beating material.

I always had to stand a bit of legpulling from Mrs Allen, a jolly talkative woman; on previous visits she had ribbed me mercilessly about being a slowcoach with the girls, the disgrace of having nothing better than a housekeeper to look after me. I knew she would start on me again today but I bided my time; I had a devastating riposte up my sleeve. She had just opened the oven door, filling the room with a delectable fragrance, and as she dumped a huge slab of roast ham on the table she looked down at me with a smile.

'Now then, Mr Herriot, when are we going to get you married off? It's time you found a nice girl, you know I'm always at you but you take not a bit o' notice.' She giggled as she bustled back to the cooking range for a bowl of mashed poatoes.

I waited until she returned before I dropped my bombshell. 'Well, as a matter of fact, Mrs Allen,' I said airily, 'I've decided to accept your advice. I'm getting married tomorrow.'

The good woman, mounding mashed potatoes on to my plate, stopped with her spoon in mid-air. 'Married tomorrow?' Her face was a study in blank astonishment.

'That's right. I thought you'd be pleased.'

'But . . . but . . . you're coming back here to read the test on Thursday and Friday.'

'Well of course. I have to finish, the test, haven't I? I'll be bringing my wife with me — I'm looking forward to introducing her to you.'

There was a silence. The young men stared at me, Mr Allen stopped sawing at the ham and regarded me stolidly, then his wife gave an uncertain laugh.

'Oh come on, I don't believe it. You're kidding us. You'd be off on your honeymoon if you were getting married tomorrow.'

'Mrs Allen,' I said with dignity. 'I wouldn't joke about a serious matter like that. Let me repeat — tomorrow is my wedding day and I'll be bringing my wife along on Thursday to see you.'

Completely deflated, she heaped our plates and we all fell to in silence. But I knew she was in agony; she kept darting little glances at me and it was obvious she was dying to ask me more. The boys too, seemed intrigued; only Mr Allen, a tall, quiet man who, I'm sure wouldn't have cared if I'd been going to rob a bank tomorrow, ploughed calmly through his food.

Nothing more was said until I was about to leave, then Mrs Allen put a hand on my arm.

'You really don't mean it, do you?' Her face was haggard with strain.

I got into the car and called out through the window. 'Goodbye and thank you, Mrs Allen. Mrs Herriot and I will be along first thing on Thursday.'

★ ★ ★

I can't remember much about the wedding. It was a 'quiet do' and my main recollection is of desiring to get it all over with as soon as possible. I have only one vivid memory; of Siegfried, just behind me in the church booming 'Amen' at regular intervals throughout the ceremony — the only time I have ever heard a best man do this.

It was an incredible relief when Helen and I were ready to drive away and when we were passing Skeldale House Helen grasped my hand.

'Look!' she cried excitedly. 'Look over there!'

Underneath Siegfried's brass plate which always hung slightly askew on the iron railings

338

was a brand new one. It was of the modern bakelite type with a black background and bold white letters which read 'J. Herriot MRCVS Veterinary Surgeon', and it was screwed very straight and level on the metal.

Siegfried had said something about 'You'll see my wedding present on the way out.' And here it was. Not many people got a partnership as a gift, but it had happened to me and was the crowning point of three years of magnanimity.

I looked back down the street to try to see Siegfried but we had said our goodbyes and I would have to thank him later. So I drove out of Darrowby with a feeling of swelling pride because I knew what the plate meant — I was a man with a real place in the world. The thought made me slightly breathless. In fact we were both a little dizzy and we cruised for hours around the countryside, getting out when we felt like it, walking among the hills, taking no account of time. It must have been nine o'clock in the evening and darkness coming in fast when we realized we had gone far out of our way.

We had to drive ten miles over a desolate moor on the fell top and it was very dark when we rattled down the steep, narrow road into Ellerthorpe. The Wheat Sheaf was an unostentatious part of the single long village street, a low grey stone building with no light over the door, and as we went into the slightly musty-smelling hallway the gentle clink of glasses came from the public bar on our left. Mrs Burn, the elderly widow who owned the place, appeared from a back room and scrutinized us unemotionally.

'We've met before, Mrs Burn,' I said and she nodded. I apologized for our lateness and was wondering whether I dare ask for a few sandwiches at this time of night when the old lady spoke up, quite unperturbed.

'Nay,' she said, 'it's right. We've been expecting you and your supper's waiting.' She led us to the dining-room where her niece, Beryl, served a hot meal in no time. Thick lentil soup, followed by what would probably be called a goulash these days but which was in fact simply a delicious stew with mushrooms and vegetables obviously concocted by a culinary genius. We had to say no to the gooseberry pie and cream.

It was like that all the time at the Wheat Sheaf. The whole place was aggressively unfashionable; needing a lick of paint, crammed with hideous Victorian furniture, but it was easy to see how it had won its reputation. It didn't have stylish guests, but fat, comfortable men from the industrial West Riding brought their wives at the weekends and did a bit of fishing or just took in the incomparable air between the mealtimes which were the big moments of the day. There was only one guest while we were there and he was a permanent one — a retired draper from Darlington who was always at the table in good time, a huge white napkin tucked under his chin, his eyes gleaming as he watched Beryl bring in the food.

But it wasn't just the home-fed ham, the Wensleydale cheese, the succulent steak and kidney pies, the bilberry tarts and mountainous Yorkshire puddings which captivated Helen and me. There was a peace, a sleepy insinuating charm about the old pub which we always recall with happiness. I still often pass the Wheat Sheaf, and as I look at its ancient stone frontage, quite unaltered by the passage of a mere thirty years, the memories are still fresh and warm; our footsteps echoing in the empty street when we took our last walk at night, the old brass bedstead almost filling the little room, the dark rim of the fells bulking against the night sky beyond our window, faint bursts of laughter from the farmers in the bar downstairs.

★ ★ ★

I particularly enjoyed too, our very first morning when I took Helen to do the test at Allen's. As I got out of the car I could see Mrs Allen peeping round the curtains in the kitchen window. She was soon out in the yard and her eyes popped when I brought my bride over to her. Helen was one of the pioneers of slacks in the Dales and she was wearing a bright purple pair this morning which would in modern parlance knock your eye out. The farmer's wife was partly shocked, partly fascinated but she soon found that Helen was of the same stock as herself and within seconds the two women were chattering busily. I judged from Mrs Allen's vigorous head-nodding and her ever widening smile that Helen was putting her out of her pain by explaining all the circumstances. It took a long time and finally Mr Allen had to break into the conversation.

'If we're goin', we'll have to go,' he said gruffly

and we set off to start the second day of the test.

We began on a sunny hillside where a group of young animals had been penned. Jack and Robbie plunged in among the beasts while Mr Allen took off his cap and courteously dusted the top of the wall.

'Your missus can sit 'ere,' he said.

I paused as I was about to start measuring. My missus! It was the first time anybody had said that to me. I looked over at Helen as she sat cross-legged on the rough stones, her notebook on her knee, pencil at the ready, and as she pushed back the shining hair from her forehead she caught my eye and smiled; and as I smiled back at her I became aware suddenly of the vast, swelling glory of the Dales around us, and of the Dales scent of clover and warm grass, more intoxicating than any wine. And it seemed that my first three years at Darrowby had been leading up to this moment, that the first big step of my life was being completed right here with Helen smiling at me and the memory, fresh in my mind, of my new plate hanging in front of Skeldale House.

I might have stood there indefinitely, in a sort of trance, but Mr Allen cleared his throat in a marked manner and I turned back to the job in hand.

'Right,' I said, placing my calipers against the beast's neck. 'Number thirty-eight, seven milli-metres and circumscribed,' I called out to Helen. 'Number thirty-eight, seven, C.'

'Thirty-eight, seven, C,' my wife repeated as she bent over her book and started to write.

We do hope that you have enjoyed reading this large print book.

Did you know that all of our titles are available for purchase?

We publish a wide range of high quality large print books including:
Romances, Mysteries, Classics
General Fiction
Non Fiction and Westerns

Special interest titles available in large print are:
The Little Oxford Dictionary
Music Book
Song Book
Hymn Book
Service Book

Also available from us courtesy of Oxford University Press:
Young Readers' Dictionary
(large print edition)
Young Readers' Thesaurus
(large print edition)

For further information or a free brochure, please contact us at:
Ulverscroft Large Print Books Ltd.,
The Green, Bradgate Road, Anstey,
Leicester, LE7 7FU, England.
Tel: (00 44) 0116 236 4325
Fax: (00 44) 0116 234 0205

Other titles published by Ulverscroft:

IF ONLY THEY COULD TALK

James Herriot

They didn't say anything about this in the books, I thought, as the snow blew in through the gaping doorway and settled on my naked back. I lay face down on the cobbled floor in a pool of nameless muck, my arm deep inside the straining cow . . . 1937: Newly-qualified veterinary surgeon James Herriot takes up a position in the Yorkshire Dales, and plunges into a working life of infinite variety — from calving recalcitrant cows in freezing byres (at two o'clock in the morning) to becoming 'Uncle Herriot' to a pampered Pekingese (and receiving Fortnum & Mason hampers from his doting canine nephew) . . .

IT SHOULDN'T HAPPEN TO A VET

James Herriot

When taking a cow's temperature the old-fashioned way, never let go of the thermometer . . . James Herriot has settled happily into life as a Darrowby vet, tending to livestock and pets alike — not to mention dealing with his mercurial boss Siegfried and his irrepressible, puckish vet student brother Tristan. Day to day, he finds himself testing entire herds of cattle for tuberculosis; acquiring another generous animal nephew alongside Tricki Woo the Peke (this time, Nugent the pig); fending off a ferocious Great Dane with a rickety chair — and attempting to court a farmer's daughter, the lovely Helen Alderson . . .

VET IN HARNESS

James Herriot

With his wife Helen by his side, and a partner's plate on Skeldale House's railings, James Herriot thinks the Yorkshire dales have never seemed more beautiful. Despite farmers who think nothing of calling him out to freezing fields at three o'clock in the morning, then drunkenly serenading him as he tends to a ewe in labour. Or vicious pigs who have to be bribed into their pens with biscuits. But there are bright moments too: pulling off a miracle cure with the new sulphonamide drugs; and saving a stray kitten — who finds a most unusual mother in the form of a sow . . .